The Asbury Theological Seminary Series in Christian Revitalization Studies

This volume is published in collaboration with the Center for the Study of World Christian Revitalization Movements, a cooperative initiative of Asbury Theological Seminary faculty. Building on the work of the previous Wesleyan/Holiness Studies Center at the Seminary, the Center provides a focus for research in the Wesleyan Holiness and other related Christian renewal movements, including Pietism and Pentecostal movements, which have had a world impact. The research seeks to develop analytical models of these movements, including their biblical and theological assessment. Using an interdisciplinary approach, the Center bridges relevant discourses in several areas in order to gain insights for effective Christian mission globally. It recognizes the need for conducting research that combines insights from the history of evangelical renewal and revival movements with anthropological and religious studies literature on revitalization movements. It also networks with similar or related research and study centers around the world, in addition to sponsoring its own research projects.

In this title, Professor Kwon offers a definitive, documented study of the global intercultural impact of the *Jesus* film. The most influential film production of the life of Jesus Christ, its impact includes being the impetus for the formation of some 14,000 new Christian congregations. From this perspective, the study finds an appropriate home in the Intercultural Studies sub series of this study project devoted to movements of revitalization of persons and cultures in contemporary Christianity.

J. Steven O'Malley
General Editor
The Asbury Theological Seminary Studies in Christian Revitalization

Foreword
Intercultural Studies Sub-Series

The behavioral science approach to the study of revitalization movements has a long history that has developed several models. Anthropologists, among others, observed that people responded to colonialism and the expansion of the West in various ways: armed resistance, selective acceptance and passive resistance, among others. The problems of the colonial frontier led to a memorandum on acculturation written by Robert Redfield, Ralph Linton and Melville Herskovits in 1936. Elsewhere in the world, anthropologists observed "nativistic" or "cultural renewal" movements as well: cargo cults in Melanesia, messianic movements in South Africa, and political revolutions in Latin America. Anthony F. C. Wallace brought some order to this area of study with his 1956 article where he named the stages and subsumed the movements under the name of "revitalization movements." Harold Turner contributed the notion of New Religious Movements to focus on the indigenous responses to mission work seen in every continent. This can be seen as part of a larger development, from the 1960s on, to develop Social Movement Theory where people are seen as agents intentionally acting to renew and reform society by organizing others to resist or dethrone the powers that be. Such movements develop a culture and social organization that give meaning and impetus to action on behalf of the leader and/or the program.

In this book, Bill Kwon explores the reception of *The Jesus* film as an evangelistic and revivalistic mission strategy, not by critiquing the film itself, but rather by examining the film's reception amongst an indigenous group in the Philippines, the Mangyan tribes of Mindoro Island. *The Jesus* film itself has become a movement, a media representation of Jesus translated into over 1000 languages and viewed over the last four decades by nearly 6 billion people. Yet, this movement is problematic. Kwon explores such issues as the identification with Western technology and the construction of the image of a Westernized Jesus. However, Kwon's main concern is with the audience and their ability to construct different readings of the film. The people's appreciation of Jesus' concern for the poor and marginalized ends up in tension with their inability to deconstruct the dominant Western themes of the showing.

Michael A. Rynkiewich
Editor for the sub-series on Intercultural Studies.

Westernized Visual Representation of Jesus and the Construction of Religious Meanings

A Reception Analysis of the Jesus *Film (1979) among the Mangyan Tribes*

Dong Hwan (Bill) Kwon

Emeth Press
www.emethpress.com

Westernized Visual Representation of Jesus *and the Construction of Relgious Meanings: A Reception Analysis of the* Jesus *Film (1979) among the Mangyan Tribes*

Printed in the United States of America on acid-free paper

Library of Congress Cataloging-in-Publication Data

Kwon, Dong Hwan.
Westernized visual representation of Jesus and the construction of religious meanings : a reception analysis of the Jesus film (1979) among the Mangyan tribes / Dong Hwan (Bill) Kwon.
pages cm – (Asbury Theological Seminary series in world Christianity revitalization movements. Intercultural Studies).
Includes bibliographical references and index.
ISBN 978-1-60947-068-5
1. Motion pictures in evangelistic work. 2. Jesus (Motion picture) 3. Evangelistic work–Philippines–History–20th century. 4. Jesus Christ–Art. 5. Mangyan (Philippine people) I. Title
BV3793K96 2015
261.5'2-dc23

2013038151

Dedication

To my Wife Yun Bum Kim
and My Children
Yi Hyun, Min Ki, Min Jae, and Geum Ju

Contents

List of Figures

Acknowledgments

The following dissertation would not be possible without many contributions around me. First of all, I thank my advisor, Dr. Lourdes M. Portus, for her intellectual guidance and collegial care during tedious progress. Her encouragement was the best source of the outcome. I am also thankful for the dissertation critic and former Graduate Chair Dr. Arminda V. Santiago and panel members, Dr. Aleli A. Quirante, Dr. Raul Pertierra, and Dr. Elena E. Pernia, who provided valuable guidance on this study. I also thank my research assistants, Mr. Erwin Galino, Ms. Salarene Manongsong for translating, transcribing interview data, and Ms. Selena Salanga, for editing script.

I cannot forget the great support of my Nazarene colleagues, including Rev. David Philips, Rev. Jose Elmo Dialing, Rev. Tino, Rev. George Junio, and Ptr. Manad, who is a native of Mindoro Island. Their support and encouragement has made this dissertation progressed till its completion. Furthermore, I thank Ptr. Santi and the members of the Indigenous Christian Churches of the Philippines (ICCP), and Mangyan settlers in sitio Siyapo, Baraas, and Calamias who allowed me participate and interview them regarding the film.

I also thank the United Board of Higher Education in Asia (UBCHEA) for granting a scholarship for my doctoral studies and the Asia-Pacific Nazarene Theological Seminary for various kinds of support, including extension of dissertation expenses, supplying research assistance, and others. There are a lot of names overflowing in my mind that inspired, encouraged and supported my work in the dissertation writing process, but most of all, I would like to give thanks to the Lord who called me and led me to the end of the dissertation.

Chapter 1

Introduction

Background and Rationale

Globalized Christian Media Production

As the media today has become more powerful than any other institution in human history, the use of media is now irresistible globally for promoting ideas and views. Various media forms including print, radio and visuals are being utilized to communicate religious messages. The *Passion of the Christ* (2004, produced and directed by Mel Gibson, was a box-office hit in the United States and the rest of the world. The *Prayer of Jabez* (2000), written by Rev. Bruce Wilkinson, became a phenomenon in both hard copy and multi-media devotional material. More than thirty million copies of The *Purpose Driven Life* (2002), written by Rev. Rick Warren of Willow Creek Community Church in the United States, were sold in 2009 and became a best-seller in many countries. The music albums of Don Moen and Hillsong appear to be favorite contemporary Christian music among global Christians. The distribution of religious media productions worldwide is the new phenomenon in Christianity.

Western Religious Icon, "Jesus"

The production of religious visual aids has a long history. Although making religious images was considered idolatry because God was divinely transcendent over creation among the early Jews and Christians (Langmuir, 2000), there has been the need and desire to have visual expressions of religious images that could be constructed as a socially accepted visual representation, particularly of Jesus. In the Medieval period in the West, the construction of the image of Jesus was transfigured into *Veronica*, known as the Vernicle or the Sudarium, in which the face was inscribed into a cloth that Jesus used for wiping his sweat on the way to Golgotha. The image of Jesus (see Figure 1) was already being constructed as a long-haired and bearded Anglo-Saxon man.

Figure 1. *The Painting of Master of Saint Veronica*

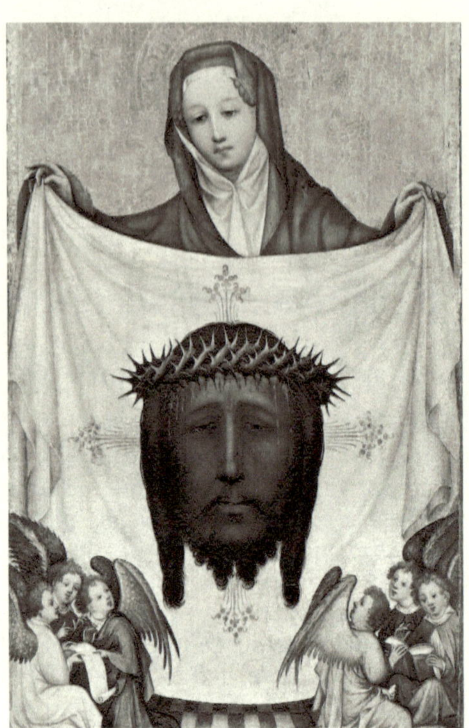

Source. *St. Veronica with the Holy Kerchief.* Retrieved July13, 2007 from http://www.wga.hu/frames-e.html?/html/m/master/veronica/index.html

In the twentieth century, the Westernized face of Jesus (see Figure 2) was transplanted into Warner Sallman's *Head of Christ* painted in 1941, which became a symbol in modern Christianity, selling more than 500 million copies. Morgan argued that the social and political needs of the particular context promoted Sallman's *Head of Christ* as a "cultural icon" (1998). Considering that Christianity has been nurtured in the West, the figure of Jesus in various forms of visual expression has been constructed as the "Western" Jesus.

Figure 2. *Warner Sallman's Head of Christ*

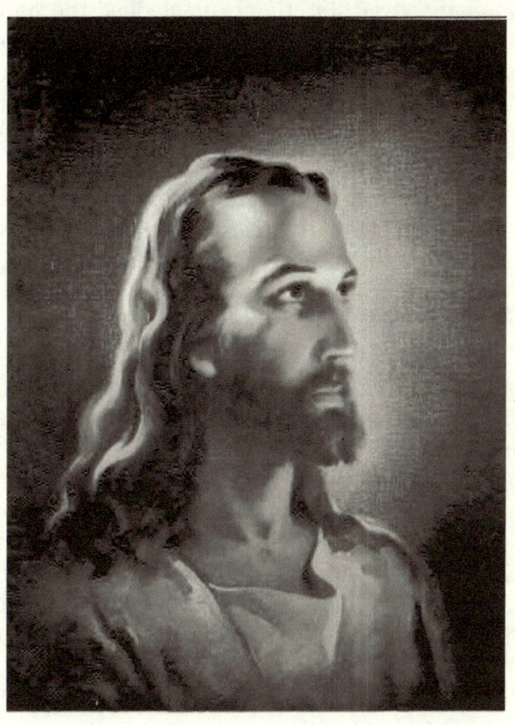

Source. *Head of Christ.* Retrieved September 10, 2009 from http://en.wikipedia.org/wiki/File:The_Head_of_Christ_by_Warner_Sallman_1941.jpg

The construction process of the Western Jesus also appeared in film. Soon after the Lumière brothers invented the cinematograph in 1895, Western Christians began to investigate film as a medium to express the Christian belief. As early as 1897, a short French-produced film based on a passion play, *La Passion,* was considered the first Jesus-figure film (Tatum, 2004), and film production has continued through the box-office hit *Passion of the Christ* by Mel Gibson. In just a century of visual depiction of Jesus in Western motion pictures, the portrayal of Jesus in this film has been widely exported throughout the world. The film and the figure represented as Jesus has surely become a "cultural icon" representing the image of Jesus.

Jesus (1979) Film and Evangelism

To understand the great influence of media with the representation of the visual Jesus, a particular film called *Jesus*, is a good example. Advertised as the most historically accurate Jesus-figure film, the film was released in October 1979 through the joint efforts of two Protestant evangelical Christians. The founder of Campus Crusade for Christ, Bill Bright, had a passionate vision for an evangelical film. He acknowledged the powerful effect of the visual medium and wanted to use a film that portrayed the life of Jesus.

On the other hand, John Heyman later had a similar vision of making the entirety of Genesis into film, but it was just a dream without a clear financial plan. Both men agreed to produce together a film that portrayed the life of Jesus for evangelical purposes. Bright raised a total of six million United States dollars to fund the film under the direction of John Heyman. He requested a systematic and scholarly investigation to a group of theologians, biblical scholars as well as archeologists to lay out the historical foundation of early Jewish tradition in the interest of making the *Jesus* film historically accurate. As a result, the film has often been cited as the most historically accurate Jesus-figure film in Christian history (Tatum, 2004).

The film begins with the birth narrative of a young Jesus, which serves as the prologue of the main part of the story. The prologue and epilogue both begin with the title and the narration of John 3: 16 that explicitly propose the evangelical standpoint of understanding Jesus as the Son of God and the Savior. The whole film is composed of thirty-five scenes (see Appendix D.).The film ends with an epilogue that is a presentation of highlighted scenes with narration that explain the theological meaning of Jesus and his life. The main body of the film rigidly follows the narratives of the book of Luke. This is a typical Jesus-figure film that describes the private and public ministry of Jesus as Christ.

The *Jesus* film has been considered one of the successful strategies for globalization in Protestant Christianity. Soon after releasing the film in the United States, Bill Bright had the enthusiastic vision of showing the film in all nations. He was able to distribute the film globally under the initiatives of Paul Eshleman through worldwide Campus Crusade for Christ network. For more than thirty years, Bright established a "delivery system" where the *Jesus* film ministry approached communities, seeking permission to show the film for free for evangelistic purposes. Mostly geographically rural and socially poor communities were selected, and the film was shown often in the community centers of villages. Evangelical preaching followed the showing of the film and religious conversions were made among the audience. In 2009, The *Jesus* Film International reported that approximately 5.6 billion people around the world had watched the single film since 1979. The film has been translated by 1,308 languages as of January of 2015 (http://www.jesusfilm.org/film-and-media/statistics/statistics).[1]

In terms of religious conversion of the audience from the film showing, the *Jesus* film has had significant effects. According to the World Mission department of the Church of the Nazarene, one of the major world distribu-

[1] In 2015, the Jesus Film International no longer publishes the total acculumated Cumulative Exposures in their statistics.

tors of *Jesus* film, more than forty-six million viewers have watched the film; more than two million viewers have actually attended some kind of religious meeting; and about fourteen thousand churches were established as a direct result of the film showing ministry (http://www.jfhp.org/progress/results.cfm).

Figure 3. The Website *of* the *Jesus* Film Ministry

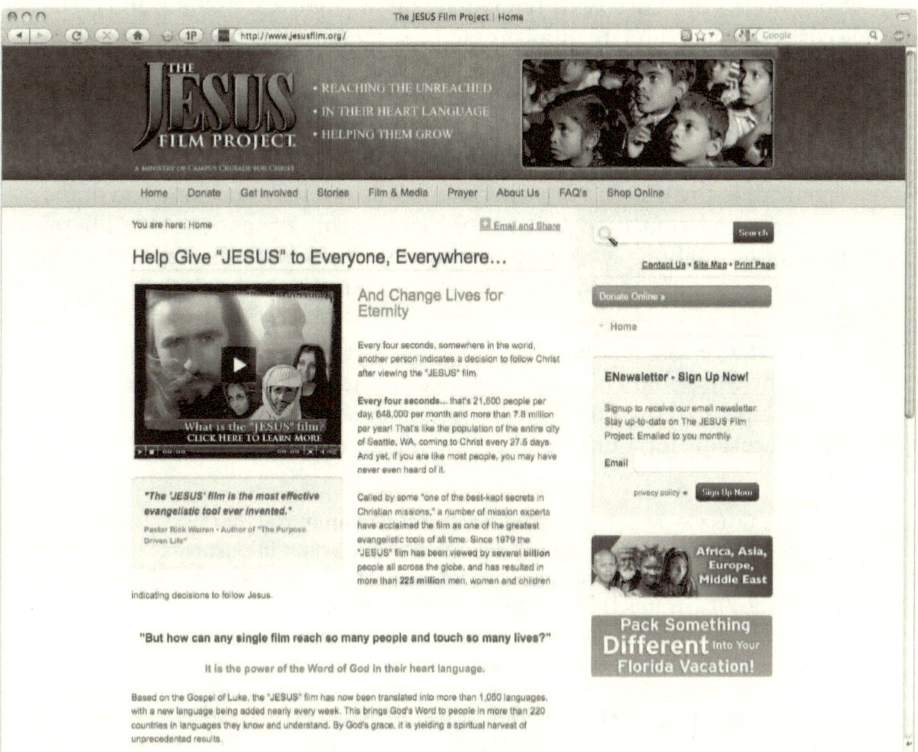

In the Philippines, film showing is clearly a means of evangelism in various evangelical Protestant denominations. Besides the Church of the Nazarene, the denomination in which this study is performed, partners cover Wesleyans, Assemblies of God, Bible Methodist, Philippine Council of Evangelical Churches (PCEC) and many more independent churches (Maano, 2000). The partners actively mobilized the use of film in various locations. In the Church of the Nazarene alone, the *Jesus* film has been shown to nearly one million people, more than one hundred thousand viewers have attended religious meetings, and more than four hundred and fifty churches were established through its systematic single-film ministry (http://www.nazareneworld mission.org/regions.aspx). From the data above, the film itself is regarded as a monumental piece that has reached the largest cross-cultural audience in the history of evangelism as well as film. And judging from by number of the converts, the *Jesus* film is one of the most powerful visual representations in Christian evangelism.

Western Ideology and Biblical Fundamentalism in *Jesus* Film

Distinctively the visualization of a historically accurate Jesus was a project developed by those with fundamentalist theological assumptions. The five core beliefs of fundamentalism can be summarized as the firm beliefs in biblical inerrancy, the second coming of Jesus Christ, as well as the virgin birth, physical resurrection, and the death of Jesus as atonement (McIntyre, 1984).[2] In reaction to the modernization and the liberalization of theology, fundamentalists (often used alternatively with conservative Christians and evangelical) in the United States became advocates for the promotion of the core evangelical stance in the face of threats from of modern and liberal churches both nationally and internationally. They were also proactive in utilizing media such as radio, television and film (Melton, 2009; McIntyre, 1984).

Furthermore, conservative evangelicals, such as Bill Bright, were close to the right-wing politicians who were concerned about communist expansion at the peak of the Cold War in the 1970s. A recent historical study on Campus Crusade for Christ and its political position was stated. Turner wrote:

> Campus Crusade evidenced an unyielding anticommunism that persisted into the 1970s and 1980s, and the activities of Bill Bright in particular illuminate the growing political influence of evangelicals during those decades. Bright also illustrates the evangelical fascination and proficiency with technology, as he sought to harness radio, records, television, movie translations, and the internet to spread his *Four Spiritual Laws* across the nation and around the world. Furthermore, since the 1980s Campus Crusade has contributed to evangelical cooperation with Pentecostals charismatics and Catholics, and Bright was a key player in the recent broadening of evangelical theology (2006, p. 11).

---

[2] Christian fundamentalism and evangelicals have been used interchangeably in the paper. The two terms share the same theological stance in that they were in opposition to liberal theory, modern biblical criticism, Darwinism, and other issues that have been attached to traditional Christian beliefs in the early 20th century. Yet radical fundamentalism and evangelicals were divided by openness to the dynamics of biblical interpretations and modern scholarship. Both of them have in common the protection of the authority of the Bible and sacredness of Jesus and the meaning of his birth, crucifixion and resurrection. Some may disagree by defining Bill Bright as a fundamentalist but, in this paper, I used the term fundamentalism in relation to the interpretation of the Bible as its major theological concern.

The rise of conservative evangelicals in political interests coincided with charismatic leaders who led massive religious "expos" in the 70s and 80s. As Turner wrote, conservative politicians such as Nixon and Reagan, Richard Viguerie and Paul Weyrich "recognized the latent potential of evangelical voters" (2006, p. 17). Clearly, Bill Bright supported the conservative and anti-communistic propaganda of the Republican politicians. Because of his reaction against communism, he had the unique privilege to raise funds for operating an evangelical parachurch organization and to be guided by United States foreign policy in the global expansion of Campus Crusade for Christ and the *Jesus* film ministry. With the threats of communist expansion in the 1970s, Bill Bright used Campus Crusade for Christ and the *Jesus* film as a means of evangelizing the world, and right-wing politicians supported him and his organization in making a global youth network to preserve Western ideology. The campus ministry and global expansion was, therefore, the result of the evangelical missional zeal of fundamentalist evangelicals alongside political allies in the context of post-war anti-communist concern in mainstream United States politics (Harvey, 1976; Israel, 2009; Turner, 2006).

The interpretation of Western Christianity in the film conceived a colonial mindset toward non-industrialized, primitive cultures. Using this technological and Western-oriented medium implied the superiority of the West over non-Western developing countries. In the 1970s, when the film was produced, United States media production dominated the world media market. Scholars cried out against their perception of this media and cultural domination in the worldwide media industry (Schiller, 1976, 1998; Hamelink, 1993; Waters, 1995; Parameswaran, 2002). Critics argued that United States-based media productions manipulated local cultural experiences. This media domination has become a significant ideological tool of the United States mass media. I have argued that the *Jesus* film was produced in a context that is centered on Western technology and capital by conservative Protestants with a great passion for evangelism. However, the image of Jesus in films propagates the Western image of Jesus and presents a Westernized construction of Christianity to the world.

Particular interest in the *Jesus* film lies in the fact that it is still an ongoing process of social construction of the Western Jesus in visual representation. Although the various Jesus-figure films have propagated a historically accurate portrayal of the life and work of Jesus, the portrayal of the Western Jesus image has been continuous from the very early production on a Jesus-figure film up to the most recent one, *Jesus of Montreal*. As already noted, Jesus was born in Jerusalem and biologically a Middle Eastern Asian, but he has been transformed into a white Anglo-Saxon figure which, I will argue, is the very process of social construction of reality as explained by Berger and Luckmann (1966).

Foucault (1980) similarly claimed that social discourse is the dominating power of society. In Foucault's understanding, discourse ordered things in a given society. Discourse was a way of talking about a certain object that constructs the object and thus creates reality. In other words, the power of discourse is produced by repeated social interactions, and reality is produced by this process. Althusser (1971) argued that dominance, in Marxist terms, is created by "Ideology" (Marx, 1859/1977) and could be achieved through the Ideological State Apparatus (ISA). The process of Western visualization through Jesus-figure films was the very act of constructing dominant "discourse." When the Westernized visual images constructed the face of Jesus, this was an example of how knowledge was socially positioned and constructed. The ongoing process is in the center of hegemonies' power struggles (Gramsci, 2005).

The context of film audience in a non-Western, socially dislocated, and economically poor country is the focus of this study. Instead of a critique of the film text, this study examines the reception of the *Jesus* film by a non-Western audience and how film mediates and constructs religious meanings.

In pursuing this research, the Philippines has a unique context in Asia. The Philippines has experienced long colonial domination by Western countries, first by Spain and then later by the United States. As a consequence the country became the only Christian country in Asia and possesses more than ninety percent of the total Catholic population in Asia. When the United States took over colonial domination after Spain, various colonial and post-colonial influences from the United States were introduced and its political, economical and social systems penetrated the Philippines (Abinales & Amoroso, 2005; Hidalgo & Patajo-Legasto, 2005; Hunchcroft, 2000; Go & Foster, 2005; Goda, 1999, 2003). Various United States Protestant denominations have carried out missionary efforts and evangelism in the country for more than a century. With the social and political, as well as religious influx of foreign and Christian influences within Philippine context, it seemed to be a good place to examine Westernized Christian visual media effects on non-Western people.

In searching for the locale of the study, I encountered one of the indigenous groups, called the Mangyans, in the Philippines. Known as swidden agriculturalists in the island of Mindoro, the name Mangyan is the generic term for the native people who settled in the island of Mindoro six hundred to seven hundred years ago (Postma, 1974). They are geographically closer to Palawan with the group of Malaysia and Borneo during prehistoric times than Luzon and Visayas (Mandia, 1987). The recent classification of Mangyan ethnic groups divided them into eight groups: Iraya, Alangan, Tadyawan, Tau-Buid, Bangon, Buhid, Hanunoo and Ratagnon. The eight groups differ in physical status, settlement and dwellings, utensils or implements, social and political organization, and more importantly, use of oral and written language, although they use Tagalog as a "lingua franca" (Maceda, 1967) in the lowland settlement. Only the Hanunoo have a written language (Postma, 1988).

The justification for the locale of this study among the Mangyans was obvious in that it was the only indigenous tribe included in the *Jesus* film showing. The film showing in Mangyan community had been planned for the year of 2008. Furthermore, a local contact, a native Mindoro pastor, Ptr. Meynard Barrales (henceforth Manad) had good communications with some of Mangyan groups. In addition, Rev. Faustino M. Roranes (henceforth Tino), the district superintendent of the Southern Tagalog district of the Church of the Nazarene, was highly recommended as the best supporter of my study. Later, I found out that he was one of my classmates during my study at Asia Pacific Nazarene Theological Seminary (APNTS). It seemed that the natural flow of the research procedure itself was beneficial for this study.

More importantly, no literature has dealt with the spirituality related to mediation through visual media and its reception of Christianity. Some studies have focused on religion and spirituality from indigenous aspects, which were also deeply related to rituals and social life (Leykamm, 1979; Mandia, 1987, 2003; Miyamoto, 1988; Pennoyer, 1975, 1976, 1977, 1980a, 1980b; Gibson, 1983, 1985, 1994), but none of the studies have paid attention to the effects of modern media on eligious life, particularly Protestantism, among Mangyans.

To this extent, the reception and the effects of the Westernized representation of Jesus will be more distinctive among the audience of an indigenous culture, the Christianized Mangyans in the study. I was able to interpret the religious meanings of the film receptions focusing on the three particular Christian Mangyan settlements (sitio Siyapo, Baraas, and Calamias), particularly the Iraya and Alangan-Mangyan tribes.

Significance of This Study

This study questions the effects of a globalizing, Western ideological, media-oriented, and massive capital-driven mission strategy. For a few decades, Protestant evangelicals have been actively mobilizing multi-media to be able to deliver religious messages throughout the world. This new tendency has accelerated with the rapid development of information and communication technology, which has been heavily dependent on Western resources. Evangelicals have especially propagated the active use of media technology into missions without much careful investigation of its ideological impact on audiences, but none of these studies has endeavored to understand the effect of the multi-media use on contemporary Christianity from a cultural point of view. This study believes it is significant to examine the evangelistic endeavor and to evaluate the in-depth and often unintended effects of the multi-media oriented, mission strategy.

Through this in-depth qualitative analysis on the *Jesus* film audiences, multiple meanings will be unpacked. During the four decades of this film ministry, there have been numerous testimonials of conversions and other accounts that have been produced for the purpose of fundraising to support the operation of the mission. This one-sided fundraising motivation does not properly reveal multi-faceted aspects of the reception of the film in cross-cultural audiences, especially in indigenous cultures, such as that of the Mangyans.

The reception of the film could also contribute to continuing discussion of the fascinating theological analyses of films that directly depict the life of Jesus, called, "Jesus-figure film" and the films that the religious meanings and themes implicitly embedded in Christ-figure films. From the literature reviewed, it was observed that several research studies focused on the themes and messages embedded in Jesus-figure films as well as Christ-figure films. Yet the analyses of the films are heavily dependent on textual film analyses, which ignore the other side of the communication process, the "audience." Current research trends should be balanced with the voices of multi-vocal audience studies.

This study is a critical and cultural analysis of the *Jesus* film ministry of the Church of the Nazarene, to which denomination I belong. This particular denomination has been the only one that has partnered with Campus Crusade for Christ for the *Jesus* film ministry since 1997. Hundreds of groups of film ministers were formed and poured tremendous resources, including finances and personnel, into this project. Yet there was a lack of research that dealt with the effects of the film among the various audiences cross-culturally. This study could be one of the ways to evaluate the mission strategy that has been systematically implemented in the denomination.

Beneficiaries of This Study

Evangelical Christians and Missionaries

This study will benefit evangelical Christians and missionaries by providing a possibly different point of view in understanding the effects of film showing. The study will also provide a critical and cultural approach in understanding the use of visual media in the cross-cultural mission. Evangelical media producers should be aware of the deep cultural and political effects of media productions for religious purposes in a cross-cultural context.

Scholars

The study will benefit scholars by providing an exceptional opportunity for the study of missions in a technologically-centered society including meaningful data regarding the current ICT and mass communication situation among Mangyans on the Occidental Mindoro Island. ICT and communication scholars might discover interests in future research. Also, besides practical and social benefits, this study contributes to Mangyan studies in Philippine studies, particularly the Mangyans in Northern Occidental Mindoro. In addition, this study hopes to stimulate further studies in various topics in this area.

Policy Makers

This study provides the rationale for future community development projects as a part of ICT development for the social integrity and welfare of cultural minorities. From a political and social point of view, Mangyans in the research area (Northern part of Occidental Mindoro) have been greatly neglected in modern technology development and information sharing.

Community Workers

The study also challenges community development social workers from both government and non-government organization, as well as social and religious workers, for future plans to facilitate various developments for Mangyans in the area.

Research Problems and Objectives

Research Problems

How do the Alangan and Iraya Christian Mangyans in Sta. Cruz, Mindoro construct religious meanings from the reception of the *Jesus* film, which contains Westernized visual images of Jesus?

Research Objectives

This study seeks to analyze the constructed religious meanings on the reception of the *Jesus* film, which contains the Western figure of Jesus, by the Mangyan Christian group. Employing ethnographic methods, with in-depth observations and interviews, to understand the reception of the film in a particular Mangyan community, the general objective can be broken down into specific objectives. This study particularly seeks to:

1. Describe the current social, religious and media contexts of the Iraya and Alangan Mangyan tribes,
2. Find out how the film showing ministry takes place, particularly among Iraya and Alangan Mangyan tribes,
3. Analyze how the film showing constructs the religious meanings of Iraya and Alangan Mangyan tribes,
4. Analyze the perceptions of the film and the Western figure of Jesus in the film among Iraya and Alangan Mangyans.

Scope and Delimitation

Geographically, this study was located in the three sitios (sitio Siyapo, Baraas, and Calamias) of Iraya and Alangan Mangyan communities in Occidental Mindoro, Philippines. The location of this study limited findings to the particular understanding of a specific ethnic group in a given situation. This study was based on the reception of the *Jesus* film as located in the social, religious and media contexts of the Mangyans in the given three sitios. Generalization of the findings into other locations and audiences is not the purpose of this study. These locations were recommended by the District Superintendent of the Church of the Nazarene, Rev. Tino, in consultation with a local *Jesus* film coordinator, Ptr. Manad, a native of Mindoro Island. After a discussion of the purpose of the studies, the three sites were chosen and there was a schedule for film showing.

This study was also limited in its selection of interview informants. The premise of the research was that Mangyan audiences were willingly expressing their perceptions and their religious meanings of the *Jesus* film. In order to receive relevant answers, the informants were limited to those who were willing participate in the interviews. The interviews were not limited to adults but included those who were old enough to adequately verbalize their ideas to me.

Due to the design of the research, I had to follow the pre-planned *Jesus* film showing and had to depend upon the interviewees who were willing to answer the questions. Although I was able to interview a few non-ICCP members and non-Mangyan Christian workers, this setting caused a heavy dependency on the Indigenous Christian Churches of the Philippines (henceforth ICCP) members.

Finally, I had to admit that my language capability to communicate with the Mangyans in their native language and Mangyan culture was limited in this study. To address this limitation, I hired two Filipino research assistants, Erwin Galino and Salarene Manongsong, who were second year students at Fairbanks International School of Communication. Both successfully completed a research methods class and were competent in Filipino and English language. They interpreted the interviews with Mangyan tribes during the field research, transcribed the interviews that were recorded, and translated the Tagalog transcription into English.

In addition to my research assistants, several key informants were very supportive in compensating for my limited language capacity. Rev. Tino made initial contact with the pastors of the community. Ptr. Manad guided the whole research process and negotiated in various situations in the Mangyan communities. In addition to the support mentioned here, a group of Mangyan pastors from the ICCP was also very helpful in coordinating the *Jesus* film ministry and interviews with the audiences.

Chapter 2

Review of Related Literature

Introduction

In this chapter, the current literature dealing with Jesus-figure and Christ-figure films, film and media reception studies, media, religion and culture dialogues, and Mangyan studies are examined. Many theologians have significant interest in the representation of Christianity and Christian values in film. Similarly, some media scholars are interested in the current media representation of certain religious issues in relation to national and cultural identity. The studies also provide the theoretical frame of multiple meanings and interpretation.

The literature review proved that British cultural studies, which I have used in the theoretical framework, have been deeply interconnected with the development of reception studies in both film and media studies. Finally, Mangyan studies and literature provided distinct cultural aspects of the historical and social development of the Mangyans in the Philippines.

Jesus-figure Film and Christ-figure Film Studies

Despite the dominant negative impression among mainstream Christian circles regarding the use of visual media, some theologians have taken a step beyond the simple good and evil dichotomy. Some have tried to compare the series of films that described the life of Jesus, called Jesus-figure films, to determine different messages and meanings (Walsh, 2003; Stern, Jefford & DeBona, 1999; Tatum, 2004). Although these publications certainly provided descriptive information of the Jesus-figure films, in-depth analysis of theology and contemporary society in the films was absent. Others delved into the meanings and values implicitly embedded in the secular films in the literature as reviewed below.

An Italian theologian, Baugh (1997), tried to balance his analysis of both Jesus-figure films and Christ-figure films that contained rich meanings of the salvation and messianic message in films. Because of his European background, his analysis was more focused on historical and European film production, which was different from that of American theologians on film studies.

A cultural critic and historian, Miles' (1996) early work attempted to see film as a text in a particular historical moment. Taking a cultural studies approach to film, she firmly rejected typical negative perception on the effects of films on the religious community, and analyzed how films interpreted religion and its values. Similar works followed on the analysis of understanding theological themes in commercial films (Marsh & Ortiz, 1997; Johnston, 2000; Stone, 2000; Barsotti & Johnson, 2004).

Flesher and Torry (1998) justified the use of filmic interpretation of the filming Jesus story as what the Targum added from Hebrew Scripture. The Targum is an Aramaic translation of Hebrew Scripture. The authors explained that the Targum translation had added a word or a phrase to several paragraphs from the original text to help early Jews who did not speak Hebrew understand the Hebrew Scripture. In their argument, the theological and doctrinal representation was an unavoidable insertion. Instead, they argued the insertion served to strengthen the meaning of the life and ministry of Jesus that the directors intended to convey.

Clearly identified as a Jewish New Testament scholar, Reinhartz (2006) discussed the portrayal of Jewish heritage and Judaism in different Jesus-figure films. Analyzing six Jesus-figure films in this article, he asserted that each film constructed different depictions of the Jewish heritage of Jesus for the purposes of the films. In doing so, he argued that the Holocaust experience was critical for the depiction of anti-Semitic portrayal in the films.

Kozlovic (2004) tried to construct the list of structures found in Christ-figure films in popular culture, which included tangible, central, outsiders, divinely sourced and tasked, alter egos, special normal, twelve associates and others. Yet the structures were severely criticized as a mere shopping list of Christ figures (Deacy, 2006). He argued that the lists of the Christ-figure structures imposed in popular films would eventually misguide the essence of theological meanings in the films.

Interestingly, social scientist Reysen (2006) studied the different fan behaviors between religious groups and secular groups. He questioned the similarity of fan behavior between religious and secular groups toward what they liked or believed. His study showed similarities between the receptivity of fans interested in religious and secular media, but other differences emerged later. Religious devotees and secular fans appeared similar but were different in nature.

From the reviews on Jesus-figure and Christ-figure films, it should be noted that the majority of the literature work has been done by theologians without consulting cultural critics. This tendency was helpful to expand theologians' hermeneutical practice to the abundant visual text in the 21st century, as exemplified by Miles' (1996). Theologians' descriptive and exegetical studies on secular films are considerably significant, and eventually connect theological studies to countless secular films.

Yet this theological attempt of textual exegesis on content paid little interest to, and had little influence on. The audience reception of both Jesus-figure and Christi-figure films. Similar to both cultural studies in media and film studies, this heavy inclination towards textual analysis showed a lack of variety in cultural understanding of the religious films as well as its meanings for both religious and non-religious audiences. At the same time, it is also crucial to understand the interpretation of religion or religious values in secular films that construct meanings in both religious and non-religious audiences.

Furthermore, scholars paid little attention to the Western representation of Jesus in the Jesus-figure and Christ-figure films. Understandably, most scholars and the research context are Western in orientation as well as in audience. Because of this situation, there was a lack of critical analysis of the Western perspective is therefore evident in religious film studies.

It is crucial, therefore, to identify the Western visualization of Jesus among the Jesus-figure and Christ-figure films and to pursue how the films are received by cross-cultural audiences with a non-Westerner's perspective. This study fills the gap between the theological interests on the topic of Christianity and media by providing media studies from a social scientific approach. At the same time, this study is focused on the non-Western audience's reception of Western religious media represented by the critical and cultural point of view.

Media and Film Reception Studies

The origin of reception studies in both television and film are the same: the interest in people's use of media. In television studies, the term "audience" was often used as an alternate to "spectators" by film scholars. In the lineage of the development of an active audience, the uses and gratifications theory came to mass communication. This theory was not developed until Paul Lazarsfeld started radio audience research in 1937 in New York as a response to the cultural critiques of Adorno, Marcuse, and Horkheimer of the Frankfrut School, who stated that media had immeasurable power over society. Under Lazarsfeld, Herta Herzog then proved that the audiences of daytime serials, called soap operas, had certain preferences in listening to programs (Katz & Lazarsfeld, 1955). Merton (1948) and others criticized the work of critical scholars on the notion of Culture Industry (Adorno & Horkheimer, 1977) by implementing social scientific quantitative methods and data to show the personal influence in the mediated message.

The interests of the audience might result from audience research, particularly uses and gratifications, research in the 1970s. A few decades later, Katz and others revised the active audience thesis by presenting the uses and gratifications theory based on Maslow's idea of basic human needs. Katz and others proposed the premise of the theory, that audiences were actively seeking gratification to satisfy certain needs in its exposure to the media (Katz, Blumler & Gurevitch, 1973). Based on the empirical and positivist stance in studying media consumer patterns in media studies, the uses and gratifications theory turned turned the interests of media producers and critics from media texts back to the audience's receptivity. Yet as the theory gained significant popularity, scholars such as Schroder suggested the need for a new paradigm negotiating between active and passive audience studies. Webster (1998) proposed the concept of "structure of agency" for the justification of overemphasizing the activity of the audience.

In Europe, this same development of an active audience thesis occurred in the critical tradition. As mentioned in the previous chapter, British cultural scholars, such as Hall, began to think of the media effects on the perception of the audience in the formation of the contemporary culture in the early 1970s in England. The Center for Contemporary Cultural Studies (CCCS) in the University of Birmingham became the center for audience studies by the work of Hall's encoding/decoding theory (1980).

Later, a series of audience and reception studies followed. Besides Morely, Hobson's study on the women consumers of a televised soap opera, *Crossroads*, was a well-cited audience study in the cultural studies' tradition. Hobson took a feminist stance on cultural reception studies and provided feminine readings of *Crossroads* (1982) with in-depth interviews of a number of office workers. Besides Hobson, Modelski's study (1984) on female viewers of soap operas, and Radway's (1984) study on female romance readers, also distinguished particular female readership toward particular media messages.

A few scholars took a different view than British scholars who focused on ideological struggles in receptivity studies. Scholars such as Ang, Jhally, Lewis and others extended their interests in global media consumption and the audience's interpretation. The audience study began its endeavors with the consumption of global media and their cultural meaning. Ang studied the audience of the TV serial, *Dallas* (1985); Jhally and Lewis studied the audience of the *Cosby Show* (2003); and Liebes and Katz (2003) uniquely studied the consumption of American TV fiction, such as *Dallas*, among cross-cultural audiences. Similar to the previous cultural scholars, the studies discovered significant meaning-making processes based on different cultural moral values. The meanings created through American media were not unified enough to transplant American values, but global audiences were actively engaged in interpreting the media messages based on their own cultural values. Cross-cultural media reception studies have argued that there are notably different readings of cross-national media productions. It is argued that the media messages are plural in the cultural context where the media texts are consumed. The messages are culturally structured pattern that media make meanings.

In previous studies, there has been a strong notion of media effects on perpetuating Christian values and meanings embedded in the media message, and it is still important to note the media's power over consumers. The strong media effect theory states that the purpose of utilizing the ideological perspective in this research is to identify the production of the Western image of Jesus. By illustrating the existence of the dominant perspectives or power of the image of Jesus in the film, we seek to find out whose "frame" or "window" is perceived in the media-reality of Jesus in film. These binary conflicts would entail Western vs. non-Western, Caucasian vs. Asian, Christian vs. non-Christian, industrialized vs. indigenous and others. This post-colonial standpoint provided a clear perspective in reading how non-Western Christians understand and make religious meanings out of the Westernized visual image of Jesus.

Yet, further findings of scholars in the cultural studies tradition provide multiple cultural meanings made of the media experiences among the indigenous audience in this study. Although the media are bound to the ideological and "dominant" meanings, Ang and others argued that there might be different "negotiated" and "oppositional" readings than Hall (1980) proposed. In the new trends in media audience studies context, the current study further explores the cultural meanings of global media text in the Christian context.

Religion, Media and Culture

Similarly, some researchers in the fields of media studies, cultural studies, religion and sociology, or religion have tried to provide insights into the convergence of religion and media in the construction of contemporary culture in less than two decades. Starting from the synthesis of studies on the sociology of religion and mass media, particularly audience studies, *Religion and Mass Media: Audiences and Adaptations* (Stout & Buddenbaum, 1996) provides clear margins and potentials of the study on religion and mass media in contemporary society. Alongside this attempt, a series of conferences and journals has provided development in the field of study, religion media and culture.

The first and the most leading body of scholars in the converging field of media, religion and culture was formed at the international conference, "Media, Religion and Culture" held at the University of Uppsala, Sweden in 1993. This conference was able to significantly stimulate those scholars who were interested in the three interplaying topics both in United States and Europe. The conference played a key role in publishing the book, *Rethinking Media, Religion and Culture* (Hoover & Lundby, 1997). The second conference was held at the University of Colorado, Boulder, and the papers presented in the conference were included in the chapters of the book, *Practicing Religion in the Age of the Media: Explorations in Media, Religion, and Culture* (Hoover & Clark, 2002). The Divinity School of the University of Edinburgh then hosted the 3rd conference and directed the book, *Mediating Religion: Conversations in Media, Religion, and Culture* (Mitchell & Marriage, 2003). The latest book, *Belief in Media: Cultural Perspectives on Media and Christianity* (Horsfield, Hess & Medrano, 2004), was released through the collaborative work of the International Study Commission on Media, Religion and Culture (ISCMRC). The fourth conference was held in Louisville in 2004, followed by the fifth conference, which was held again at the University of Uppsala, Sweden from July 6-9, 2006.

These series of collaborative books, which were a compilation of the works in both international conferences on media, religion and culture, provide a foundational understanding to guide exploration of the interdisciplinary areas of religion, media and culture. To identify the field of studies and update the literature on the study of media, religion and culture, each of the four books provides comprehensive and bibliographic overviews (Clark & Hoover, 1997; Clark, 2002, 2004; Hoover, 2003). In the articles, both authors have pointed out the significant scholarly endeavors of the study of media in the context of changing religion in contemporary society.

The World Association for Christian Communication (WACC) has been one of the pioneering Christian (both academic and activist) bodies to participate in exploring the relationship between religion and media since the 1970s. The primary concern of WACC has been the response of ecumenical Christians to the mediated world as the very nature of the contemporary society. WACC sponsored *Religion and the Media: An introductory reader* (Arthur, 1993). The association also produced three media journals, titled *Media Development*, *Media & Gender Monitor*, and *Media Action*. These journals continue to serve as a platform for the voice of the South, women, and marginalized social groups to speak about human dignity in relation to the issues on media and communication. WACC hosted another international conference on media, religion and culture again in August 2008 in Brazil.

Among other research topics, newspaper representation of religion has stimulated the interests of media scholars. The book *Quoting God: How Media Shape Ideas about Religion and Culture* (Badaracco, 2005) can serve as a guide for textbooks on the power of news media in shaping religion in society. Buddenbaum and Mason (2000) also collected newspaper writings on religion in the United States in *Readings on Religion as News*. Buddenbaum (1996), a former newspaper religion reporter, continued to research on the newspaper coverage on the topic of religion in the United States

With the rapid development of Internet technology, the virtual community is one of the growing research topics in the study of religion. Dawson and Cowan (2004) collected and guided the growing interests in the topics from a sociological and theological perspective. Clark (2003) continues to write about religious meanings among adolescents online. Hoover, with Park (2005), shifted his interests from newspapers to virtual communities upon the emergence of the Internet. Horsfield (2005) provides thoughtful insights on how media is a powerful force in the construction of contemporary society and religion.

Morgan, with Promey, has deepened his interests in the visual image in religious expression (Morgan, 1998, 2002, 2004; Morgan & Promey, 2001). From the constructivist point of view, he argued that the visual image is "construction and maintenance of everyday life" (Morgan, 1998, p. 203). Other historians are focused on the figure of Jesus in American history (Fox,

2004), the materialistic culture of Christianity in America (McDannell, 1995), and the history and theory of art in religious images (Freedberg, 1989).

Lindlof (1996) studied the community's reaction toward the film *The Last Temptation of Christ* as a way of doing audience analysis. He chose Lexington, a city in Kentucky, in July 1988 that successfully persuaded the cancelation of the film showing in town. He analyzed 164 oppositional letters made by the community members to the *Lexington Herald-Leader*, the city's only newspaper. In his conceptual frame, the letters represented the constructed interpretation of the community as a discourse reflecting both pros and cons. In his conclusion, he stated that the film violated a fundamental value of the city's concept of God with this imaginary film medium.

Stout, Scott, and Martin (1996) also studied interpretive community views on mass media. They carefully studied Mormon communities to understand their views on mass media. Two interpretive communities, the traditionalists and independents, emerged, showing different positions and views on secular mass media. In this study, the two religious perspectives of the communities were clearly identified and the interpretive community showed close reliance within the community members in their views on secular media.

The series of seminarial scholarly attempts in the study of media and religion took a cultural approach which has guided this current study. Horsfield argued that the cultural approach of media in the 1990's broadened the evangelical use of media communication from an "instrumental approach" to cultural plurality of meanings (2005, p. 27). He further argued that the cultural and reception theory in media studies could challenge the dominant functional understanding among theologians and church leaders. The current study takes a cultural approach in the study of media and Christian mission. By taking a cultural approach, the study problematizes the reception among religious communities in dealing with the film-form of the Jesus story.

Due to the unique and dominant context of Catholicism and relatively secure religious freedom in broadcasting, Philippine media students have studied religious media topics such as market-oriented media structure, religious program content, and audience of religious programs. This topic of audiences has dominated the students' attempts to understand the related topics of media, religion and culture. Research shows the emphasis on the practical aspects of research data on the viewership (Obordo, 2001; Jonson, 1994, Ispuruyanto, 1999; Velarde, 1999) and content of religious broadcasting in the Philippines (Arinto, 1999; Kooran, 2000).

Besides the series of Philippine studies on religion and media, Pernia, Pascual and Kwon's (2006) study analyzed broadcasting content in the Philippines in order to focus on how personal and interpretive communities played key roles in understanding religious television content. In their study, religious programs were the second most popular format after animation/children's shows and equal to news/current events/ public affairs.

Interestingly, in this research, audiences watched religious programs for entertainment, curiosity and spiritual needs in order to to compare and learn more about religions other than their own.

These findings demonstrated the importance of cultural background in the reception of religious content and active engagement in the construction of meanings of the religious message in the Philippines. Followed by the emerging dialogues in the current religion media and culture, this study takes a cultural and constructive perspective in the understanding of media intertwined with the religious aspects of media. The study further questions how religious audiences, in a different context, have acted upon religious visual messages.

Furthermore, the study distinctively demonstrated the usefulness of the conceptual framework of the interpretive community in the study of Philippine audiences. The emerging fields of study of media, religion and culture actively employ various research methods including ethnography, in-depth interviews, online discourse analysis and others to interpret the perception of religious audiences and non-religious audiences toward supernatural power. Several studies, including Pernia, Pascual and Kwon's (2006) have framed a group of religious audiences as an interpretive community (Fish, 1980). This constructive notion of epistemology that I actively employ in the current study provides new insights on audience reception other than those that are positivist in orientation.

Mangyan Studies

Japanese scholars are noted among the leading scholars in Mangyan studies. Kikuchi (1973a, 1973b, 1974, 1979, 1982) began his study on the leadership and kinship system among the southern ethnic groups in Batangan, Oriental Mindoro, which was based on the Muradake's theory of a cognatic society. He argued that the Batangan-Mangyan group confirmed the bilateral social organization theory that formal political leaders do not exist. It was a "caretaker" and "magico-religious leader" who took primary leadership among traditional Batangan groups (Kikuchi, 1973a, p.7). Miyamoto continued to explore ethnographical studies among the Hanunoo Mangyan group on kinship, leadership, funeral rituals, cosmology, law and other interesting subjects (1975, 1978, 1985, 1988).

The community development work and research of Postma, a Dutch missionary to Hanunoo Mangyan in Oriental Mindoro, needs to be stressed. With more than forty years of missionary service to the Hanunoo Mangyan ethnic group, Postma articulated the social problems and how his mission improved the lives of the people (1974), studied mission history of the land (1977, 1981) and translated into English the only written form of communication, called *Ambahan*, of the Hanunoo Mangyans. With other bibliographic accumulation of written documents regarding Mangyans (1988), the *Ambahan* is it a valuable tool for sociolinguists and anthropologists as they analyze other bibliographic documents.

Socio-historical studies were also conducted by both foreign and Filipino historians. Lopez (1976) provided local perspectives on ethno-historical studies on Iraya and Hanunoo Mangyans. Later, a German historian, Schult (1991) studied the social history of the island of Mindoro. He argued that the various foreign interventions and invasions of the islands caused the "delay in the development of the island in the modern history of the country." With Swedish anthropologist Helbling (2004), they pursued the study of the peaceful nature of the people among Alangan Mangyan in Oriental Mindoro and concluded that the peaceful nature shown throughout the history of the Mangyans is the very survival strategy they used in the face of various threats from outsiders including the Spanish colonizers, Moros, American colonizers and lowland Christianized Filipinos.

Pennoyer, a son of a long-term Protestant missionary, did extensive anthropological research on plants and the rituals of cosmology among Hanunoo Mangyan (1975, 1977, 1980a, 1980b). Later, ethnobotanical studies were continued by the Filipino scholar Mandia (1987, 2004) on the Alangan group in the Northeastern Mindoro. Both researchers argued that the role and the use of plants in the communities are deeply related to social and spiritual life.

Before and after Mandia, there was a group of Filipino scholars who provided an inner perspective on the study of Mangyans. Maceda (1967) did the first descriptive study among the Mangyans in the northern part of Oriental Mindoro. Yet due to the lack of articulated research areas on the topic, the study was rather descriptive and unfocused. Leykamm (1979) studied the diseases and the remedies of the Alangan Mangyan in Oriental Mindoro. Similar to the findings of Pennoyer and Mandia, the researcher argued that the Alangan Mangyans believed the work of evil spirits in various illnesses and depended on the intervention of magico-religious leaders in the remedies. A more scientific study on health-related disease was done by Osteria (1985) among Hanunoo Mangyans in Oriental Mindoro. The research discovered common diseases among the group and proposed suggestions for remedies. Navarro (1993), on the other hand, studied the legal aspects of the land as the ancestral domain of Alangan Mangyans in Oriental Mindoro, while Quiaott (1997) and Feraro-Banta (1985) compared the life and the culture as well as the concept of land between traditional and acculturated groups of Alangan Mangyans. Both confirmed that modernization through the government, foreign missionaries and other factors made significant changes in the life and social structure of the people.

Mangyan studies clearly provided cultural diversity of the Mangyan indigenous groups in Philippine studies. Mangyan indigenous groups have communicated with the lowland Christians and continued to be influenced by them for over four centuries. While previous Mangyan literature provides cultural identities, worldviews and coping strategies in their lives, it is evident that further research is needed in Occidental Mindoro and on the ethnic groups in the Northern part of Mindoro. Furthermore, with the deep religious exchanges with lowland Christian groups, little study has been done on the cultural and religious influences from both Catholic and Protestant Christian groups. This study, therefore, focuses on the distinctive cultural plurality of Mangyan indigenous groups while examining how they contstruct religious meaning as a result of the influence of religious media in modern society.

Synthesis

Based on the literature review, this research is situated in the larger context of contemporary cultural studies in religion and media dialogues. Varieties of studies have discussed the cultural aspects of either religious or media, but have not linked these together. These emerging cultural studies in both religious and media studies still lack focus on the construction of religious meanings (Horsfield, 2005) and the influence of modern media, which in this study is the Jesus-figure film. In the context of globalized media production and its distribution, religious meanings are more questionable in the cross-cultural context of Mangyan indigenous Protestant audiences.

Furthermore, the Horsefield study pointed out the usefulness of the conceptual framework of interpretive community in the study of Philippine audiences. Several studies, including Pernia, Pascual and Kwon's (2006) and Lindlof (1996) have framed a group of religious audiences as an interpretive community (Fish, 1980).

Besides the series of Philippine studies on religion and media (Obordo, 2001; Jonson, 1994; Ispuruyanto, 1999; Velarde, 1999), Pernia, Pascual and Kwon's (2006) study also focused on how personal and interpretive communities played key roles in understanding religious television content. Notably, the study pointed out the importance of cultural context in the reception of religious broadcasting for constructing religious meaning in Philippine context.

Compared to the reviewed literature, the uniqueness of this study is its examination of the local construction of religious meanings over globalized media forms in the religious minority group of the Mangyans in Mindoro of the Philippines. Mangyan studies clearly identify the Mangyan cultural identity as an indigenous group in Philippine studies. Mangyans are considered as the cultural group that has been least studied in the Philippine studies.

Further research is needed in the area of Northern and Occidental part of Mindoro. Furthermore, existing religious studies on indigenous religious practices in the Philippines do not consider the influence of Protestant Christianity, which is significant in contemporary Mangyan culture. Furthermore, religious studies in the Philippine studies are also focused on indigenous religious practices rather than Christians or Protestant influences, which is obvious in the contemporary culture of Mangyans. Therefore, this study is focused on the Protestant religious understanding of Jesus as portrayed to audiences of a Jesus-figure film, the *Jesus* film.

Chapter 3
Study Framework

Integrated Theoretical Framework

This study is rooted in the constructionist perspective understanding of the meaning-making process, which was spontaneously constructed from media exposure within a particular context. The theoretical frames that were used in this study were 1) social construction of reality by Berger and Luckmann, 2) encoding/decoding theory of Stuart Hall, 3) discourse, ideology and 3) the interpretive community of Stanley Fish. Social construction of reality provided the way that the message has been constructed, and at the same time, gave clues to how the message was received. From the theoretical frameworks, the message constructed was bound by the social context of the message creator as well as reception of the audience in the communication process. On the other hand, the interpretive community theory that Fish (1980) proposed provided a useful theoretical framework for how the reception was being constructed. In his theory, the meanings were created when the reader/audience consumed the text.

Social Construction of Reality

Berger and Luckmann (1966) turned their interests to the process of how the reality of everyday life was constructed in a society where the traditional sociology of knowledge focused on philosophical and ideological inquiries on the validity of knowledge and history:

> Since our purpose in this treatise is a sociological analysis of the reality of everyday life, more precisely, of knowledge that guides conduct in everyday life, and we are only tangentially interested in how this reality may appear in various theoretical perspectives to intellectuals, we must begin by a clarification of that reality as it is available to the common sense of the ordinary members of society (p. 19).

The authors saw social and interpersonal interaction as the crucial mode in the process of the construction of reality in everyday life. They borrowed the concept of social interaction theory from symbolic interactionists, saying that through interaction, the members of society negotiate the identification or typification of daily activities (p. 31). They emphasized the use of linguistic signs and symbols in the social negotiation process. Interpersonal interaction among human beings became the process of the objectification of the knowledge of everyday life by subjective intention through language.

In maintaining subjective reality, the authors pointed out the roles of maintenance and power which were required to make this possible. They emphasized the role of language and conversation as the most important vehicle in maintaining subjective reality (p. 152). In media studies, scholars attempted to see the conversational role as interactions between audiences and the media messages. The interactive feature of human action supported the intersubjective sequence of institutionalization and the legitimation process. In power to maintain reality, the power of elite again creates the monopoly of the power and knowledge. As a consequence of the elites' power, pure theory developed and the stability of the society creates a tendency to become stable as long as no significant threat occurs.

As to what was widely criticized, the social construction of reality was super-theoretically framed, which was difficult to operationalize into specific empirical research. As reviewed throughout the paper, the theory has often borrowed ideas from several authors from several traditions. Instead of construction of a theory or frame, social construction of reality was indeed a compilation of existing theories and thoughts primarily from the sociology of knowledge.

Yet, the theory sounds theoretically and conceptually reasonable and provides a visual flowchart of the process of knowledge and reality building. This social construction of knowledge theory provides a conceptual frame that interprets the production process of the *Jesus* film in a mass-mediated Christian context. The Christian media produced within a Western social and religious context and the epistemological input made a great deal of impact on the creation of the Western Jesus in the medium of film.

Encoding/Decoding Theory in British Cultural Studies

British cultural studies was born and developed as a result of the long struggles and debates of ideology, which was a dominated way of thinking, and nurtured by various interdisciplinary discourses. Beginning in the 1960s in Britain, "culturalism" or "culturalist" has been developed as one of three "contending paradigms" in Marxist media theory (Gurevitch, Bennet, Curran, & Woolacott, 1982, p. 8). The three paradigms used by structuralist and political economists have articulated their distinctive perspectives on the culture correlating and interacting with each other. These traditions are inter-affected, accepting and rejecting particular ideas and theories within each other.

British cultural studies have focused on the analysis of ideological domination and is still critical in its stance. It emphasizes the critical interpretation of the various forms of ideology in contemporary society, especially in the form of media. Hardt argues:

> Critical Studies is a specifically British critique of contemporary culture within Western Marxism; reminiscent of the Frankfurt School in the United States more than thirty years ago, it represents the quality and intensity of an intellectual commitment to a critique of ideological domination and political power (1992, p. 173).

The purpose of cultural studies is to reveal the ideological force in society and to interpret the dominated ideology to disfranchise that ideology. Therefore, action is necessary to realize the belief in society. But post-Marxists are reluctant to push physical revolution; instead, only suggesting ideological struggle to provide alternate suggestions to society (Littlejohn, 2001, p. 232). Hall himself also suggested that media is a "public forum" in which various ideas and ideologies can meet and shape popular culture in consensus (qtd. in Baran and Davis, 1995, p. 322).

In the formation of British cultural studies, there were a few theoretical backgrounds. Specifically, the tradition began with a series of literary and sociology scholars in England, who focused on understanding culture as human activities that have participated in making human history (Hoggart, 1958; Williams, 1975, 1977; Thomson, 1978). They were later called "culturalist," which was a distinction from "determinist" from early Marxism. The founding figure of British cultural studies, Stuart Hall, agreed to "culturalist" in the notion of culture as dominated by the prevailing ideology of society from the early critical tradition, the Frankfurt School, but diversified his notion from the "hypodermic" effect of the media on audiences. Hall leaned more towards the uses and gratifications theory in which the audience actively participated in the reception of the powerful media text. In his notable polygamy audience reception theory, the "encoding/decoding" model was built on the semiotics of Barthes, Frank Parkin's meaning systems, and Louis Althusser's media as ideological state apparatuses (Hall, 1980).

British scholars such as Paul Gilroy, Dick Hedige, Angela McRobbie and David Morley further developed culturalist perspectives in cultural studies, particularly in reception studies (Curran, Morley & Walkerdine, 1996). Contrary to the early screen theories that emphasized textual analysis, proponents of reception theorists turned their attention to the complicated audiences' interpretation of the texts. Furthermore, various advocates of cultural studies have been scattered around the world to analyze their contemporary cultures, which have been deeply interested in the projection of media messages.

British cultural studies has contributed to the diversification of humanity's understanding of what makes a culture. Hall (1997) problematized the anthropological concept of culture as a political notion, saying that culture was ideological and political. He discussed the ideological and political effects of reception on active or passive audiences. Surely, British cultural studies attempted to identify one Ideological State Apparatus (ISA), which media brings significant impact on in the serious attempts on the process of Westernizing the visual icon of Jesus in contemporary society.

The theoretical tradition of popular and sub-cultural arguments from mainstream mass culture can provide a significant foundation from which to analyze contemporary Christian culture in a cross-cultural context. As mentioned in the introduction, a new paradigm of Western-oriented, mediated and massive capital-oriented missions aggressively transported the visual message throughout the world. In this context, British cultural tradition provides a clear theoretical foundation, which gives a clear framework to understand the Westernized ideologies of Christian culture in contemporary times.

Yet the British cultural studies tradition does not provide a firm ground for cross-cultural media studies in indigenous culture. The cultural context that British cultural scholars delved into has been industrialized society and the audiences whose lives have matured outside of technology and media. Hall's negotiated or preferred reading of the text may or may not be consistent with the indigenous audience that has never been exposed to media messages during their entire lives. How does this indigenous audience perceive religious meanings from this Western-oriented and ideologized media message? Furthermore, how does the reception of the visualized religious message play a role in the construction of religious meanings, which is intertwined with social and religious contexts? This series of questions supports and directs this study.

British cultural scholars, such as Hall, began to think of the media's effect on the perception of the audience in the formation of contemporary culture. Among the early scholars in British cultural studies, Hall presented sound theoretical formulation toward a critical notion of great media effects theory in a neo-Marxist response to the functionalist understanding of gratification over media use. That is called the encoding/decoding theory (Hall, 1980).

Under Hall's theoretical guidance, this theory provided abundant empirical testing grounds for how audiences have actively engaged in the meaning-making process during the 1980s. One of his followers was Morley, who further tested the different decoding process of British audiences based on the social strata on the "Nationwide" program (1980). Morley focused on how readers of the ideological text interpreted the typical text in their experiences. Therefore, Morley (1980, 1992) researched different social levels of audiences for TV, tested with whom they would react, and how they interpreted the same message on TV. In his study, he utilized the theoretical conception of Hall's (1980) encoding and decoding model using the empirical method. The result was interesting in that readers from a variety of social classes reacted to and interpreted the same same ideological text differently. Although he admitted that the research exaggerated the oppositional reading of those audiences later, the ideological struggles taken part in the situation of Television viewing was significant in sparking a series of research projects in the years to come.

Hall's encoding/decoding theory began with the a series of British literary and sociology traditions that focused on understanding culture as human activities that have participated in making human history (Hoggart, 1958; Williams, 1975, 1977; Thomson, 1978). Named as "culturalist" that distinguished it from "determinist" from early Marxism, Hall agreed to "culturalist" in the notion of culture as dominated by the prevailing ideology of the society from the early critical tradition, the Frankfurt School. Yet he disagreed with the notion of the "hypodermic" effect of the media on the audiences in the functionalistic sense. Hall leaned more toward the uses and gratifications theory that the audience was actively participating in the reception of a powerful media text. Yet Hall tried to overcome micro-level media effects as well as direct responses and understood media reception as socially structured and culturally patterned. In his polygamy audience reception theory, the "encoding/decoding" model was influenced by the semiotics of Barthes, which attempted to decode the social meanings of signs and symbols, particularly in the mythologies in contemporary culture (Barthes, 1972).

Hall provided his encoding/decoding process of the reception theory. He understood the aspects of television production in three different layers of structure: technical infrastructure of broadcasting institutions; relations of production, using Marx's terminology, the labor in production; and frame of knowledge, which meant the pre-structured knowledge in the production of content. He further explained that the production was encoded through meaning structure, which was also called the "discursive process" in which ideological meanings are created (p. 129). So the end product of the television program became a meaningful discourse that also became the source of multiple meanings for audiences by the decoding process. Yet he never forgot to mention that the decoding process was passed through the preexisting ideological structure of a particular audience, and the meanings were located within, again, the structure of audience that were frameworks of knowledge, relations of production, and technical infrastructure (See Figure 4).

Hall's model conceptualized the three theoretical ideological positions that the audience could take. The first was the "dominant-hegemonic" position, which represented the ideological perspective of the dominant elite and is interpreted by the viewer accordingly. The second was the "negotiated" position that the audiences participated in the dominant ideological impulse to negotiate the meaning of specific situations. The third was that the audiences took an "oppositional" position that disagreed with or decoded the ideologically driven message in order to provide an alternative frame of reference (Hall, 1980, p. 136-138). The possible degrees of reception of the audience provided groundwork for various reception studies afterwards.

Figure 4. *Hall's Encoding/Decoding Model*

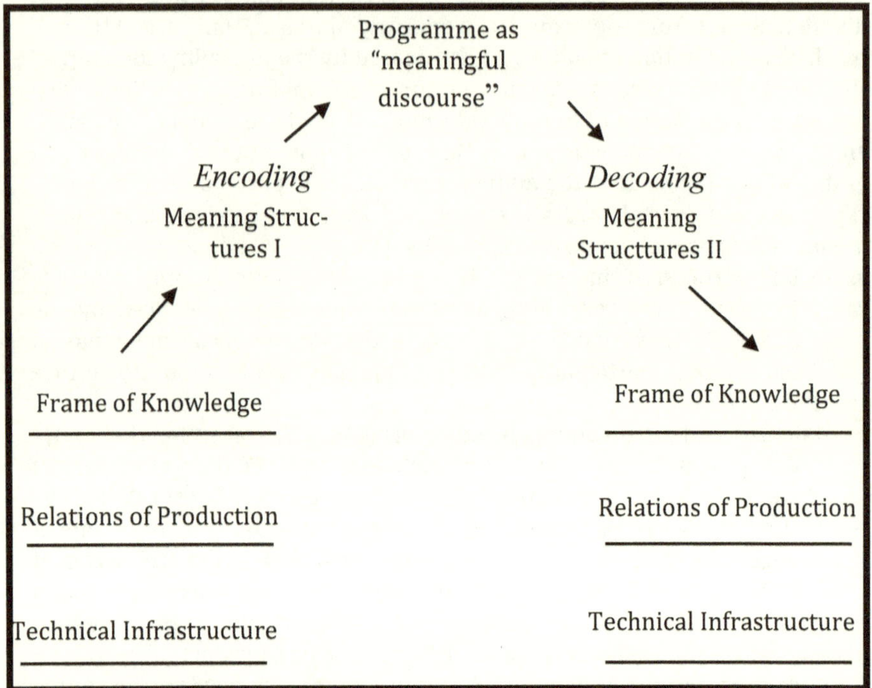

The current study is based on the ideological notion of media texts as meaningful discourse set by Hall and potential multiple meanings among Mangyan audiences. It has been clear that the film has been produced from a Western ideological and Protestant frame of knowledge within the technology of film and DVD authoring infrastructure. This study then focuses on the receptive process of multiple meanings that could be constructed by Mangyan audiences.

Discourse

French philosopher and critic Michel Foucault (1980) proposed the term "discourse" as a systematic knowledge that dominated the power of a society. In his understanding, discourse ordered things in a given society. Discourse was a way of talking about a certain object that constructed it and made its reality. In other words, discourse was produced by repeated social interaction, and then reality was produced by this process.

Discourse is a term referring to "utterances beyond the unit of the sentence and to passages of dialogue" (Brooker, 2003, p. 78). The term was originally used in linguistics to analyze a group of thematic structures that superimposed particular usages in everyday life. Foucault used the term "discourse" or "discursive formation" to refer to a superstructure that dominated the present mode of thought that directly influenced members of society. In his book, the *Archaeology of Knowledge* (2002), Foucault tried to present the existing structure of knowledge, laws, and rules. He argued that the knowledge the society accumulates was the very center of the power that was formed with the social discourse in his series of interviews, *Power/Knowledge* (1980). Foucault further elaborated on his notion of discourse in several of his writings: the creation of prison as a systematic confinement in *The Birth of the Prison* (1975/2003), and the enslavement of sexual pleasure in the *History of Sexuality* I, II, and III (1984, 1988, 1990).

Discourse, in this research, can be interpreted as the process of the Westernization of the visual image of Jesus in Christian history, which has been reflected in film media in the contemporary society. Brooker further explained discourse as a social "episteme" (2003, p. 79); thus, the visualization of Jesus was the very construction of religious episteme that has been nurtured over hundreds of years. The collaborative works of Western Christian churches in history have come out of constructing the "Western Jesus" in numerous ways. There has been a systematic construction of the Western Jesus as a cultural icon, evidenced by paintings, murals, stained glass on the church walls and windows, visual drawings on devotional materials, pictures of Jesus on the walls of Christian houses, and other places (Morgan, 1998; Morgan & Promey, 2001). In a visually oriented society, Western-based Christian film industries have also presented a series of Jesus-figure films in the episteme-making process. Using discourse theory, I argue that the process of a systematic visual production system of Western Jesus, which is represented in the *Jesus* film, is a way of discursive formation, as what Foucault termed in a Christian context. This theory provides a framework to understand the message of the reception process.

Ideology

The term "ideology" was first developed by Karl Max and Friedrich Engels to refer to the "ideas of the ruling class" that were perpetuated in every epoch (Marx, 1846/1995, p. 47). The ruling ideas purposely maintained the prevailing social order in order to manipulate the social mode of production. Therefore, from the perspective of the working class, ideology was the "false consciousness" that distorts their reality. Marx's idea of ideology was further developed by the neo-Marxist, Louis Althusser, who said the way of understanding the world and reality was a social "practice" in which everyone in the society participated to some extent (1971). Gramsci then used the term ideology for a social struggle that maintained and enlarged consensus at a satisfactory level (2005). The term ideology was first articulated as a false consciousness to blind the eyes of the working class and was later broadened to define a perspective that was formed by society as a window to understanding the world.

With Foucault's use of the term discourse, ideology was used to construct a system of reality. It was a systematic force that mediated the Westernization process of Christian religion. In contemporary visual society, various Christian practices were formulated by the Western churches. The ways in doing systematic theology, hymnals or PowerPoint, traditional and contemporary Christian music, religious icons and visuals, and devotional materials were the systematic ways of forcing Western Christianity, which Althusser explained as ISA. These apparatuses mediated Western-oriented Christianity, which was used as a Western Christian ideology in this study.

The concept of ideology provides the theoretical framework to position the *Jesus* film in the dominant Western construction of Christianity. Western ideology has been the center of criticism in critical studies in media studies. In this study, the Western representation of Jesus in the film was problematized as a way of Western construction of Christianity, which became the dominant ideology in contemporary Christianity.

Figure 5 explains the integrated theoretical framework. Based on Hall's encoding/decoding theory, the aspects of television production (in this study, film production) are structured in three different layers: technical infrastructure of broadcasting (in this study, film) institutions; relations of production (using Marx's terminology, the labor in production); and frame of knowledge, which refers to the pre-structured knowledge in the production of content that is located on the production side in this reception process.

Production, then, was encoded through meaning structures I, which was also called the "discursive process" in which ideological meanings are created (p. 129). This discursive process was interpreted from the notion of discourse by Foucault on page 44. So the end product of the television program became a meaningful discourse that also became the source of multiple meanings for audiences by the decoding process, which is meaning structures II. The decoding process was passed through the pre-existing ideological structure of a particular audience, and the meanings were located within, again, the structure of audience: frameworks of knowledge, relations of production, and technical infrastructure (See Figure 5).

Yet Hall's model conceptualized the three ideological positions that the audience could interpret. The first was the "dominant-hegemonic" position, which represented the ideological perspective of the dominant elite and is interpreted by the viewer accordingly. The second was the "negotiated" position that the audiences participated in the dominant ideological impulse to negotiate the meaning of specific situations. The third was that the audiences took an "oppositional" position that disagreed with or decoded the ideologically driven message in order to provide an alternative frame of reference (Hall, 1980, p. 136-138). The possible degrees of reception of the audience provided groundwork for various reception studies afterwards.

Represented as arrows from production to the audience sides, the reception process was interpreted as the construction process for creating the social reality. The construction process was that of social and interpersonal interaction in everyday life, including situations involving mass communication. Interpersonal interaction became the process of the objectification of the knowledge of everyday life by subjective intention through social sign and symbols.

Figure 5. Integrated Theoretical Framework

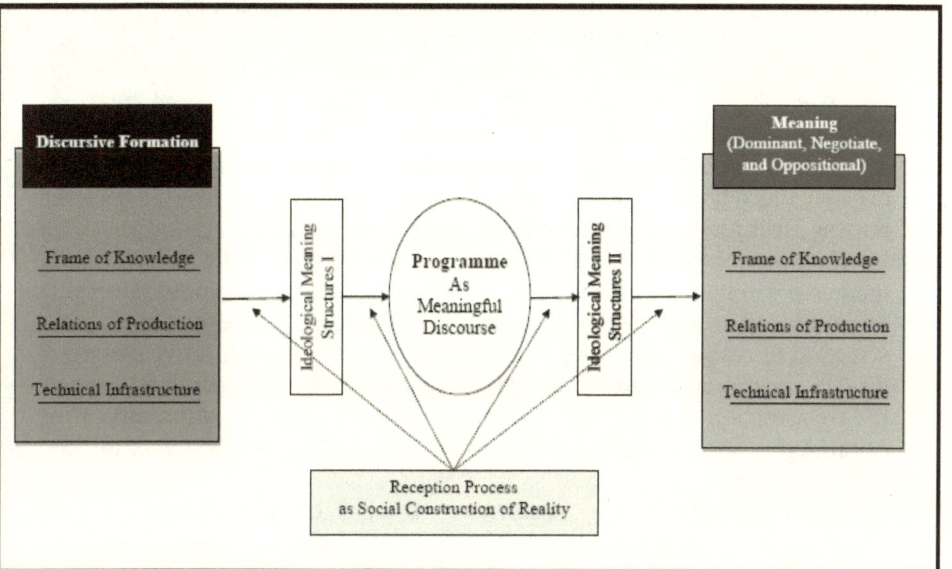

Integrated Conceptual Framework

Evangelical Christians have emphasized communicating cross-culturally. Jesus, born in the Jewish religion, proclaimed that his salvation message was to be communicated to the world (Matthew 28:19-20; Acts 1:8). In the center of cross-cultural communication in Christian mission, missionaries have gradually realized that "cultures" are crucial elements for their purposes of communicating cross-culturally. Several anthropological studies in Christian mission have developed the concept of "contextualization" based on the deep understanding of culture in the communication process (Nida, 1954, 1960, 1968; Hiebert, 1985; Kraft, 1986; Hesselgrave, 1989). These studies evaluated past missionary efforts and concluded that missionaries lacked an understanding of cultures in different contexts.

Global Protestant mission is being challenged by globalized and mass-mediated society. The development of information and communication technology directed by Western countries, the United States in particular, has accelerated Christian missions more than ever in Christian history. With the financial power of United States-based mission agencies, visual images of Christianity have been created in the Western context that have caused the construction of a Western image of Jesus as an ideological apparatus for over a century. Therefore, the construction of the Western face of Jesus is considered as the discursive formation of the Christian image of Jesus that has gradually been constructed in Christian history.

The effect of a Westernized Christian message on a non-Western audience seemed to be irresistible by state of the art media technology. The perceived message was somewhat bound to the message perpetuated through mass media. The two elements, globalization through mass media, played as two axes of the transmission of Christian message. The globalized strategy of the Christian message led to a Western articulation of Christian message. Through the globalized expansion of Western culture, ideology and a Westernized visual image of Jesus and construction of the life of Jesus, a certain message was then received by non-Western audiences.

The model (see Figure 6) provides the integration of the theories and models presented above. Borrowing Hall's encoding and decoding process of multiple meanings, the model has been modified to include social construction of reality, discourse, and ideology, as well as interpretive community, to conceptualize the research framework as a way of understanding the construction of religious meanings within a particular community. The community certainly plays a considerable role in the construction of meaning of its members.

Media production in a Western context has been formulated in the structure that Hall has provided: frame of knowledge, relations of production, and technical infrastructure. The structure consisted of the discursive formation that constructs the Westernized image of Jesus and his life. This construction process provides the *Jesus* film as a meaningful discourse to the audiences in Mangyan Christian communities.

On the other hand, Mangyan audiences have decoded the discursive text through the established Christian beliefs system in their media, social and religious contexts, which construct the religious meanings (interpretation of the film). The meanings can be, based on Hall's theory, diverted with dominant, negotiate and oppositional meanings.

Considered to be an anti-formalist and post-modernist, Fish (1980) argued that construction of meaning took place within the reader's interpretation of the text. It was epistemologically different from the traditional approach in textual analysis in literature circles. Fish further articulated that the interpretation of the text is within the community in which the reader was located. Understanding of the text was not purely within the self but constructed within the interaction and communication taking place in a particular context (Lang, 2007).

The concept of interpretive community has been influential in media studies, especially in the study of audiences (Littlejohn, 2001). In subcultural groups, the communal construction of meanings was more distinctive than personal interpretation such as African-American reading of the comedy, *Cosby Show* (Jhally & Lewis, 2003), the reading of African-American women of *The Color Purple* (Bobo, 2003), the national difference in reception of *Dallas* (Liebes & Katz, 2003), and the reading of *The Last Temptation of Christ* by the religious community (Lindlof, 1996). According to Lindlof, media audiences became an interpretive community forming a consensual discourse that shares the group experience:

> What seems as the key to the interpretive community is the idea of a special discourse made up of the appropriate social occasions and rules of using them. The discourse grows out of people's experiences with the histories, pleasures, and problems of social collectivities in which media use is a core activity. Notions of audience and community merge in such a way as to lose the disadvantages of social isolation in the former and locational fixity in the latter (Lindlof, 1996, p.152).

In the study of religion and media interconnections, religious communities often naturally become interpretive communities. The members of any religious group have easily formed a certain degree of religious identity. Lindlof's study (1996) on the community's reaction toward the film *The Last Temptation of Christ*; Stout, Scott, and Martin' study (1996) on Mormon views on the perception towards mass media; and Pernia, Pascual and Kwon's (2006) study also borrowed the concept of interpretive communities in understanding religious television content. All of these studies agreed to conceptualize the media reception as collective interactions within the context where the media reception took place.

In this reception study, Fish's interpretive community was adopted as the communal interpretation of the mediated message. The reception of religious message was being interpreted by the community of the Mangyan ethnic group. The religious meanings that were constructed out of the exposure to the film were inevitably a shared experience within the community.

It was also noted that the reception of religious meanings could be plural and collective perceptions of the community of believers. Fish's interpretive community provides a useful frame for understanding the collective reading of the *Jesus* film as a perception of the religious groups. It was, based on Fish's theoretical frame, the collective construction and understanding of the community members in the reception of the message.

Figure 6. Integrated Conceptual Framework

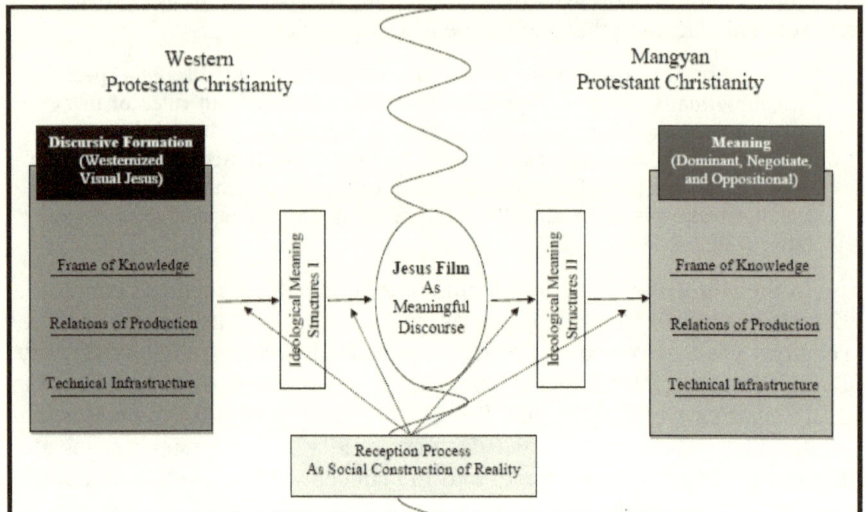

Operational Framework

The model (see Figure7) shows the operational level of the conceptual frame of this study. Media production in a Western context has been formulated in the structure: frame of knowledge, relations of production, and technical infrastructure. Globalized media productions have been equipped with current film production and digital authoring technology (technical infrastructure) that has enabled digitalization of the Westernized image of Jesus (frame of knowledge) in a mobile format; with technology and human resources (relations of production) constructing the Westernized Jesus in film media. The structure consists of the discursive formation that constructs the Westernized image of Jesus and his life. This construction process, which was encoded into film format, provides the *Jesus* film as a meaningful discourse to the audiences in Mangyan Christian communities.

On the other hand, Mangyan audiences have decoded the discursive text of film through established Christian beliefs system in their media, as well as social and religious contexts that construct the religious meanings (interpretation of the film). Although the effects of the Westernized visual image of Jesus and construction of the life of Jesus through mass media was inevitable, there was no such guarantee that the message was to be retrieved as it had been projected. The reception process was placed within the religious, social and media contexts in which the audience was located. These meanings can be, based on Hall's theory, diverted with dominant, negotiate and oppositional reading. Yet it is important to note that the religious meanings have been constructed through the particular religious, social and media contexts in which the Mangyan audiences were situated.

In this study, the Mangyan Protestant religious group on Mindoro Island was chosen to be the non-Western audience in the reception process. Particularly placed within unique religious, social and media contexts, the Mangyan audiences provided the religious meanings that they constructed from exposure to the *Jesus* film. In a community that has been influenced to a certain level by the Catholic religion, yet also contained indigenous religious beliefs and practices, the social situation, as well as the level of media exposure that were interpreted by media acquisition and use, will certainly affect the reception of the film. Familiarity with the use of modern technology may be other indicators for understanding the level of technical acceptance among Mangyan audiences. The Protestant community of selected Mangyan audiences who were particularly placed in the religious, social and media context constructed multiple meanings about their religiosity and the Western Jesus out of the projected message via the *Jesus* film.

Figure 7. Operational Framework

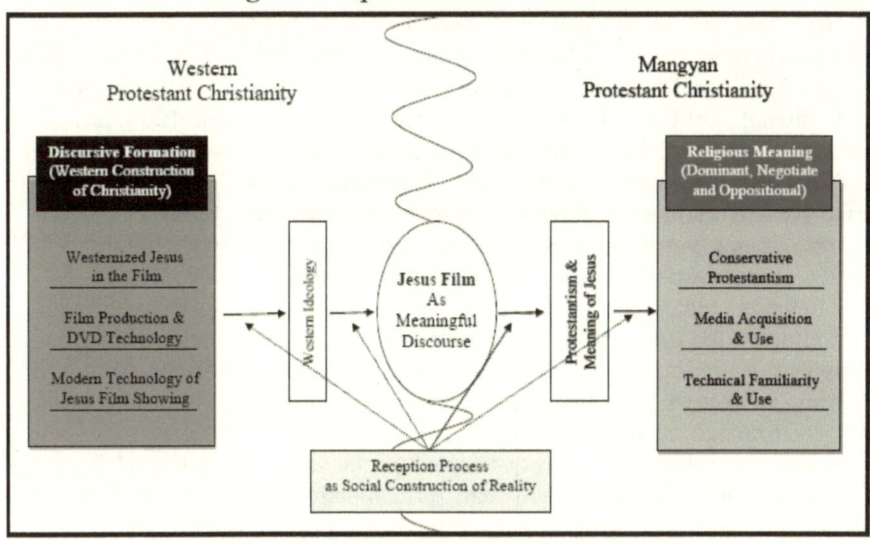

Operational Definition of Terms

Religious Community

Religious community is a coherent group of people that has come to form a shared meaning of any religious beliefs. The definition of community means the ideas of what people have *in common*, as in common goods, interests, customs, identity and faith (Williams, 1983, quoted in Lindlof, 1996, p. 150). Lindlof further explained that the members of a certain community have obligations to fulfill and maintain the community, which is in contrast to the concept of audience.

This study took the interpretive community of Fish (1980) as a framework to define the religious community. He argued that the meaning being understood from a text was constructed in the process of reading and interacting with readers (in visual text, it was the audience). Contrary to the extreme post-constructionists and post-modernists notion of meanings, he also argued that the meanings constructed in the individuals were influenced by the context of the community in which the individuals were located.

Therefore in this study, the term religious community was used to refer to a group of sitio Mangyans who shared a religious identity that had been influenced by the social and religious context.

Religious Meanings

Over the course of several decades, scholars have come up with different definitions of religious experience according to their theoretical and philosophical traditions. In sociology, Durkheim saw religion as a "social thing" that represented "collective realities" (1912/1995, p. 9 & 44). In contrast, Weber argued that "understanding of this [religious] behavior could only be achieved from the viewpoint of the subjective experiences, ideas, and purposes of the individuals concerned" (brackets added, 1963, p, 1). In this apparently different approach to defining religion and the religious experience, Berger tried to negotiate the space for the integration of the two paradigms by providing an inductive method that stands in the Weberian stance, yet he also made an attempt to include Durkheimian social and collective aspects to study religion and religious meaning.

Religious meanings, in this study, are defined as the constructed understanding of God through the external visual mediation, the *Jesus* film and its implication for one's life. "*Verstehen*" (understanding), derived from Weberian subjective meanings, were constructed through interaction and shared practice within the society. It was assumed that the constructed and practiced meanings were surely affected by the social and religious context in which people belonged. Through the collective action of watching the *Jesus* film, the Mangyans, as a community audience in a remote culture, would attempt to perceive religious meaning intertwined with the prestructured social and religious experience to create a new religious experience and meaning for Jesus and the Christianity.

Jesus-figure and Christ-figure Film

Jesus-figure film is the term that describes a group of films that explicitly deal with the life and the ministry of Jesus in its content. In a sense, it was inevitable that Jesus's life would be portrayed. Tatum listed 15 representative Jesus-figure films chronologically using the term "Jesus-story" films

(2004, p. 19). Some of well known Jesus-figure films include *Ben-Hur* by William Wyler, *King of Kings* by Samuel Bronston, *The Greatest Story Ever Told* by George Stevens, *The Gospel According to St. Matthew* by Pier Paulo Pasolini, *Jesus Christ Superstar* by Norman Jewison, *Godspell* by David Greene, *Jesus of Nazareth* by Franco Zeffirelli, *Life of Brian* by Monty Python, *Jesus* by John Heyman, *The Last Temptation of Christ* by Martin Scorsese, *Jesus of Montreal* by Danys Arcand, and the most recent film, *The Passion of the Christ* by Mel Gibson.

In this listing, the *Life of Brian* and *Jesus of Montreal* are somewhat problematic. In the *Life of Brian*, Jesus is not the main character, but Brian, who is portrayed as a contemporary of Jesus and who encountered the life and ministry of Jesus serves as the main character. It was called a biblical comedy and unique in its treatment of some of the important biblical accounts (Tatum, 2004). Meanwhile, *Jesus of Montreal* is also problematic in belonging to the classification of Jesus-figure films as the film is about a story of a young drama actor, Daniel Coulombe, who battles a social and racial dilemma in the 20th century in Quebec. Tatum pointed to this film as a Jesus-figure film because it "was re-visualized, but paralleled to - and intersected with - modern story" (Tatum, 2004, p. 195). However, Baugh (1997) classified the film as a Christ-figure film. This confusion reflects the ongoing discussions and trials in defining the fields of study in theology and film as well as Jesus-figure films and Christ-figure films.

Christ-figure film is the term used to describe films that portray the implicit theme of the Christ in addition to savior-like themes or figures whose message could be compared to the life and ministry of Jesus. This term was developed by theologians whose interest lay in the exegesis of theological themes from secular and commercial films. Due to the wide variety of film genres and its offshoots, the definition and classifications are somewhat problematic and unclear. For instance, Kozlovic described twenty-five structural characteristics of the so-called Christ-figure films, arguing that the Christ-figure film could be a "legitimate pop culture phenomenon, and that as a living genre, its usage was undiminished in the foreseeable future" (2004). Recalling the very article of Kozlovic, Deacy (2006) severely criticized the structure as artificial and based on false assumptions. Baugh (1997) listed the models of the Christ-figure films including the saint, the priest, women, and some other extreme figures such as clown, fool, madman, the child, dramatic role of Jesus, and the popular adventure hero. All of the models have abundant examples in popular films.

Chapter 4

Methodology

Research Design

Using a qualitative ethnographic approach, the reception study was intended to understand the religious construction of meanings and the meanings constructed from the Western representation of the visual Jesus in the film among ethnic groups in Mangyan communities in Mindoro, where the *Jesus* film was shown and systematic activities have been implemented to achieve the goal of evangelization.

The interpretive paradigm has guided this study, which allows the researcher to interact in the process of constructing meanings that Denzin and Lincoln (2000) modeled as interpretive researchers. An interpretive researcher tries to find different materials and methods to assemble the elements in order to make a complete artwork to construct multiple meanings (Geertz, 1973) that spontaneously flow from the interactions and encounters with people and events in this media audience and film text. This research process was a progressive construction of meanings from the reception of acculturated Christian Mangyans by observing participation in the actual film showing and interviewing the audiences as well as the coordinators.

Methods

The reception method was used in this study for effective and relevant audience evaluation of a particular media. In British cultural studies, it was Morley (1986) who implemented this in his study of television reception among English households. He participated in television consumption by direct observation and conducted interviews in the households where media consumption took place in order to interactively gather meanings from different audiences in their everyday lives.

> The value of ethnographic methods lies precisely in their ability to help us 'make things out' in the context of their occurrence - in helping us to under-

stand the television viewing and other media consumption practices as they are embedded in the context of everyday life (Morley, 1986).

The distinctive feature of this reception study from other audience studies was the interactivity and dynamics between audience and text. Some functional approaches such as the uses and gratifications method in audience studies tended to focus on the reactions and perceptions of audiences and neglected the influence of the presence of an ideological impulse in media texts. For this reason, Pernia (2003) argued that the reception method was the method developed within mass communication studies that could usefully analyze audience perception within the presence of the media and text interactively. Focused on the interactivity and context of the audience in the media environment, this method was a vehicle to provide extended analysis beyond direct effects of the perception from the text.

Numerous methods were added in order to weave the audience reception into a final "quilt." At the initial stage, several interviews were conducted with Mangyans, the *Jesus* film coordinators, pastors of the community and others, which contributed to the meaningful patterns in the quilt making. Following the schedule and the ministry of the film team, participant observation was possible for this study. During field study, photographs were taken for visual documentation and interpretation.

Interviews were conducted during the film showing and in the houses of the audiences on the following day. Interview informants were primarily chosen with the help of Ptr. Santiago Lekwenyan (henceforth Santi) and *datu* Mr. Rodolfo Sambutan (henceforth Roding), who facilitated the film showing in the two sitios. Besides the interviews on the ministry site, additional interviews with the audiences, the *Jesus* film ministers, facilitators, and seminary students were targeted to take multiple layers of meaning (Geertz, 1973). (See Appendix A-1, 2 and 3 for interview guides).

Observation was intensively used during three consecutive film showings in the community and during field work. Tedlock (2000) argued the use of "observation of participation" as the method more inclined to the subjective and interpretive strategy compared to the term "participant observation," as objective and positivist researchers have used. The observation of participation method allowed me to observe the viewing behaviors of the Mangyan audience and to make more vivid descriptions (See Appendix B).

Participating in the film showing, the audiences were inevitable in the study. The reception of the Mangyan groups was a good example of community interpretation (Fish, 1980). In the film showing, Mangyans formed small groups of five to ten people and constantly interacted with the scenes showing from the screen. Children, women and men sat together without much order on the ground. Naturally, they formed various interpretive communities in which the research was framed. Careful observation was used to detect reception patterns, reactions, words and even gestures of the people. Ptr. Santi and Erwin were helpful whenever interesting reactions and short discussions occurred in the audiences. Ptr. Santi and his brother Erning M. Lekwenyan (henceforth Erning) helped translate the audiences' conversation into English. In times of difficulty, Erwin also helped in translating Tagalog into English during the film showing.

Visual methods were used to vividly capture the description of Mangyan contexts, as well as to describe the film showing ministry and the reception of Mangyan audience. Payne and Payne said, "visual methods cover all uses of images, with or without accompanying words, such as photographs, video, film, television, or hand-drawn artwork, whether pre-existing or generated as part of the research process, as data for social research purposes" (2004, p. 238). This was one of the methods that recently gained popularity among cultural scholars and anthropologists to overcome the positivist notion of empiricism and to reflect the visually oriented world (Harper, 2004; Pink, 2004). The visual ethnography of David (1978) studying street life in Manila provides an excellent example of how visual methods were used in interpretive sociological analysis. In addition to photography, the film clips were captured and used for analysis of the reception of the Mangyans.

In this study, the reception of the film was considered as the visual method of elicitation and interpretation with the visual images in order to stimulate the perceptions and meanings of the interview informants (Harper, 2000, 2004; Pink, 2004; Ball & Smith 1992, p. 314 quoted in Marvasti, 2004). The *Jesus* film was the very stimulation of the elicitation in the study of religious meanings among Mangyan community members.

Research Instruments

For the nature of in-depth observations and interviews in this study, the primary research instrument was my personal observation before, during and immediately after the *Jesus* film ministry. An observation guide was prepared based on the problems and purposes of this study (See Appendix B).

In the interviews with Mangyans and coordinators and the *Jesus* film ministers, an open-ended interview guide was used to make the interview smooth, flowing and focused (See Appendix A-1, 2 and 3). Yet the main role of the guide was to support and let the interview informants actively express their experiences of the *Jesus* film ministry in the past.

In addition to the interviews, the previous focus group discussion with seminary students held in 2005 was also added. For the previous research, the primary attempt was to understand how seminary students who came from different national and cultural backgrounds perceived the Western Jesus from the film. Theological students in the focus group discussion came from the Philippines, Thailand, Taiwan and Japan. This focus group discussion data will be further analyzed to strengthen this study (See Appendix B).

Research Area

The research was done in the three sitios of Siyapo, Baraas and Calamias, which are located in the northern part of Occidental Mindoro. The first local contact in this study, Ptr. Santi, proposed six places as the target of his ministry area (see Red dots on Figure 8). Barangay Barahan was the place where Ptr. Manad lives, and sitio Siyapo was where Ptr. Santi lives. In sitio Siyapo, Ptr. Santi proposed sitio Landing, Baraas, Dapdap and Ranao. Considering the accessibility, convenience and needs of the film showing, Ptr. Santi decided on sitio Siyapo, Baraas and Dapdap for this showing, while sitios Landing, Dapdap and Ranao were dropped due to the complexity in the schedule.

Figure 8. Locale of the Study

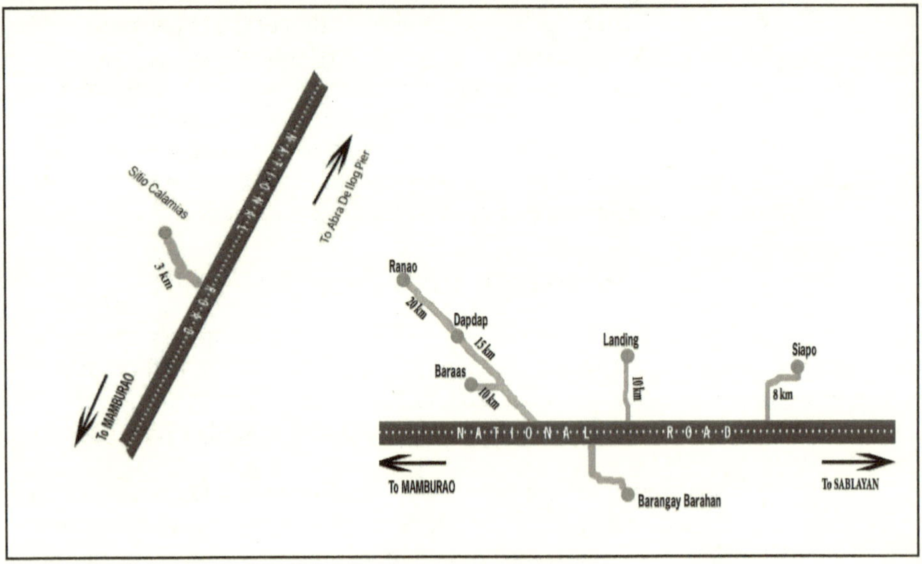

Research Procedures

Besides Ptr. Santi's contact, Ptr. Manad had established another contact with the Iraya Mangyan settlement called sitio Calamias, which was located in Barangay Cabacao in the Municipality of Abra de Ilog. Ptr. Manad strongly wanted to spend one day for this group, since he was establishing barangay Bagong Silang. Ptr. Manad was sure of the evangelical effects of the film showing on this group. As was usual in the negotiation process, Rev. Tino rightly accepted this suggestion and agreed to investigate the Siyapo Calamias for the last the *Jesus* film ministry among Mangyans in Occidental Mindoro.

Unlike typical ethnographic studies, the process for choosing the research site was a bit different from the usual research pattern. The search for the site began during the early conceptualization process. Contact with the *Jesus* film ministry in the Philippines was made in early 2007 through the Philippine Field Office of the Church of the Nazarene. Yet the communication was not made until the Field Strategy Coordinator, Rev. David Philips, an American missionary to the Philippines, was involved. He granted me permission to do this study under his jurisdiction and called a meeting with the National *Jesus* film coordinator, Rev. Elmo. During the meeting, the *Jesus* film coordinator presented a year-round showing plan and briefed me on the sites and their conditions. After a careful discussion, everyone agreed that the Mangyans in Mindoro would be the best research subjects for the period of this study, which was scheduled for February 2008.

The next step that Rev. Philips and Elmo recommended was to meet DS Tino and his *Jesus* film team, who have worked for the ministry for some time. For background understanding, some initial interviews were done with the experienced local *Jesus* film coordinators during the Southern Tagalog District Assembly. Interviews were recorded and later translated. In the meeting, DS Tino and Ptr. George Junio (henceforth Junio) agreed to be the part of their *Jesus* film team and allowed this research during their film showing.

Due to the tight schedule of the film showing plan, an immediate preliminary visit to the places where the *Jesus* film ministry was to be shown was not an option. As a qualitative researcher, the research should not have been limited by time. But in this study, the nature of research in which the schedule was set forced the research period to be limited to before and after the film showing, which was scheduled for February.

For the first field visit made on January 2008, DS Tino guided me and my research assistant, Erwin Galino, who helped me translate Tagalog to English and took photographs in the field. Travel time for the visit took more than twelve hours. Erwin and I left Antipolo at 3 a.m. and arrived at Batangas port at ten minutes before 6 a.m. We were able to take a boat going to Abra De Ilog at Occidental Mindoro by 6 a.m. The ferry boat that we boarded was called "RoRo", which meant "Roll On, Roll Off" and carried vehicles across bodies of water. However, Tino pronounced the word as if it meant "slow" in Tagalog. The ferry boat brought us down to Abra by around 9 a.m. and we had to take a bus going to Bgy. Barahan for another two and a half hours where the informant, Ptr. Manad, lived. By driving another ten minutes by tricycle from the bus stop at barangay Barahan, we arrived at Ptr. Manad's house.

On this visit, I also had a chance to meet key informants for this research and was able to interview some of them. Ptr. Manad was one of the key coordinators for this showing. Other key Mangyan pastors; Ptr. Santi and his assistants were helpful to guide to other possible two sitios for film showing. Named as Indigenous Christian Churches of the Philippines (henceforth ICCP) and Ptr. Santi also agreed to guide and also participate in the group interviews (see Figure 9, Ptr. Santi is the one in the middle of the group looking at the camera).

Interestingly, the *Jesus* film team and I encountered some challenges with the "*kuyay*" (elder) of the sitio. At this time, little was known about the procedure for getting permission to enter the Mangyan community. The *kuyay* of this sitio carefully approached Ptr. Santi and the team to ask about their permission to enter the sitio. Later, Ptr. Santi told that he was the leader of a Catholic group, Pantribong Samahan Sa Kanlurang Mindoro, (henceforth, PASAKAMI) which was strongly opposed to the work of Ptr. Santi and his church in this community. This interruption made the team aware of the opposition that was possible at any of the film showings, and so I tried to secure the legal permits to allow this study in these areas. Later, a permission letter to the National Commission on Indigenous peoples (NCIP) was sent and permission was granted from Atty. Arthur K. Herman, OIC of the Regional Director's Office (See Appendix C).

Figure 9. *Ptr. Santi and His Church Members Discussing Possible Places for the Jesus Film Showing*

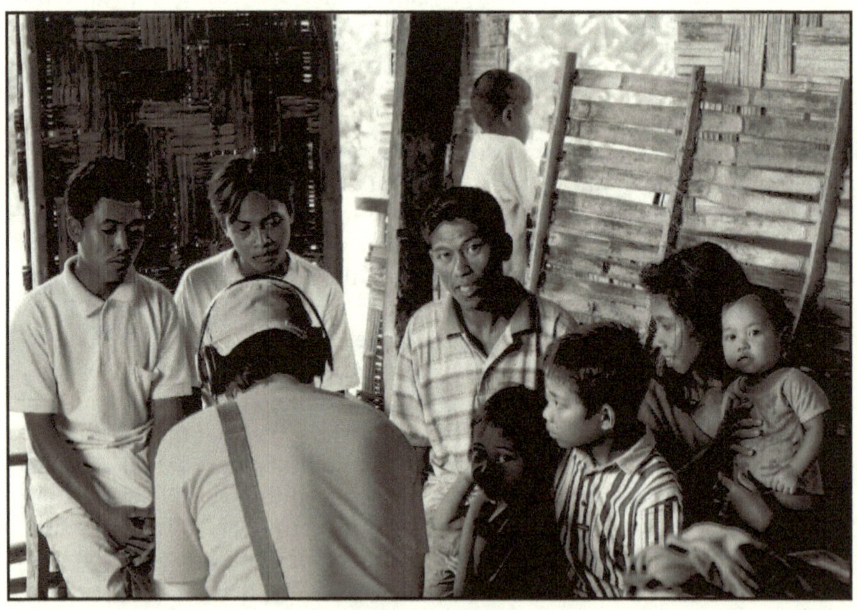

The second visit to the place was made soon after the first visit. At that time, stronger rapport with the local Mangyan Christians was made as well as with the area investigation of the three sitios where the *Jesus* film was to be shown. On this visit, a trip to sitio Dapdap was made for the prospect of the film showing. Although the sitio was not included in the final film showing, the visit helped me to know more about the Protestant mission work of the Overseas Missionary Fellowship (OMF) and its local organization,

Mangyan Tribal Christian Association (MTCA). Further explanations were made in the religious context in Chapter 5. Several interviews were done during this visit, which were recorded and then later transcribed. During our stay with the Mangyan community, Erwin and I stayed at the house of Ptr. Santi, which was attached to the church. The next morning, I was able to attend a dawn prayer meeting at four o'clock in the early morning. With the Sunday worship service at sitio Calamias, the experience helped me understand more of religious aspects.

With the understanding of the importance of preparation in the film showing, which was a part of my description of the research procedure above, the actual showing took place from February 14-17, 2008 as scheduled. I came with Erwin and, instead of DS Tino, Ptr. Rex, former *Jesus* film coordinator in this district, was leading this showing. Local contacts, Ptr. Manad, Santi and others guided the team. The film showing usually took place at night due to the location and projection of the movie. Observation by participation was done before, during and after film showing. Interviews were done right after film showings and in the following days.

Selection of Interview Informants

The selection of interview informants purposefully used snowball methods. Rev. David Philips and DS Tino introduced me to Ptr. Manad in Mindoro, and Ptr. Santi was the one who guided the future selection of interview informants. The interviews were done before, during and after film showing. Members such as DS Tino, Ptr. Junio and Manad were included in the research because they could provide different perspectives on the reception of the film. An initial interview was done with Ptr. George Junio, who was a former *Jesus* film showing coordinator in the Southern Tagalog District. Major interviews were done during and after the showing with key informants with Ptr. Santi's help. More interviews were continued the next day. The interviews were more or less spontaneous in their actual showing places. Naturally enough, the informants were shy to express what they thought and looked to their friends for help. All interviews were recorded and later translated by Erwin Galino and other research assistants.

Concepts and Indicators

Social, religious and media context of the three Mangyan sitios (Alangan and Iraya) in Sta. Cruz, Mindoro

1. Analyze Social, Religious and Media Context of the Three Mangyan in Sta. Cruz, Mindoro.
    A. General Description of the Research Site
        1. General Description of the Island of Mindoro
        2. General Description of the Mangyans
        3. General Description of Alangan and Iraya Mangyans

4. And Specific Description of the Three sitios (Siyapo, Barras and Calamias)
5. Geographical Description of the Research Site
6. Demographic Profile of Respondents and/or Informants (Age, Gender, Religion, and Area of Living)

B. Social Context of Three Sitios
1. General Social Description of Three Sitios
2. The Structure of Settlements
   a. Ethnic Origin and Dress
   b. Family and Kinship
   c. Marriage
   d. Residence (Home) and Church Structure
3. Community Development
   a. Education and Schools
   b. Electricity and Modern Technology Use
4. Leadership Patterns
5. Food and Cultivation
6. Ancestral Domain and Land Struggles
7. Interactions with Outsiders

C. Religious Contexts of three Mangyan sitios
1. Christianization and Modernization
2. Indigenous Religious Beliefs and Rituals in the Three Sitios
3. Protestantism
   a. Indigenous Christian Churches in the Phil ippines (ICCP)
   b. ICCP at sitio Siyapo and Baraas
   c. ICCP Prayer Meetings
   d. Episcopal Church

D. Media Context
1. Media Acquisition and Use
2. Visual Media and Television
3. Mobile Phone
4. Graffiti as a Form of Expressive Media

2. Observation on how the film Showing Takes Place in the Three Sitios

A. Initial Contacts and Negotiations

B. Preparation for Film Showing

C. Actual Showing
1. Composition of Audience
2. Exhortation

D. Follow-up Strategy after Film Showing

3. Construction of the Religious Meanings of Mangyan audiences,

   A. Analysis on the *Jesus* Film Scenes
      1. Scene numbers, Time
      2. Name the Scenes and Short Description
   B. Responsive Scenes and Negotiated Meanings
   C. Perceived Image of Jesus
   D. Other Meanings
4. Analyze the Perceptions of the film and the Western Figure of Jesus.
   A. The Awareness of Western figure
   B. Familiarity of Western Jesus
   C. Materialization of Christianity through film

Units of Analysis

The basic unit of analysis in this study was the individual and community members' account of religious meanings among community members in Iraya and Alangan-Mangyans as parts of an interpretive community. Since a religious community had been formed in three sitios, the reception of the film was based on the previous religious experience of the Mangyans.

Besides direct personal accounts as a basic unit of analysis, the individual and communal aspects of watching the film were worth observing. The mediated religious meanings were directed through the place of film showing. The moment of film showing was an important unit in this study.

In addition to the interviews of Mangyan audiences and direct observations, the perceptions of the *Jesus* film coordinators and ministers were made available for another unit to be analyzed. As much as possible, close attention was given to how the coordinators were experiencing religious meanings through the perception of the film. This data was significant to support the primary units.

The Researcher and the Team

Born in an ethnic Korean family, I lived in Korea until the age of 26. After marrying a Korean woman, I decided to go to the Philippines for further study and ended up studying communication and media instead. During my doctoral studies, I was appointed by the Instructor of Asian-Pacific Nazarene Theological Seminary, Taytay Rizal, Philippines as a missionary intern for the Church of the Nazarene. I was soon promoted to assistant professor and director of the Fairbanks School of Communication. These ten years of studies, work and experience in the Philippines have nurtured me in significant ways to perceive the culture and people of the Asia-Pacific region.

In my course of studies, I began my early secondary education through theater arts in performing arts school. The school was a two-year junior and professional college with the diploma in theater production. Later, I worked at a professional drama company called Wagon Stage Inc. for three years before becoming involved in television production through a national cable television network, GTV. Seven years later, I earned a B.A. in English Language and Literature through Korean Open University and a M.A. in Christian Communication. During my studies at APNTS, I was able to gain a theological background and missiological understanding. My current doctoral program is funded by financial support from the United Board of Christian Higher Education in Asia (UBCHEA)

During my doctoral studies, significant research in cross-cultural studies and reception studies in the areas of media, religion and occured. With Prof. Deza, I conducted research on third cultural identity among missionary kids at an international school in the Philippines, and authored *Living in a Yellow Submarine: Third Culture Missionary Kids at Faith Academy* (Plaridel 2, 2005), and with Pernia, and Pascual, *Religion in the Box: Viewership of Religious Television Programs in the Philippines* (*Journal of Communication and Religion* 29, 2006). Another reception study was of Korean telenovelas and the Filipino experience: *Is It Too Early to Talk About "Hallyu" in the Philippines? Korean Telenovela and Its Reception Among Filipino Audience* (*Asian Communication Research Journal, 2007*). In the conference, *Media Culture and Industry in Asia* (Seoul and Choon Cheon, Korea, 2007), the initial paper of the current dissertation, *Westernized Visual Representation of Jesus and the Construction of Religious Meaning: The Jesus Film and Its Reception among Asian Audiences* (Kwon, 2007) was presented. This series of research projects stimulated further development of this current dissertation topic in the growing field of religion, media and culture.

Two Filipino research assistants helped with this study. Erwin Galino and Salarene Manongsong were second-year students at the Fairbanks International School of Communication, APNTS. Both of them successfully finished research methods classes and were competent in Filipino and English. They assisted this study by interpreting interviews with Mangyan tribes during field research, transcribing the interviews that were recorded, and translating the Tagalog transcription into English. Also, three more part-time research assistants helped transcribe the interview data and translated in English

In addition to the two research assistants, Ptr. Manad and Santi were key informants who also served as facilitators and interpreters during the field work. Since Ptr. Manad was born in Mindoro and possessed many years of various ministerial experiences, he was very helpful during the initial investigation and actual research process. He facilitated negotiation when it was needed. Pastor Santi, a native Mangyan pastor who studied for two years at a Bible college in Oriental Mindoro, was able to speak in English. He translated and worked with the research assistants and the interview informants when necessary. Pastor Santi's assistance was crucial to get this research into the Mangyan communities.

Chapter 5

Results and Discussion: Social, Religious and Media Context

Introduction

This chapter presents the interpretation and construction of data from the field research. The general description of the research site begins with the description of the island of Mindoro, the Mangyans, and the three sitios (Siyapo, Baraas, and Calamias). The research, then, proceeds to the social, religious and media contexts, which provides a broad and deeper understanding of the research informants and areas. By understanding the context in which the audiences are located, the reception of the *Jesus* film and their construction of religious meanings could be related to their religiosity.

The research areas have been significantly evangelized by Christian institutions such as Catholic, Protestant and Episcopal churches and other denominations. Due to the developmental nature of Christian missions in Mangyan communities, Christianization has coincided with the modernization and acculturation process. Furthermore, the acculturation process has appeared similarly to media exposure and acquisitions among the Mangyans in the three sitios. Even without a regular supply of electricity, various types of media including video, television and radio have been introduced and used in the lives of acculturated Mangyans. Notably, devoted religious members have intentionally chosen to use radio and visual media for religious purposes.

General Description of Research Site

The Island of Mindoro

Mindoro is considered to be the seventh largest island of the Philippines, 90 kilometers long and 15 kilometers wide with a total land area of more than 10,000 square kilometers. There are a few mountains spread throughout the island, including Mt. Halcon, which is the third highest mountain (8,481 feet high) in the Philippines, and the home of the Iraya and Alangan Mangyans (see Figure 10).). The three particular Mangyan settlements (sitio Siyapo, Barras and Calamias) in this study are located in the northern part of Occidental Mindoro, which is located south of Manila, west of Bicol and north of the Palawan islands.

Figure 10. *The Map of Mindoro*ource.

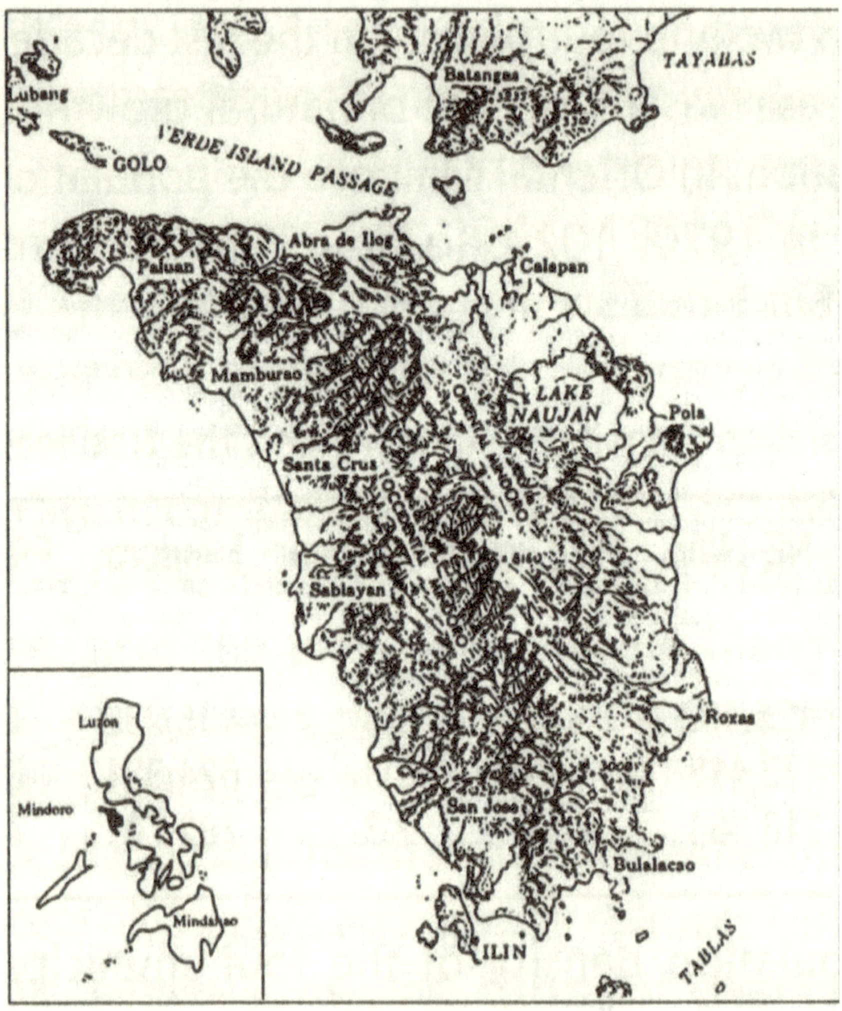

Helbling J. & Schult, V. (2004). *Mangyan survival strategies.* Quezon City: New Day Publishers.

Without much attention to the welfare of the native Mangyans, Republic Act No. 505 divided the island into the Oriental and Occidental provinces of Mindoro in 1950. In the ethnographic map of Mindoro (see Figure 11), except for Tadyawan Mangyan, other Mangyans were divided by the two provinces. Occidental Mindoro is composed of 5,897.8 square kilometers, and Oriental Mindoro is 4,364.7 square kilometers. In contrast to the geographical division, the present population of Oriental Mindoro is about 450,000, which is double the population of Occidental Mindoro (Schult, 1991). This figure confirms the unbalanced development of Occidental Mindoro compared to Oriental Mindoro. Besides the literature, the unhinged development of the two sides of Mindoro, and even between Mangyan settlements, were clearly noted in field work.

Due to constant threats from other ethnic groups from Luzon, Visayas and others, the island of Mindoro is no longer that of native Mangyans. The population of the island consists of two-thirds Tagalogs, ten percent Visayans and seven percent Ilocanos. As a result, the natives of the land, the Mangyan population, make up only ten percent of the total population of the island, which is approximately 60,000-80,000 individuals. The influx of Filipino migrants searching for land and prosperity have become major threats to Mangyans, and have caused conflicts with Mangyans over the Ancestral Domain given to them (Navarro, 1993).

The Mangyans

Known as the swidden agriculturalists of the island of Mindoro, "Mangyan" is the generic term for the native people who settled on the island 600-700 hundred years ago (Postma, 1974). During the sixteenth century, the Mangyans gained the attention of the early Spanish colonial Catholics. Several reports regarding Mangyans were made by the missionaries assigned to the island. Yet, the Catholic mission was not able to continue due to aggressive attacks from Moro Islamic groups that tried to protect their previously occupied island. It was in the early twentieth century when ethnographers again searched for new ethnic tribes in Mindoro and the origin of the Mangyans (Blumentritt, 1940; Worchester, 1899). Interestingly, the Mangyans were geographically close to Palawan with the group of Malaysia and Borneos during prehistoric times (Mandia, 1987). Estel (1952, 1953) again argued that Mangyans are certainly not Negrito but a mixture of Veddoid (Indo-Australoid and Dravidian, and the Sakal group) and Borrio ethnic groups.

Although Mangyan is the name for all proto-Malayan ethnic groups found in northern Oriental Mindoro (Maceda, 1967), there are some differences in the linguistic and cultural diversity among Mangyans. Early scholars classified the Mangyans into nine groups (Estel, 1952) and some narrowed it down to seven groups (Conklin, 1949; Gibson, 1983). The recent ethnographic map of Mindoro published by Mindoro Mission Center (2006) again classified them into eight groups: Iraya, Alangan, Tadyawan, Tau-Buid, Bangon, Buhid, Hanunoo and Ratagnon (See Figure 11). The eight groups differ in physical status, settlement and dwellings, utensils or implements, social and political organization, and more importantly, use of oral and written language, although they use Tagalog as a "lingua franca"

(Maceda, 1967) in the lowland settlement. Only the Hanunoo have a written language (Postma, 1989).

Figure 11. *The Ethnographic Map of Mindoro*

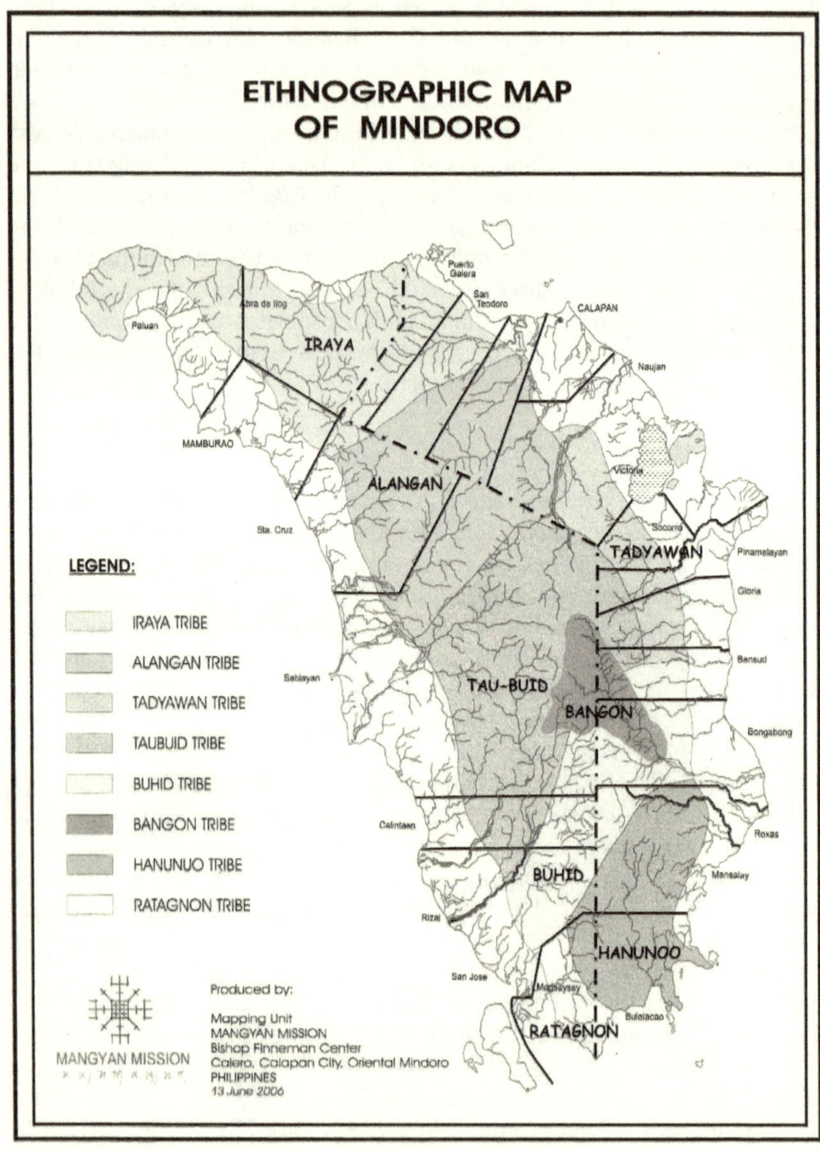

Source. Ethnographic Map of Mindoro (2006) produced by Mangyan Mission Center, Calapan, Oriental Mindoro.

Alangan and Iraya Mangyans

Alangan and Iraya Mangyans are widely spread throughout the inner northern part of Mindoro, yet their habitats are differentiated linguistically and culturally, and also differ in the degree of acculturation. Classified as northern Mangyans (Conklin, 1971), both Alangan and Iraya Mangyans mostly inhabit the hills and mountains of northern Mindoro. Alangan refers to the people living on Mt. Alangan. In Mindoro Oriental, Alangan Mangyans mostly live in the municipalities of Baco, Naujan and Victoria that are adjacent to Mt. Halcon. In Mindoro Occidental, they widely range among municipalities of Sablayan, Sta. Cruz and Mamburao, which are also close to Mt. Tallalan and Mt. Pamucuban. Iraya Mangyans mainly live in the area of Puerto Galera in Oriental Mindoro and the Municipalities of Mamburao to Abra De Ilog in Occidental Mindoro. While traditional Mangyans tended to live deeper in mountainous areas due to the colonial and foreign invasions of the Spaniards, Moros, Japanese and the United States (Scholts, 1991, see also Leykamm, 1979), acculturated Mangyans have lived close to or near lowlanders that are connected by roads.

Unlike most traditional Mangyan communities, three acculturated Mangyan settlements in this research were close to the national road and seacoast. Sitio Siyapo was about 20 kilometers south of the municipalities of Sta. Cruz and a tricycle ride away from barangay Pinagtulian along the national road. Within a ten-minute walking distance, there were several lowland Tagalog sitios from which I could get help and support, such as toilets and water in case of need. Sitio Baraas is closest to the base camp, barangay Barahan, which is about five to seven kilometers away from the municipality of Sta. Cruz. Although it was rocky and hilly, the tricycle was able to bring me and the *Jesus* film team from the national road to the sitio Baraas in ten minutes. Sitio Calamias is rather far from Sta. Cruz but close to municipality of Abra De Ilog, which is the gate of Occidental Mindoro with the ferry boat dock (see Figure 12).

Figure 12. *The Location Map of Three Sitios*

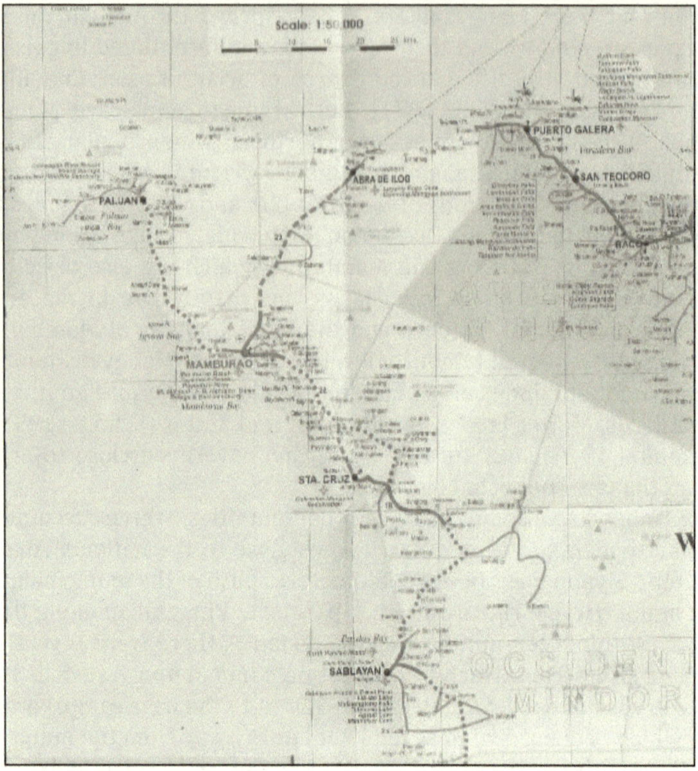

Source. Adapted from EZ Map Mindoro (2006) produced by United Tourist Promotions, the Philippines.

Although Calamias was close to the dock, the sitio was the farthest place from the national road, about thirty minutes from the Barangay Barahan. The team had to cross two small creeks to reach the sitio Siyapo. It took about thirty minutes by tricycle and another thirty minutes by walking. Some variations and differences were shown in the location of the three sitios tricycle access and relatively easy accessibility provided sufficient commonalities to identify acculturation process in the three sitios, which resulted in significant differences from traditional Mangyans.

Three sitios (Sitio Siyapo, Baraas, and Calamias)

This study was located in three Christianized and acculturated Alangan and Iraya Mangyan settlements. Although major ethnographic studies have focused on the culture of traditional Mangyans, Feraro-Banta studied on the life and social aspects of Christianized and modernized Iraya and Alangan Mangyans (1985). He compared the settlements described and the three sitios in Occidental Mindoro draw these differences. In his study, the Christianized settlements had well-established schools and churches, political leaders, water supplies, roads, basketball courts and cooperative stores. In spite of the longitudinal gap from the previous to the present study, most aspects that were indicated in Feraro-Banta's study appeared in the three sitios. The aspects were significant indicators to identify the three sitios in the frame of the Christianized and acculturated group of Mangyans.

The three sitios showed distinctive modern settlement patterns. Interestingly, religious institutions have become the major agent of acculturation and modernization process in addition to the local government. Settlement sizes were relatively large compared to the traditional villages, with the numbers between 200 and 350 individuals. Yet, in contrast to the large settlement sizes, family size has also become smaller compared to the traditional Mangyan groups, which range from four to six members in a family and the average settlement was composed of forty to sixty households. Modern education and water systems were partially introduced. Traditionally, Alangan and Iraya Mangyans did not have a written language, but modern education systems such as elementary and high school have allowed some sitio members to speak and write Tagalog as a lingua franca. At least one water pump was installed in each sitio, which was able to establish the settlement. Both Catholic and Protestant churches were established in all the sitios, with the existence of traditional and modern political and religious leaders. Outdoor basketball courts were established in sitio Calamias and Baraas, and even sari-sari stores existed only in sitio Baraas, although members of all sitios had direct and indirect access to the stores of the lowlanders.

Demographic Profile of Interview Informants

In this research, I was able to interview Mangyans and non-Mangyans who were *Jesus* film ministers, local pastors or part of the audiences in the film showing. A total of 60 informants were actively engaged in the various interviews (see Table 1). Among the 60 respondents, nearly half of the respondents were in their twenties and the others were similarly distributed: six members of ages over 60 years old; five members of ages between 40 to 59; and four members of ages younger than 19. All informants were religious and Protestant Christians. Due to the fact that local Mangyan coordinators of the film showing were leaders of the Indigenous Christian Church of the Philippines (ICCP), most interview informants were members of ICCP that included pastors and leaders of the organization. A few non- ICCP members were also included in this interview, yet few were from sitio Calamias. Lastly, the informants mostly lived in the sitios in which the film was shown but there were some Mangyans who came to visit the sites with the community members. The sitios were sitio Dapdap, Ranao, Bagong Silang and Kamanpugan.

Table 1. *Profile of Respondents* (N=60)

Age	Frequency
60 and above	6
40 to 59	5
20 to 39	28
19 and below	4
Total	60
Gender	
Male	23
Female	37
Total	60
Note: there are nine non-Mangyan interview informants, including seminary students and the *Jesus* film coordinators.	

Social Context

General (Sitio Siyapo, Baraas and Calamias)

Sitio Siyapo

Sitio Siyapo is located about 20 kilometers south of the municipality of Sta. Cruz and within tricycle-reach from barangay Pinagtulian along the national road. The settlement was located on the outskirts of the hilly mountain and a large corn field was located in front of the sitio. This settlement was developed and organized by the joint efforts of the local government and the Catholic Mangyan Mission, Pantribong Samahan Sa Kanlurang Pantribong Samahan Sa Kaulurang Mindoro (PASAKAMI). The local government agreed that the religious NGO PASAKAMI would encourage various Alangan Mangyans to move to the new sitio Siyapo from neighboring settlements who had a hard time with their previous living conditions.

The community has grown to more than 350 members with more than 50 families. Near the entrance of the sitio, an elementary school and a community health clinic were built with concrete and hollow-block walls to accommodate sitio Alangan for education- and health-related matters. Personal and private water pumps have been installed at Siyapo and bring enough water for the whole community throughout the year. The sitio is an example of how modern structures were able to attract the scattered Alangans to reside in an organized acculturated settlement (see Figure 13).

Figure 13. *Life in Sitio Siyapo*

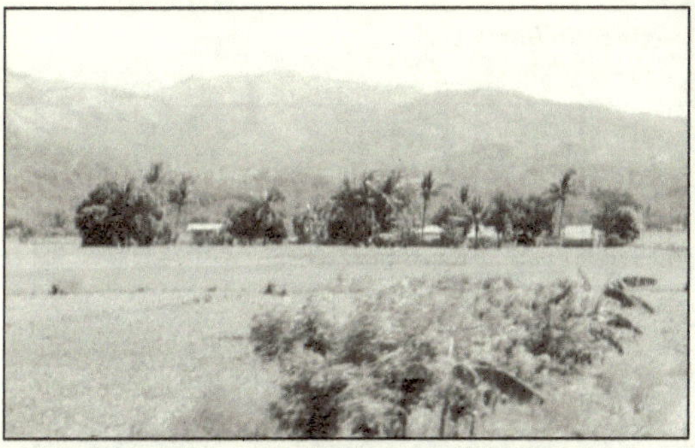
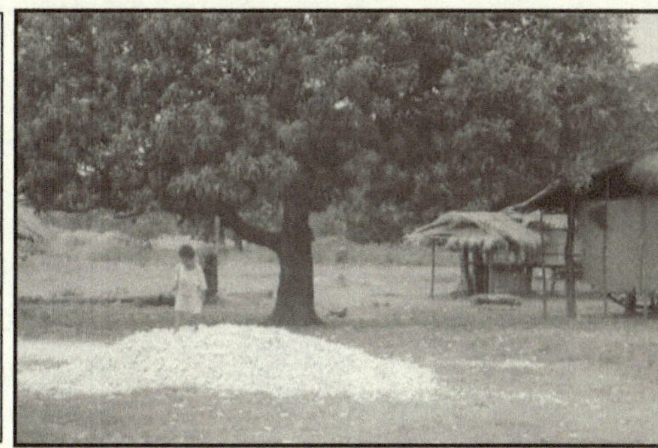
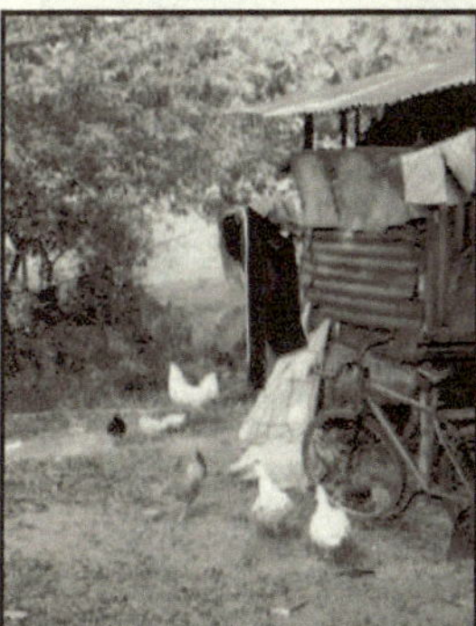
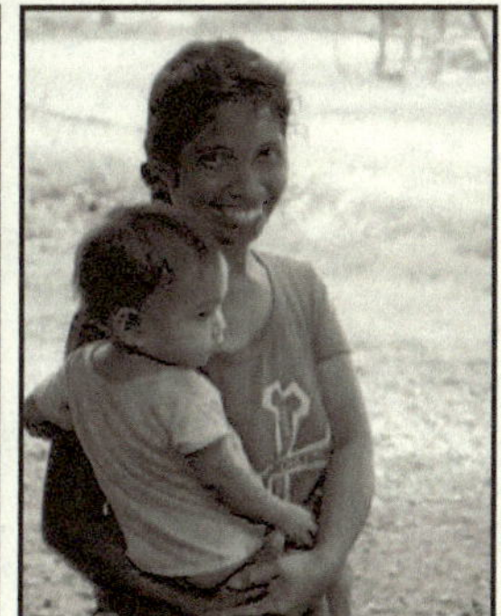
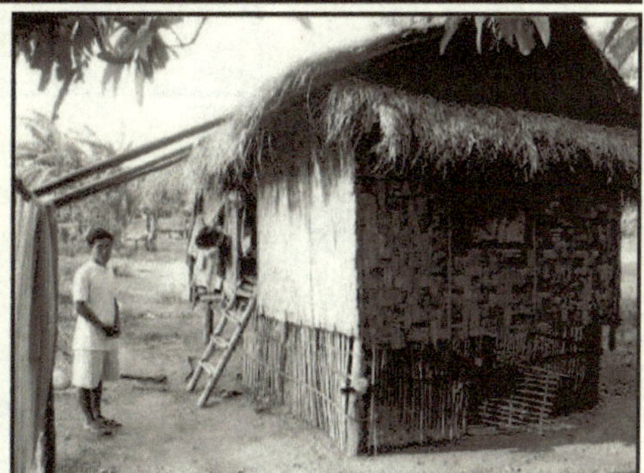

Clockwise, from top left: Sitio Siyapo is located around a huge corn field; a boy playing on the pile of harvested corn in the center of the sitio; sitio ICCP church; the wife and a son of Ptr. Santi; and a Mangyan house in the sitio.

Sitio Baraas

Sitio Baraas was the closest settlement to the base camp of this research, barangay Barahan, which was about five to seven kilometers from the municipality of Sta. Cruz. Although it was rocky and hilly, a tricycle was able to bring the *Jesus* film team and equipment in ten to twenty minutes from the national road to the sitio. The location of sitio Baraas was similar to that of sitio Siyapo in that the settlement was located on the outskirts of the hill and a vast cornfield near the settlement. Most members of the settlement worked in the cornfield, which was owned by the lowland Tagalogs and Visayans who had moved to the settlement (see Figure 14).

Figure 14. *Life in Sitio Baraas*

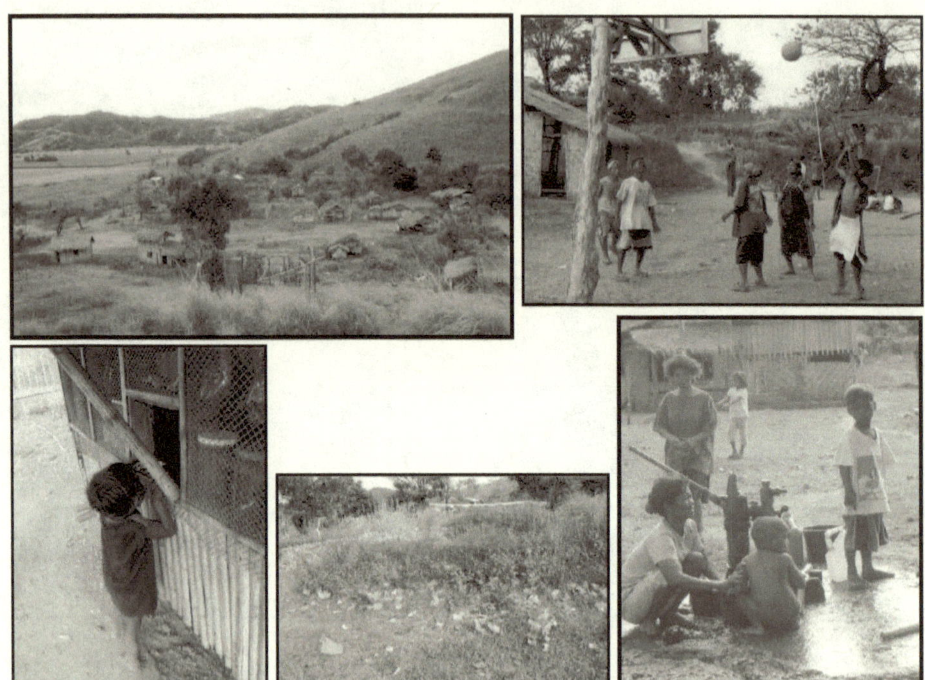

Clockwise, from top left: Sitio Baraas from the hill; adolescents at Baraas playing basketball; a child bathing at the one and only water pump; garbage in the yard of sitio; and a child buying chips from the sari-sari store that is owned by a Visayan family at sitio Baraas.

Including children, there were about 300 members of this village settlement, which was similar to sitio Siyapo . Notably, eleven Visayan immigrants had moved into the compound of Baraas and had already intermarried with Iraya Mangyans in the settlement. The Visayans had purchased part of the Ancestral Domain of the Iraya Mangyans in the sitio. They cultivated corn, rice and other crops as they moved into the settlement, and opened a sari-sari store that sells modern products from lowlanders to members of the settlement.

While no Catholic mission was organized in sitio Barras, two Protestant churches were organized by MTCA and ICCP. The MTCA church had been established in the settlement a long time ago. The ICCP church was relatively new with only 15 members, yet it was religiously viable in terms of the commitment of the members to religious activities and their financial self-support. Most of the members of the settlement attended either MTCA or

ICCP churches, yet several families attended Catholic mass and local sects in the nearby lowland communities.

Sitio Calamias

Sitio Calamias was close to the pier of the municipality of Abra De Ilog where shipping ferries went to Batangas port. Although Calamias was close to the pier, the sitio was the farthest place from the national road, and the *Jesus* film team had to ride a tricycle for about thirty minutes from the lowland community. It took about another thirty minutes to walk from the end of the road and cross two small creeks before reaching sitio Siyapo.

This settlement was a part of three small Iraya sitios (sitio Lipawin, Burburuan and Calamias) that were spread across five kilometers. The settlement was located on the outskirts of a hill yet covered by trees that protected the community from being seen by outsiders. This settlement was hard to find from outside without prior knowledge of the location (see Figure 15). Organized as a small sitio, Calamias had only fifteen households, with the total of fifty-five members lived in the three sitios where traditional leadership *kuyay* (Iraya leader) and a *chieftain* (political leader in the modern Mangyan settlement) who was often called the "mayor of the settlement."

Figure 15. *Life in Sitio Calamias*

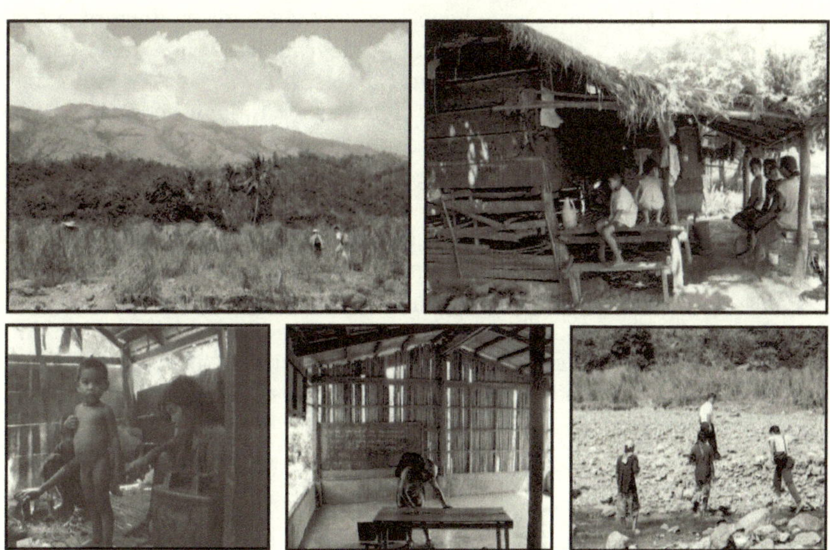

Clockwise, from top left: Sitio Calamias entrance; Iraya Mangyans in front of a house at Sitio Calamias; The team crossing a creek going to the settlement; Inside of the Community center, "Aplan"; and a family cooking inside a Mangyan house.

Due to the division of three small sitios, the sitio Calamias was composed of only fifteen households, including nine children. Each family was given a division of the Ancestral Domain of Iraya and planned or leased the land to the lowlanders for corn and rice cultivation in return for cash. Due to the cash returns from their labor and land lease, the settlement members were able to purchase some goods from lowland markets such as secondhand clothes, cooking utensils, rubber shoes, and even some canned goods, that led them to a way of modern living.

The Structure of Settlements

Ethnic Origin and Dress

Ethnic and linguistic differences among Mangyan varied from the ethnic origins of the Mangyans. Notably, Estel (1952, 1953) argued that Mangyans were certainly not Negrito but a mixture of Veddoid (Indo-Australoid and Dravidian, and the Sakal group) and Borrio ethnic groups. Mandia also argued that the Mangyans were geographically close to Palawan with the group of Malaysia and Borneo in the prehistoric period (Mandia, 1987) rather than Luzon and Visayas. Maceda (1967) also argued that the Mangyans are generally referred to as the proto-Malayans in northern Oriental Mindoro, although some disagreements on the linguistic and cultural differences could be found (see Figure 16).

Acculturated Mangyans have been transformed with modern manners of clothing and styles of dress. Several ethnographic studies depicted the traditional Alangan and Iraya Mangyan dresses, "*Abayen,*" or G-strings that were made out of cotton, bark clothes and rattan, although no Mangyans in the field research wore traditional dress that was shown in previous literature. Interviewers witnessed the presence of traditional Mangyans who wore the traditional G-string clothes in the mountains. Yet, acculturated Mangyans gave priority to the purchase of clothes when cash was available. Clotheing was the first and foremost modern way of living among acculturated Mangyans. Even lowland secondhand clothes dealers sometimes visited Mangyan settlements to sell clothes. Due to the lack of available cash, many children under five years old often lived without proper clothes or wore large clothes handed down from older siblings (see Figure 16 and 17).

Figure 16. *Mother with Children of an Iraya Mangyan Household*

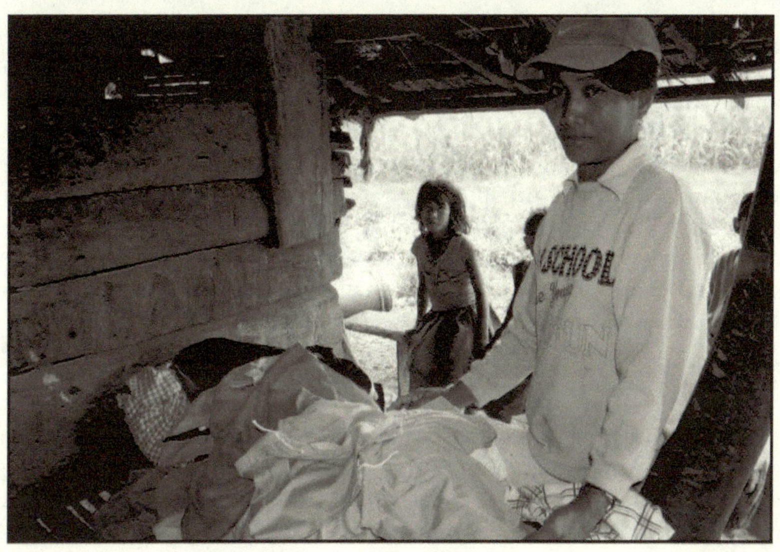

Figure 17. *A Tagalog Retailer Selling Second-hand Clothes in Sitio*

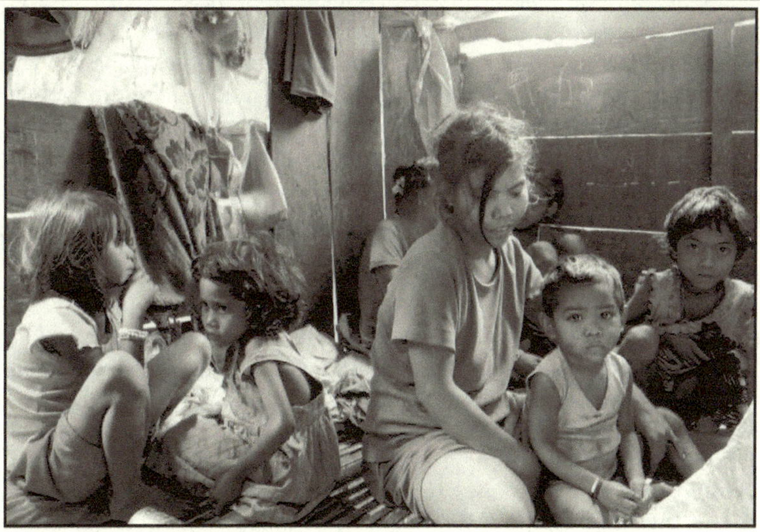

Family and Kinship

As the nuclear family is the new family shape in modern times, the family type has been similarly shown in the acculturated settlements for both Alangan and Iraya Mangyans. Kikuchi explored *balaya lakoy*, which is the large family house that can shelter more than five to ten households with more than fifty individuals, among traditional Alangan settlements. Yet it was again a different attribute that distinguished traditional Mangyans from the acculturated Mangyans. Mangyans in the three sitios had a similar nuclear family structure with parents having three to five children. Parents shared ancestral lots upon the marriage of their children and the bridegroom built a new house in the same settlements.

Marriage

The acculturated Mangyans tended to marry later than traditional Mangyans. Traditionally, Mangyans have practiced early-age marriages, beginning at the age of twelve. Early marriages arranged by parents often happened even before a child reached ten years old. Therefore, the size of the house became smaller until it was only enough for the nuclear family. The wedding feast became a big social gathering that was usually presided over by the magico-religious leader of the settlement.

The modernized marriage and wedding ceremony are still considered a central feast among Mangyans. Marriages often began with courtships among adolescents in the settlements, while arranged marriages were still commonly practiced. Courtship often became the center of life for adolescent Mangyans, probably due to the influence of media, including television and radio. The desired marrying age became older as they attended elementary school and learned about marriage customs of lowlanders. In Christian settlements, the wedding was presided over by priests or pastors and marriage contracts were signed at municipal hall.

Residence (House) and Church

As revealed in the nuclear family, the structure of Mangyan housing was smaller than traditional houses. The main material used for Mangyan houses was sliced bamboo (see Figure 18).

A family of five lived in the house in Figure 18It was made of wooden boards and covered with cogon grass on top. *Datu* Roding proudly mentioned that the nails and saws that needed to be purchased were used to construct this sort of improved-Mangyan house. The new construction method has been around since the Marcos regime and these skills for house construction were introduced by lowlanders and modified by Mangyans since then. Still, in some cases, Mangyans hired lowland carpenters to build Mangyan houses in the settlement.

Although the house in Figure 18 looked like two houses attached to each other, it was one unit that had a closed room used for sleeping and eating, as well as an open living room that was often used for storage and gathering. Usually, a Mangyan house was lifted up one foot high and the space below the house called *silong.* The function of the *silong* was to protect dwellers from the chill and humidity coming from the ground, but it was multi-purpose in that it was often used as a storage space for firewood, root crops and livestock such as pigs, dogs and chickens. The height of the house from the *silong* was usually about the height of an adult Mangyan who lived in the house. The floor was usually made of bamboo slats without a mattress. Inside the closed room there was a fireplace on which the family members often cooked, although there was another fireplace outside the house.

Figure 18. *A Mangyan Wood-Board House at Sitio Calamias*

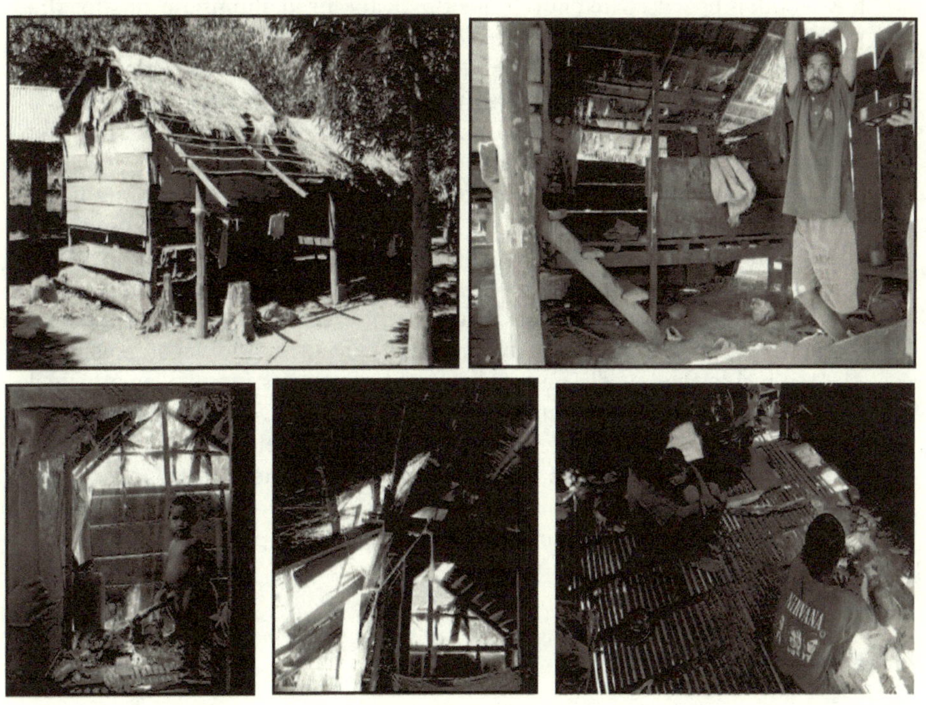

Clockwise, from top left: A Mangyan house at Sitio Calamias; Entrance of the house; closed room and a family: cogon grass roof; and a closed room viewed from outside.

The construction of the Mangyan house waws usually done by a bride-groom who was either getting married or was the father of the house. Lack of professional skills in construction was revealed in some parts of the house, such as in the roofing and flooring. When it rained heavily, family members could not avoid damages to the house and it often deteriorated, either by natural corrosion or termite infestation. Although their construction skills are slowly improving, the Mangyan house is still more mobile than a permanent residence.

Several recycling materials were used in daily Mangyan house in various ways. The door wass not present but covered with a recycled rice sack. Small and big rice sacks were used in various places in house construction. A gasoline container was transformed into a water container and various recycled cans and plastics bottles used in daily life. When I visited the house, the family was preparing lunch by boiling cassava in a small can of sardines. This modern influence from the outside did not fully equipped the lives of Mangyans, but rather has marginalized them with their use of garbage in recycling materials from the lowland communities.

The construction of Mangyan churches was somewhat similar to the Mangyan house in use of materials and structure. The main construction material was bamboo, which was sliced and woven to make a mat, and a few wooden boards. The church in sitio Siyapo used aluminum tins for the rooftop and other churches also used cogon grass, which was common roof material for Mangyan houses. The floor was not finished but consisted of just bare ground that is easily filled with water when it rains. Similar to the residences of Mangyans, the church did not have a door to close but had entrances on both sides (see Figure 19).

The outer construction of the church was not different from the usual residences of other Mangyans, except for the tin roof. The walls of the church were built with woven bamboo mats that are loosely tied with other mats as well as square boards but lacked an actual door. The church was enclosed with a bamboo fence that was different from that of the usual Mangyan house. Banana, papaya and other fruit trees and vegetables were planted inside the fence. The residence of the pastor's family was attached to the church with an entrance. Inside the church, seven pews were structured similarly to the proscenium type, which is a typical church structure. A pulpit was made of wood that holds Bible and other items for worship and discipleship training. To support various training and biblical teaching, a blackboard was made of wood and stood behind the pulpit.

Figure 19. *The Siyapo Church of ICCP*

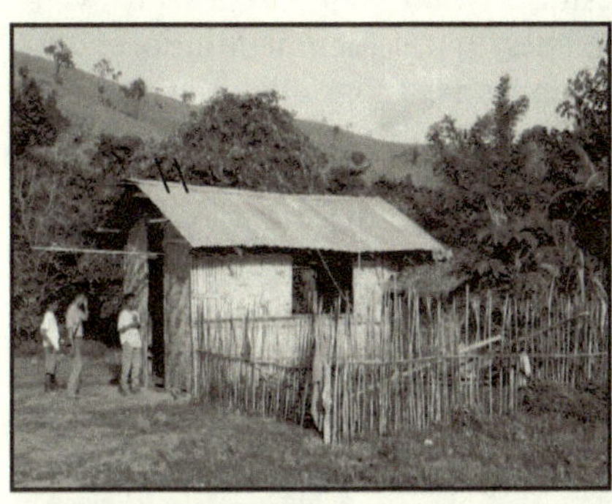

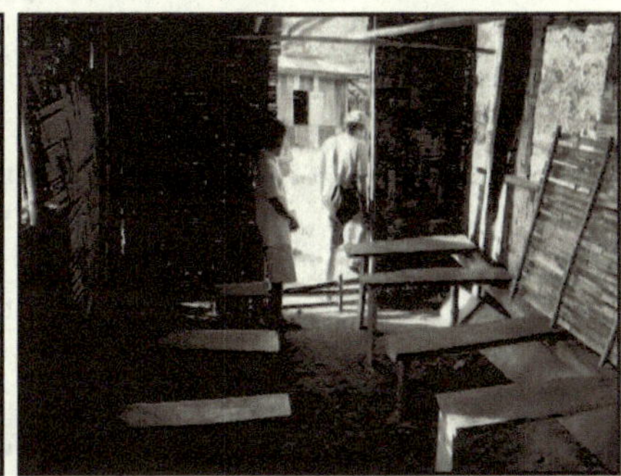

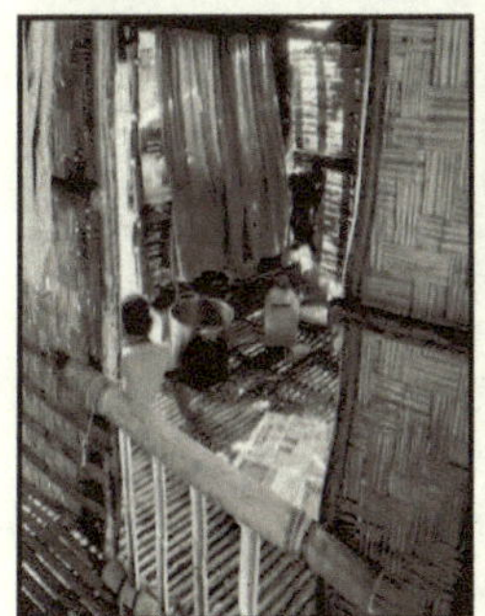

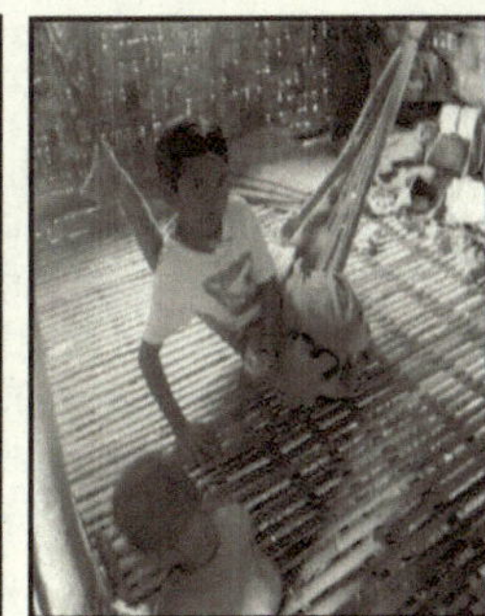

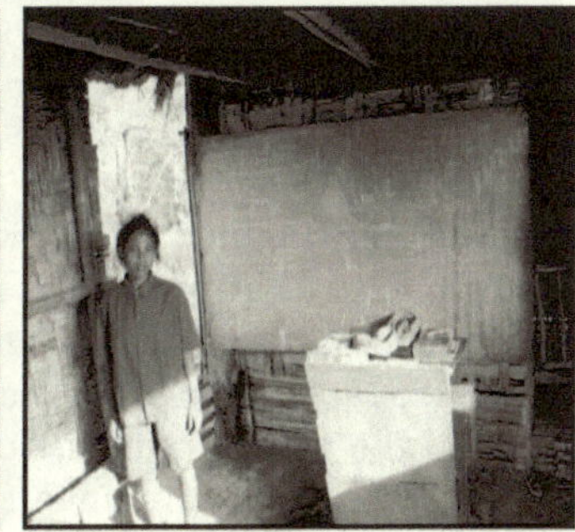

Clockwise, from top left: The building of the Siyapo Church of ICCP made of bamboos and aluminum tins; Entrance of the church and Pews; Front view of the church and back entrance; Hanging bed in the pastor's residence adjacent to the church building; And the view of the residence from the entrance gate.

Community Development

Education and Schools

Education was a vital part of the Mangyan modernization process. Acculturation has required the adoption of a modern political social system and Tagalog as a lingua franca. Most Mangyans in the three sitios had somewhat extended Tagalog language education over the past years and let their children attend elementary education either in the Mangyan settlements or lowland schools. At the time of your research, sitio Siyapo has an Alangan Mangyan elementary school that has been funded by the local government and run by the PASAKAMI. Two Tagalog teachers were hired to teach the children using a DECS-recognized curriculum but have adopted some Mangyan subjects, such as an Alangan language class. Religious institutions and workers have played a pivotal role in Mangyan education by facilitating school administration and providing teachers, support class materials and funds.

The Alangan elementary school at sitio Siyapo was a relatively well-established school unlike other settlements in Occidental Mindoro. Although an urgent need, schooling for Mangyans, especially Alangan and Iraya tribes in Mindoro Occidental, has not been sufficiently provided. Sitio Baraas did not have an elementary school for Mangyans, making it difficult for the children to attend elementary school. In sitio Calamias, an elementary school once operated a few years ago but stopped recently due to the lack of allowance for teachers. Children who once attended elementary schools at Calamias stopped schooling and were left out from much-needed modern education. Sufficient and compulsory elementary education for every Filipino child is still far from the reality of Mangyans.

Electricity and Modern Technology Use

The modernization process comes with technology development and utilization. In terms of technology use, there were no advanced places in Mangyan settlements. The first and foremost infrastructure in modern gadgets, electrical power, has not been installed in the settlements. As a consequence, information and telecommunication technologies such as television signal, landline, mobile phone and Internet have not been introduced to the members of the community. In terms of modern technology use, the Mangyans settlements are far behind the rapid development of modern life.

In the field research, I noticed that the lowland communities less than a kilometer away had been already equipped with those technologies. It was possible to extend electric power supply to the Mangyan settlements. However, it was doubtful that the Mangyans could pay for the electric bills with their limited acquisition of cash. Therefore, although this settlement has been in the process of acculturation, it is not yet fully equipped for modern living. More description of media use in the settlements will follow later in this paper.

Leadership Patterns

Emerging socio-political leadership among Mangyans is also a distinctive feature of acculturation. In the Mangyan studies from the 1970s, the presence of socio-political leaders were found as a contrast to the existing magico-religious leaders such as *kuyay* (elder) in Alangan and *datu* (elder) among Iraya Mangyans (Leykamm, 1979; Kikuchi, 1973a; Miyamoto, 1975, 1977, 1978). The emerging leadership was continually observed during field research and was quite involved, even the local administration, in their municipalities. Yet the emerging socio-political leadership was somehow separated and, at the same time, merged into the traditional *kuyay* and *datu* system.

In sitio Calamias, *datu* Roding was a traditional elder of the three sitios (sitio Lipawin, Burburuan and Calamias) with the presence of a new socio-political leader, *chieftain* Poming (Figure 20). Before the election of *chieftain* Poming as the socio-political leader, "*chieftain*" or the "*Mayor of the Barangay*" *datu* Roding had been involved in local political matters. He once served as a council member of the municipality of Abra De Ilog while he continued to serve the community as the traditional *datu*.

The case of Sitio Siyapo showed a different merging of two leaderships. The *kuyay* of sitio Siyapo was traditional leader of the settlement. But his role as an elder of the community has been transformed into a more established socio-political one as the settlement acculturated at the same time, as a traditional leader. At the same time, he also served as a leader of the Catholic parish. Interestingly, his wife At the time of your research as a magico-religious leader performing traditional rituals for community members. Instead of the separation of the traditional leadership from the emerging socio-political leadership, this case shows the integration of the two leaderships that have been handed down from ancestors within one family.

Figure 20. *Datu Roding (the left) and Chieftain Poming (the right) at Sitio Calamias*

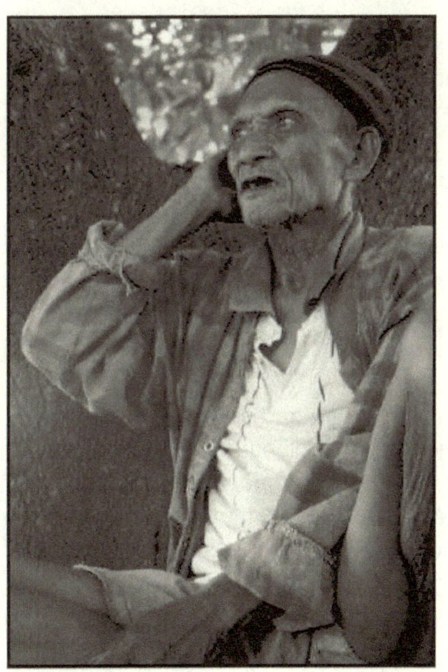

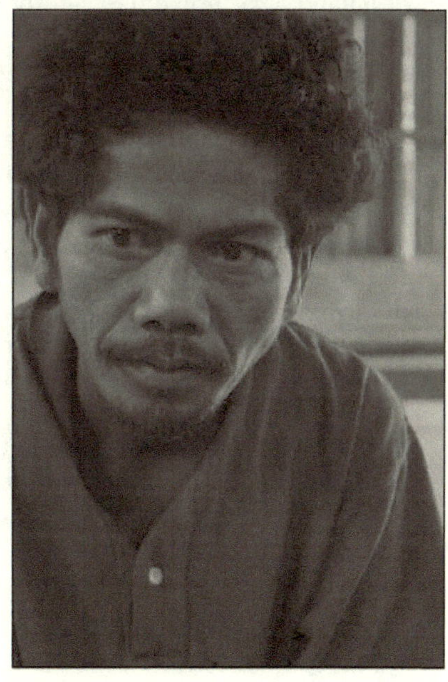

Sometimes, political leadership came into conflict with religious affiliation. *Datu* Roding confessed that he was an evangelical. His cousin became an evangelical pastor and returned to sitio Lipawin. The pastor continued to conduct evangelical worship in sitio Lipawin and visited sitio Calamias every Tuesday. However, the majority of sitio Calamias had already converted to the Episcopal church, where *chieftain* Poming led worship on Sundays. These two leaders with different religious affiliations sometimes caused conflicts in terms of decision-making on social and political matters.

Ptr. Santi and ICCP church were newly installed in the dominant Catholic community where the traditional magico-religious leader and the socio-political leader were from one family. The new insertion of the religious group caused small and big conflicts due to the different religious convictions on certain social matters as well as religious practices. Ptr. Santi strongly opposed community movie watching for a social gathering that was often held at the house of the *kuyay*. With the same conviction, Ptr. Santi and the members of ICCP did not agree with spiritual practices such as casting out of the bad spirit "*Hinang*" by the spiritist, called "*Marayawan*." The different religious beliefs due to different leaders and styles of leadership within a settlement were now seen among the acculturated Mangyans.

Food to Eat

Known as swidden agriculturalists (Conklin, 1949, 1954, 1969, 1971; Pennoyer, 1979), traditional Mangyans implemented slash and burn methods of agriculture, whereas acculturated Mangyans practiced new methods of upland agriculture. The gently sloping hillsides were ideal places for the slash and burn methods. Traditional Mangyans have practiced swidden cultivation, moving from one place to another with no concern for the environmental impact of slash and burn methods.

Sitio Siyapo is placed at the foot of a rocky hill and faces the large corn field. Lowland Tagalog communities own most of the cornfields that are within ten minutes walking distance from sitio Siyapo. According to Ptr. Santi, corn harvesting had not been widely practiced among Mangyans in Occidental Mindoro. Although cultivation seemed relatively simple, the use of farming equipment such as tractors and carabaos to plough the land, as well as the purchase of chemical fertilizer, made it impossible for Mangyans to practice the cornfield cultivation.

Major staple foods, such as cassava, camote and banana remain important to Mangyans, but acculturated Mangyans have been borrowing seeds and methods of cultivation from lowland Tagalogs, aiming to grow crops such as beans and eggplants. Nowadays, some try to cultivate corn and rice, but this is still not widely practiced. Ptr. Santi said that it was due to the lack of farming capital such as fertilizer:

> Santi: It is not enough especially when it comes to farming because all that we need like fertilizer, and the rice is taken (w.out pay) and during harvest time, we give a part of it to them and there is almost none left for us.

Mangyans also raise various types of livestock such as chickens, pigs, goats and dogs, and sometimes raise carabaos for cultivation. Chickens and pigs are major food source during wedding feasts and religious rituals. They are raised not in cattle sheds or barns but around the Mangyan houses. In most Mangyan settlements, these livestock animals are easily seen roaming around the village.

Besides swidden cultivation and raising livestock, acculturated Mangyans have begun to work for cash income. Some Mangyans worked in the corn or rice fields of lowlanders for an average of a hundred pesos per day to make cash. Acculturated Mangyans need cash to purchase clothes, rubber shoes, bolos, cooking utensils and canned goods. Selling firewood is one of the most common ways for them to make cash because of lowlanders' high demand for firewood. However, intermediary exploitation by lowland brokers prohibits the fairness of trade between Mangyans as producers and lowlanders as buyers. Chieftain Poming shared this criticism:

> For us natives, money is very hard to find... because we don't have means to get money... because we don't have products where we could get money... we are treated unfairly... we are mistreated... that is what is happening to us... The charcoal is bought for only 30 pesos from us... one peso per sack... but when they sell it, the charcoal becomes seventy to eighty pesos already... that is the market price... but the product comes from us. Wood and everything else comes from us...

Ancestral Domain and Land Struggles

Ancestral Domain is the recognized ownership of land by the central government in order to secure the land of indigenous people in the Philippines, which includes the island of Mindoro, the land of the Mangyans. DAO No. 102, Series of 1993, provided "the recognition and protection of the right of the indigenous people in their ancestral land and domain and to ensure their economic, social and cultural well-being" (http: //www. davaonorte. Gov.ph/profile/sep 2 1 4. htm). The law was enacted as the Indigenous People's Rights Act (IPRA) Law on October 27, 1997 and awarded Certificates of Ancestral Domain Claims. With the law's enactment, Mangyans began to recognize and receive ownership of physical land that had been used by their forefathers. In the distribution of the land, Alangan Mangyans were awarded 7,200 hectare and Iraya Mangyans were awarded 2,500 HA. Again, the whole domain awarded to the tribal groups was divided into small sitios as long as the inhabitants followed government protocols. *Datu* Roding explained how the ancestral domain had been divided:

> Like this land of our ancestors, I am the one who divides the land for them... like the one in bingal, they already showed a survey that their land has already been measured. That is what we also want to happen in our land because even in Alangan its finished already, its only our land that has not been measured yet... now... the way we divide the land is through the planting trees as point of divisions, or sometimes stones, or rivers, small creeks, and all of the papers of these divisions are all keep in my house...

Sitio Calamias had a land distribution process finished by *datu* Roding, although it was not officially recognized by the local government. Instead of waiting for the survey engineers to measure the land for distribution, *datu* Roding and the settlement Mangyans came to an agreement in the land distribution and divided the land with mutual consensus. They utilized a traditional way of measuring that involved taking note of the positions of creeks, trees and other natural landmarks, keeping records of these at *datu* Roding's house. Some Mangyans began to lease the land to the lowlanders for corn and rice cultivation and made lease contracts for cash return. Others also leased mango trees to the lowlanders and shared the harvests. The ancestral domain helped the settlement process of Mangyans, which has led to the acculturation process.

However, not all Mangyans have benefited from the distribution of the land and the acculturation process. Mangyans who have been experiencing acculturation also experienced the challenges of adjustment in modern economic conditions. Given the land of ancestors, Mangyans began to settle down in a permanent place and planted rice, corn and other more lucrative crops. Yet the new methods of cultivation, such as purchasing fertilizers and seeds, required a certain level of capital. They began to borrow money from lowlanders to purchase seeds and fertilizers for cultivation, having little left after paying them back. This is a widely occurring phenomenon among all tribes of Mangyans (Pennoyer, 1975). Ptr. Santi noted:

> ... It [the harvest] is not enough, especially when it comes to farming because all that we need is fertilizer, and the rice is taken [without payment]. And during harvest time, we give most of it to them, and there is almost none left for us.

Acculturated Mangyan settlers needed cash for various reasons that were other causes for losing part of their ancestral domain. In cases of food shortage and media emergency, Mangyans had to borrow cash from lowlanders at a high interest rate. They even presented parts of their ancestral domain as bond. Mangyans often ended up failing to pay the debts and, as a result, handed over their land to creditors. Many Mangyans became tenant farmers or temporary laborers working on the land they once owned.

Lack of government intervention and a self-reliance plan for indigenous groups such as Mangyans, both acculturated and settled, have left them exposed to tragic situations such as the loss of their land and becoming daily laborers.

Interactions with Outsiders

Contact with lowlanders is inevitable for acculturated Mangyans in the permanent settlements. Given the indicators provided above, the three Mangyan settlements have extensive interaction with outsiders, both positively and negatively. Christian contacts have supported the process of acculturation and modernization of the settlements as well as provided efforts toward building elementary education and community centers. However, at the same time, Christianization has meant the unavoidable disappearance of a genuine cultural heritage among Mangyans, such as their traditional birth, wedding, funeral and burial rituals. Commercial contact with lowlanders eased the life of Mangyans by providing various stencils, tools and food. Yet in reaping the benefits of commercial markets, Mangyans have exposed themselves to the danger of losing their ancestral domain to borrow cash from lowlanders. Lastly, Mangyans also began to receive modern media content for information and entertainment, religious practices, with media often introducing influences that caused undesirable behavior in adolescents and adults.

Sitio Baraas was the most open to the lowlanders among the three sitios. The Mangyans opted to go to the public market and interacted frequently with lowlander communities for purchasing commodities and food. The presence of Visayan communities has played a key role in introducing outside influences to the community, including commerce through sari-sari stores and even drinking, smoking and gambling. When the *Jesus* film was showing in the community, several members brought umbrellas to protect themselves from strong wind, not from rain. Although the evidence of modern life is still relatively unsophisticated, the interactions of Mangyans at sitio Baraas predict a certain degree of interactivity for future Mangyans.

Religious Context

Christianization and Acculturation

In the distinctive cultural and religious heritage of traditional Mangyans, the three acculturated sitios have experienced significant Christianization through the various efforts of foreign missionaries, local priests and pastors. Mangyans began to settle down in a permanent place by belonging both Catholic and Protestant Christian religions. Sometimes the settlement caused the rejection of indigenous belief, such as bad spirits causing death. The Christianization process was, indeed, a significant distinguishing feature of acculturated Mangyans from traditional groups (Feraro-Banta, 1985).

The religious context of the three sitios revealed the process of acculturation. Religious institutions such as PASAKAMI had been deeply involved in the establishment of the elementary school at sitio Siyapo, and native Mangyan priests were directly involved in teaching kids at sitio Calamias, which also happened in the work of missionaries in several settlements of Mangyan tribes (Postma, 1974). In sitio Calamias, an Episcopal priest extended his ministry to the people of Iraya, including members in Calamias. He not only provided religious services, but was also considerably involved in elementary education in the sitio by providing teachers from his parish. Religious institutions and workers were actively involved in the acculturation and modernization process of the three settlements in one way or another.

Communications media were also actively utilized by the religious activities. Only two ICCP pastors were using mobile phone units to communicate within and outside of assigned religious personnel. During initial research in sitio Daptap, the MTCA church utilized speakers, amplifiers and other modern media equipment for various religious and social gatherings. The equipment was donated by OMF, the mother organization that supported Mangyan missions. Both foreign and local missionaries brought various Jesus-figure films with evangelistic purposes, which were often the only visual exposure to the outside world of the Mangyans.

Religious workers made extensive connections with outside communities. Several Mangyan pastors in ICCP were educated biblically and professionally at Calapan, Oriental Mindoro. The pastors were able to learn Tagalog and English, which helped them learn and apply typical evangelical patterns of worship and teach songs in Mangyan churches. Churches also often served as meeting places for Mangyans to interact with lowland Mangyans. In the case of sitio Calamias, several adolescents stopped going to school but often visited Anglican churches in the lowland community. The priest who was in charge of the Anglican parish in barangay Bagong Silang regularly visited sitio Calamias and interacted with members of the settlement. The significant social development was mostly initiated by religious and government projects such as schools, community centers and water pumps, and were mainly negotiated and carried out by the religious institutions in the settlements.

Indigenous Religious Beliefs and Rituals in the Three Sitios

Christianized Mangyans did not necessarily cease the traditions that applied indigenous beliefs and rituals. Alangans in sitio Siyapo still recognized the presence of "*Apo Oraron*," the Supreme Deity. "*Apo*" in Alangan means master and "*Oraron*" refers to the Old One. Despite Catholicism being the dominant religion in the settlement, the religious spirit of Mangyans has merged with the Christian concept of God. Indigenous religious beliefs not only remained in the mind of Christianized Mangyans but were also still practiced through traditional ways in which they deal with problems and sicknesses.

For instance, Alangans in sitio Siyapo often asked the traditional magico-religious leader of the community, "*Marayawan*," to perform "*Hinang*," a ceremony that drives away bad sprits. In this ceremony, members of the settlements bring offerings such chickens and pigs, depending on what they can access, to remedy bad luck. A participant explained:

> For example, they ask the demons, they ask the faith healers, they call the bad spirits—those are the rules. If there is sickness, they will kill a black chicken, a white chicken and a pig so that they will be healed, and then they will call on a spirit.

And he continued:

> If somebody is sick, they will call the spiritist (*Marayawan*) and they will bring a yard of wood. And then they will ask if there is something wrong and if there is, they will measure it; if the wood became shorter, there was something wrong. After that, they will go to the house of the sick person and they will put something there while praying. I don't know what they are saying because they are whispering. Sometimes, they will put ginger on the head and then they will blow the head and say: The reason why your son is sick is because there is a big person in the Balete tree that you have passed and is now causing the sickness: and then the spiritist will get something and tell them that that it is the sickness that was placed on you.

The religious practice could be interpreted as a way of traditional healing. In this interpretation, even the wife of the *kuyay*, who was the community leader of the Catholic parish in the settlement, could perform the rituals.

When the investigation was not enough to find the robbers, traditional practices dealing with theft were still being carried out. A participant said that when there were times when community property, such as livestock, was stolen, the *kuyay* called all the members of the settlement and performed the rituals so that the spirits could determine who the robber was. This process was called the "*Tigi*" ritual:

> ... For example, if there is something missing, something has been stolen, the leader will prepare hot water and then he will pray and call the bad spirits, and all the people are called to participate. Then, one at a time, they will pull out things that are in the hot water and then they will pray something like: "If this person that will pull out a certain thing is the one who stole the carabao or goat, may he be burned/hurt by the hot water but if he is not the one, may he not be burned/hurt." So everyone dips their hand in the water.

However, the informants said that there were times that some of the members of the community got burned when they dipped their hands into the hot water over prayer, while strongly suspected people did not get burned during the rituals. So instead of ceasing thievery in the community, it continued without revealing the real robbers. Even so, the ritual *Tigi* and other indigenous practices continued in the Christianized Mangyan settlement.

Yet Christian Mangyans did not practice indigenous rituals such as moving away from the house of the death to avoid harm from the bad spirit in some of the settlements. Traditionally, Mangyans believed that the cause of various diseases came from bad spirits. Traditional Mangyans believed that they had to leave the house within twelve hours after someone died to avoid the bad spirit that caused the death. Before they left, they had to burn the clothes of the dead person and bury them together with the body (Leykamm, 1979). This practice made evangelical efforts very difficult among Mangyans. When Christian missionaries worked with the Mangyans and somehow were able to persuade them to go through the process of evangelism, the whole community would suddenly evacuate within the day if a death occurred. Therefore, an acculturated Mangyan settlement is a Christianized community that does not fear the harmful actions of bad spirits. Mangyans still practice quick funeral services within twelve hours from death, but they now pray over the dead body and bury it outside the settlement instead of leaving them in the place of death.

Protestantism

Christianized Mangyans were either Catholic or Protestant. It is hard to find data about the religious profile of Mangyan tribes, yet Ptr. Santi roughly figured out that twenty percent (20%) of Alangan tribes are Catholic, ten percent (10 %) are Protestant and the rest are traditional spirit believers. These figures were based on the number of small sitios and settlements of Alangans due to the distinctiveness of community of believers, which has been raised in recent theological dialogues by understanding the spirituality of settlements that are community-based in Africa and Asia (Adewuya, 2001; Hays, 1996). Mangyan religious settlements were similar to community-based religion in that all the community members experienced conversion to another religious belief. Members of sitio Siyapo converted to Catholicism, sitio Baraas converted to Protestantism, such as MTCA that are initiated by OMF, and sitio Calamias converted to Protestantism through the collective work of Western OMF missionaries. Religious conversion did not happen individually but collectively through the community leader's proposal. *Datu* Poming shared the past history of Christianization process in the sitio Calamias:

> Poming: Everybody here believes... Christ really is God... I can only say, if Jose Rizal is God I am not supporting it... because we all know that it is not written in the Bible. He is only a mere man. But if it is Christ... he is my brother... that is for sure.... Whatever kind of man... American.. Japanese... as long as he believes is Christ he is my brother because I am for Christ... that is my idea...
>
> Interviewer: When did Christianity arrive in this place?
>
> Poming: Forty years ago.. they (missionaries) were Americans... They were female Americans who taught us... That was the time when many natives learned abut the bible... because of them...
>
> Interviewer: How long did they stay? How many of them, did she stay alone or there are many of them?
>
> Poming: They were three when they arrive here, there were Americans and another from Germany. Two Americans and one German.
>
> Interviewer: How long did they stay here?
>
> Poming: Very long.... They serve for fifteen years...

One more distinctive characteristic of the three sitios was the extension of a new religious group in the collective religiosity. Sitio Siyapo was established by the work of a Catholic mission, PASAKAMI, and later the ICCP church with Ptr. Santi established a new Protestant church in the sitio. The ICCP church was established in sitio Baraas where MTCA church has existed; and sitio Siyapo once converted to Protestantism, yet later moved to the Episcopal Church with the presence of Protestant religious worship in the same settlement. The pluralistic changes of Christian context among Mangyans are the very center of religious context that this study built on.

Similar to the case of Siyapo, ICCP expanded its evangelistic endeavor to sitio Baraas, where the MTCA church has long been established. In sitio Calamias, social issues including ancestral domain have interfered with the Mangyans' relationship and connection with Protestant churches in the lowland. Later, they converted to the Episcopal Church. Although the three sitios have experienced community-based religious conversion to Christianity, they have experienced different kinds of religious beliefs, which is a modern characteristic in religious life. Religion, therefore, has become more a personal choice based on preference and religious experience.

Indigenous Christian Churches in the Philippines (ICCP)

ICCP was an indigenous Protestant organization established by the visionary Mangyan pastor, Santi. Ptr. Santi,was once a member of sitio Dapdap, which belonged to MTCA. When he had a personal spiritual experience—in Protestant terms, born again in the Spirit—he wanted to become a minister, so he attended a Bible school in Calapan, Oriental Mindoro in 1998. During his study, he was able to adopt typical Western and Protestant patterns of worship, discipleship and pastoral skills such as preaching, church administration and church finance. He came back to Dapdap and tried to apply what he had learned from the Bible college:

> That's where our group started. In 1998, that's when I studied. Then I went back to Mindoro in 2001 and had discipleship training. We discipled them; we were five, at first, and then we became 10. They became pastors, and we taught them how to lead the church, how to preach, homiletics, and evangelism, personal soul winning, until we had a lot of workers, pastors, and then we came up with a training program.

However, the members of the MTCA church in Dapdap did not agree with his plan, especially discipleship training. In their understanding, the new strategy was an overwhelming innovation that destroyed the church structure of the MTCA. Ptr. Santi did not stop his new ministry but recruited new members from different sitios who agreed with him and followed his ministry. He then created a discipleship group that named "Christian Leadership Bible School (CLBS)," which is now an organized religious denomination, ICCP. Santi continued to explain about ICCP:

> CLBS: Christian Leadership Bible School. I organized it, too, and then there is one week of training every month. They bring their own food, own fare, they go down from the mountain, and then we would be together for a week until there would be a lot of workers. We organized our group. When our group was organized, it was not yet registered. We called our group ICCP or Indigenous Christian Church of the Philippines, but we wanted to register it at the SEC. So that was our plan. It started in 2004, and we now have board members. We have a Vice President and President at the moment.

Ptr. Santi's older brother, Ptr. Ernesto Lekwenyan (henceforth Erning), later joined the group and became a pastor. Both Santi and Erning became the President and the Vice President of ICCP and tried to formally organize and register with the Security and Exchange Commission as a non-profit and religious organization. Under ICCP, more than twenty churches have been established and another twenty churches are being pioneered by the members of the group (see Figure 21).

Figure 21. *The Members of ICCP*

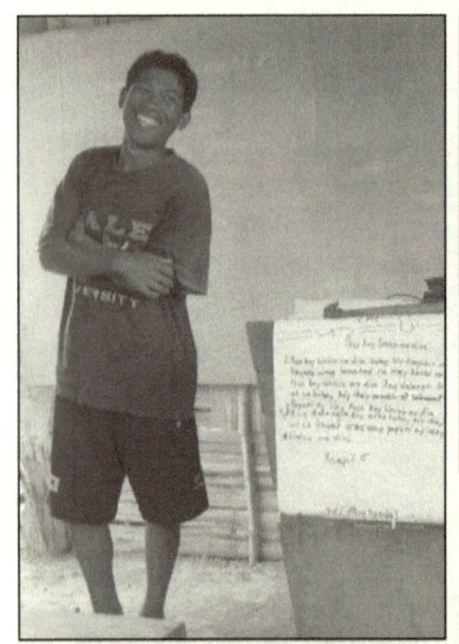

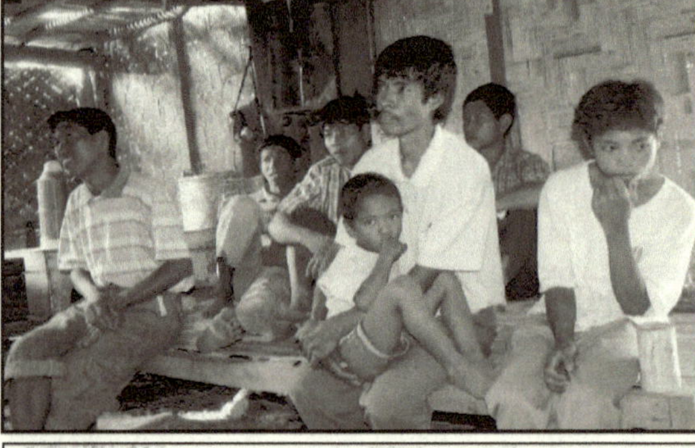

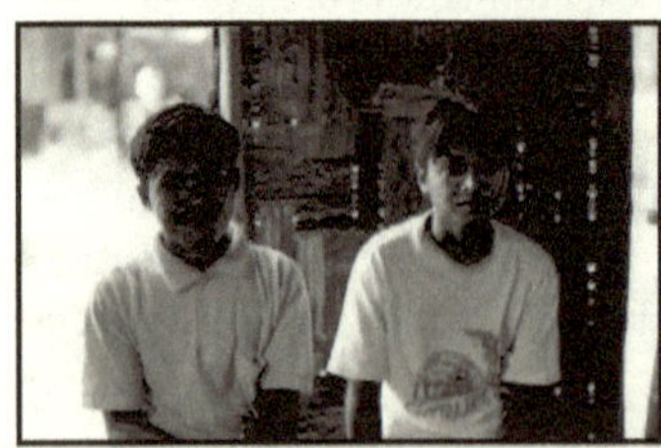

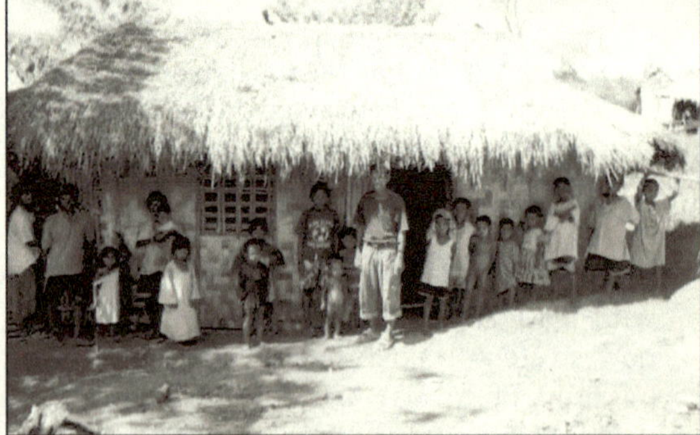

Clockwise, from top left: Pastor Santi at the pulpit in Siyapo church; the ICCP members involved in the film showing at Baraas; the ICCP church members at sitio Dapdap; and two assistant pastors at Siyapo church of ICCP.

The distinctive features of ICCP were its self-governing, self propagating and self-supporting characteristics. ICCP as an indigenous religious organization was not initiated by foreign missions but established by Mangyan Protestant Christians. Although it was not legally organized, the leadership and the administration were quite formalized. When Ptr. Santi moved to sitio Siyapo, he established the church finance system. Although the tithes and weekly offerings were not large (about 100 pesos per month), compared to urban churches, the church allotted its monthly income to church administration, pastor's salary, compassion for the members in case of financial difficulties, and missions for other Mangyan churches. ICCP also actively forced evangelism to duplicate churches among other Mangyan settlements. With regards to self-propagation, ICCP members have contacted external mission agencies such as the Bible League to obtain financial support for their mission efforts, yet the pioneering work was their own. Ptr. Santi stated:

> ...last 2007, the Bible League of the Philippines helped us and supported 21 church planters. They committed until August 2008 by giving a monthly allowance (*1,500 pesos per person per year* [italics mine]) to 21 church planters, and we hope that we will reach up to 25 local churches until August 2008. That's how our group started and how discipleships were formed until we grew bigger and bigger.

He also continued to explain the vision and the future of the Mangyan Mission:

> We are always praying that we would be able to reach the Mangyan tribes who are in the interior and don't really have hope. They will just die without Jesus in their hearts. That's our goal in ICCP, the Indigenous Christian Church of the Philippines. We want to reach all the tribes in the Philippines and we pray to the Lord that we will reach even the tribes in Palawan, tribes in Quezon, tribes in Baguio and everywhere. But we will start here in Mindoro through discipleship. That's our way of reaching them.

He dreamed of great evangelism, not only for the indigenous people of Mangyans, but also beyond ethnic boundaries. Evangelism beyond ethnic boundaries has been the favorite passage of Scripture among evangelicals as Acts 1:8 says, "But you will receive power when the Holy Spirit comes on you; and you will be my witnesses in Jerusalem, and in all Judea and Samaria, and to the ends of the earth" (New International Version, 1984). Ptr. Santi and his group were greatly influenced by typical evangelical Protestant tradition that has practiced the three-self policy and active expansion of the mission territory to other Mangyan settlements among Alangan and Iraya Mangyans.

ICCP at sitio Siyapo and Baraas

The ICCP of Ptr. Santi began its ministry two years ago at sitio Siyapo, which had been a Catholic community. Some members of the sitio were not satisfied with Catholic religious beliefs, practices and local leaders of the parish, and they tried to contact Ptr. Santi of ICCP to establish a new church in the settlement. Born in the Taubuid tribe and married to an Alangan wife, Ptr. Santi had a passion for his ministry among Alangans and received an invitation from a member of sitio Siyapo. The pioneering member donated land where their church was constructed, and a water pump was installed behind the church.

ICCP at sitio Baraas was built through joint efforts with the Bible League, which provided financial support of 1,500 pesos per month for the church. Similar to the size of the ICCP church in sitio Siyapo, it was relatively small, with fifteen regular attendees with only five family members in the settlement. The MTCA church had been established in the settlement for a long time and most households in the sitio still attended the MTCA church in sitio Barras. Neither Catholic churches nor other religious sects were established in the sitio yet—only in the nearby lowland communities. Those who did not attend either MTCA or ICCP went to other Christian churches located in the barangay proper of Lumangbayan.

The presence of a new Protestant, and simultaneously strong, evangelical church in the same compound gave the MTCA church some competitions. The presence of the ICCP church meant that the ministry of MTCA was not sufficient enough to provide the community members with spiritual leadership. Similar to pastor Santi at sitio Siyapo, the senior pastor of the ICCP church in sitio Baraas strongly felt the need for a new evangelical church in the sitio. According to him, the MTCA church was neither biblical nor evangelical.

ICCP Prayer Meetings

Ptr. Santi and ICCP members conducted a familiar pattern of evangelical Protestant religious services. Regular Sunday morning and afternoon worship as well as Wednesday morning service were held, and ICCP added a dawn prayer meeting every four o'clock in the morning. Worship was typically evangelical with the use of Tagalog Hymnals purchased at the OMF bookstore in Calapan. A guitar was the only musical instrument that was played to lead worship songs and hymnals during services, which was easily seen in typical Tagalog evangelical churches in the Philippines.

Interestingly, Ptr. Santi and his church practiced dawn prayer meeting each early morning. Ptr. Santi revealed that he derived the dawn prayer meeting not only from the prayers of Jesus, who prayed early in the morning (Mark 1: 35), but also from religious rituals of the traditional Mangyan prayer. These traditional rituals were devoted to prayers for bad and good spirits that lived in the rocks, trees, creeks and various objects that surrounded the settlements.

At four o'clock every morning, Ptr. Santi began the service by playing a tape of recorded religious music that was purchased in the OMF bookstore. In a few minutes, two assistant pastors and their spouses who lived beside the church arrived to join the prayer meeting. Members added to the congregation as the service went on. An assistant pastor rang the church bell loud enough to wake up the whole community to announce the beginning of the dawn prayer meeting. A few songs played in the solemn atmosphere as members prepared for the coming service with deep prayer and silent meditation. The oil lamp made of a recycled can of processed meat was the only source of light in the church (see Figure 22). The quiet was sometimes disrupted by the birds' singing and roosters' crows, yet I felt as if the walls and the tinned roof had been removed and the church became a part of nature.

Meanwhile, Ptr. Santi broke the deep meditative moments and carried on with the prayer meeting. He led a few Tagalog songs by playing guitar, and his wife would read a passage of the Tagalog version of the Bible. A sermon prepared by Ptr. Santi was followed by a Scripture reading for twenty to thirty minutes. Members kept adding to the congregation as the service went on. The sermon talked about faith in Christ and some members in the congregation sometimes agreed with the sermon by saying, "Amen." Although it was not quite lively, the service had interactions between the preacher and the congregation.

After the sermon ended, each individual member began to move out from the church to find their own prayer place near by the church. While Ptr. Santi was kneeling down on the first pew of the church, others went out and settled down in various places such as in front of a rock, tree and bush. Some prayed with a small voice that one could not understand even from just a few inches away. Others just kept silent. But most of them were kneeling, flat on the ground, bent forward so that they seemed to become a part of the land. The prayer went on for more than twenty minutes and the ones who finished prayers began to leave the place. The whole dawn prayer meeting lasted for more than an hour and a half that morning.

Figure 22. The *Instruments of Worship in the Siyapo Church of ICCP*

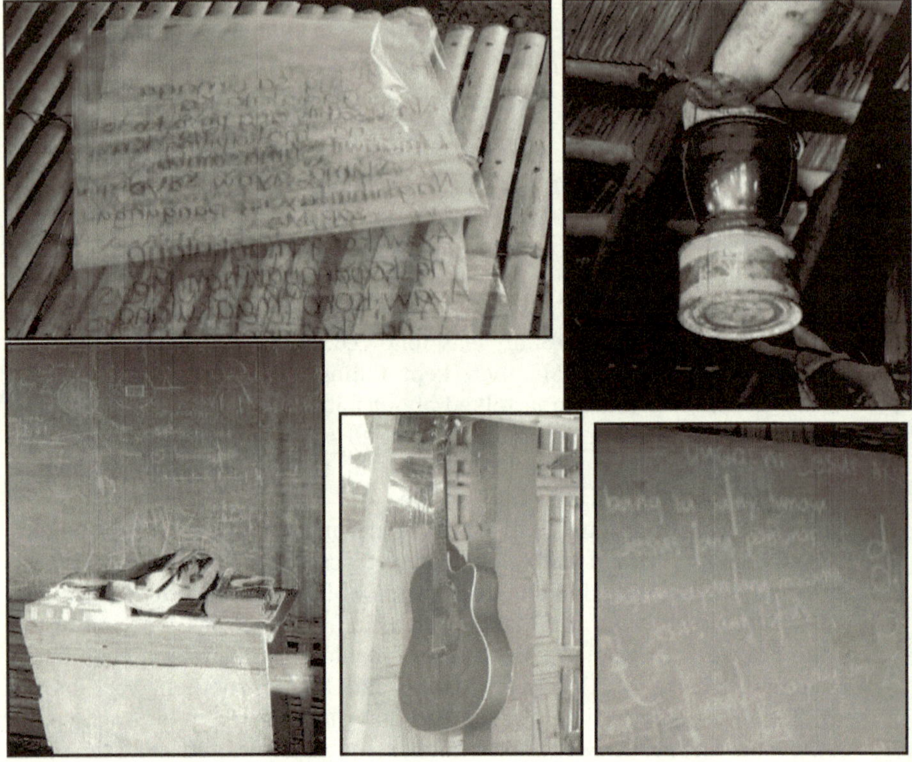

Clockwise, from top left: Tagalog songs written on the recycled plastic bag; the oil lamp made of recycled can and bottle hanging on the pillar of the church; A blackboard filled with biblical teaching; a guitar on the church, and pulpit with several Bibles and other materials.

Episcopal Worship at Sitio Calamias

Christian activities in sitio Calamias had some unique features. Without the clear distinctions between religious groups shown in the previous two sitios, the members of the settlement somewhat tolerated the plurality of Christian sectarianism. The settlement was once Christianized by Protestant missionaries. More than forty years ago, one German and two American OMF missionaries came after their China mission and subsequently arrived at the Manyan settlement. They lived in the settlement for fifteen years and taught the Bible as well as converted the whole village to Christians from indigenous beliefs.

Yet after the missionaries left the settlement, there was a dispute with regards to the ancestral domain that was given to Iraya and the members of the settlement. In 1976, lowland Tagalog evangelicals who were once communicating with the settlement negotiated the use of land given to the people of the community. The lowlanders tried to loan the land to the bank to make profit out of it, yet the land was not returned to the owners at the end. *Chieftain* Poming explained:

> Everyone in the community here owns land with a title in Pambu-an. The evangelicals pledged/pawned their lands, but did not return it to them. This means that God's purpose for us is good, but the leaders failed in their relationship with us.
>
> Actually, to our wit, it was pawned to the bank. ... And it was loaned... the proper word is "collateral," and the people who did it were actually lawyers and some Mangyan elders.

The Iraya Mangyans in sitio Calamias were upset with the calamity of losing the land and finally disconnected themselves from the Protestant group for a few years. Meanwhile, the Mangyans maintained their Protestant religious worship, which became a routine in their spiritual lives. The grandson of *datu* Roding was educated at the seminary in the municipality of San Jose and returned to the community as a bivocational pastor. He maintained offering weekly evangelical service on Tuesday in the community center. Adjacent Iraya community, sitio Burburuan, was ministered by another lay. The presence of Iraya pastors studied Bible college at Calapan, Oriental Mindoro.

Later, the members of the sitio Calamias had experienced another community conversion of religion to the Episcopal Church. During their hermit lives, an Episcopal father Sherwyn, who was assigned in a parish at a lowland community, sitio Bagong Silang, happened to find out about the presence of Iraya Mangyans. For seven years, he tried to help and contact the Mangyans. He provided foods and medicine as they were needed. He also tried to invite Mangyan adults and children to his lowland parish to participate in religious activities. Gradually, the community members accepted the Episcopal Church as the "official religion" in the sitio Calamias.

Yet the community maintained the presence of the multiple religious activities at different times, but held them at the same place, which was *Aplan*, the community center. There was no physical presence of a church building, but there was a shared multipurpose community center. Protestant worship was performed by the local Mangyan pastors at the same time as Episcopalian worship. The plural Christian presence was mundane and became a part of their religiosity. Some went to one service while other family members attended the others according to personal preference. *Datu* Roding emphasized his evangelical stance for his religious conviction but remained tolerant of any denominational division by citing a Tagalog praise song that was popular in the community:

> Si Hesus ang lahat sabuhay kaya Masaya
>
> Si Hesus ang lahat sabuhay kaya Masaya
>
> Problem ay mating kaya natig harapon

Jesus is everything in life so we are happy

Jesus is everything in life so we are happy

Problems may come, but we can face them

The community maintained this contextualized worship style that has evolved from that of typical evangelical Christians. The tradition of worship must have been inherited from the Western missionaries from OMF, yet with the absence of foreign guidance in the worship, it evolved into a more contextualized form of worship. Remarkably, the conflicts between lowland evangelical Protestant groups made the Christian members of the settlement back away from connection with the outside world, yet the disconnection with outside Christians caused the changes in the form of worship over the years.

The Sunday worship that was presided over by *chieftain* Poming and members in the settlement was more or less contextualized. The worship was observed without officiating Episcopalian priest to take charge of the worship. Chieftain Poming gave a sort of sermon in the middle of the service, and two youths played guitars and sang Iraya and Tagalog praise songs. The attitude of the informants of this service was quite different from those of ICCP members at Siyapo. They often chatted with other members while leaning against the wall. It seemed more of social gathering instead of worship in an evangelical sense (see Figure 23). No common prayers and rituals commonly offered through the Episcopal Church were present, as father Sherwyn explained.

The Mangyan Christians in the three sitios began to experience multiple religious practices and voluntarily chose one religion. Several religious groups such as Catholic Mangyan missions, PASAKAMI and Protestant foreign organization such as OMF, and indigenous group like ICCP and MTCA were involved in establishing the churches of the Mangyan settlements in the sitios. They actively constructed church buildings and conducted various worship styles. Conservative Protestant groups among indigenous groups were noteworthy, while indigenization of religious practices has been witnessed among Christian religious practices in various religious groups.

Figure 23. *Contextualized Episcopalian Worship at Sitio Calamias*

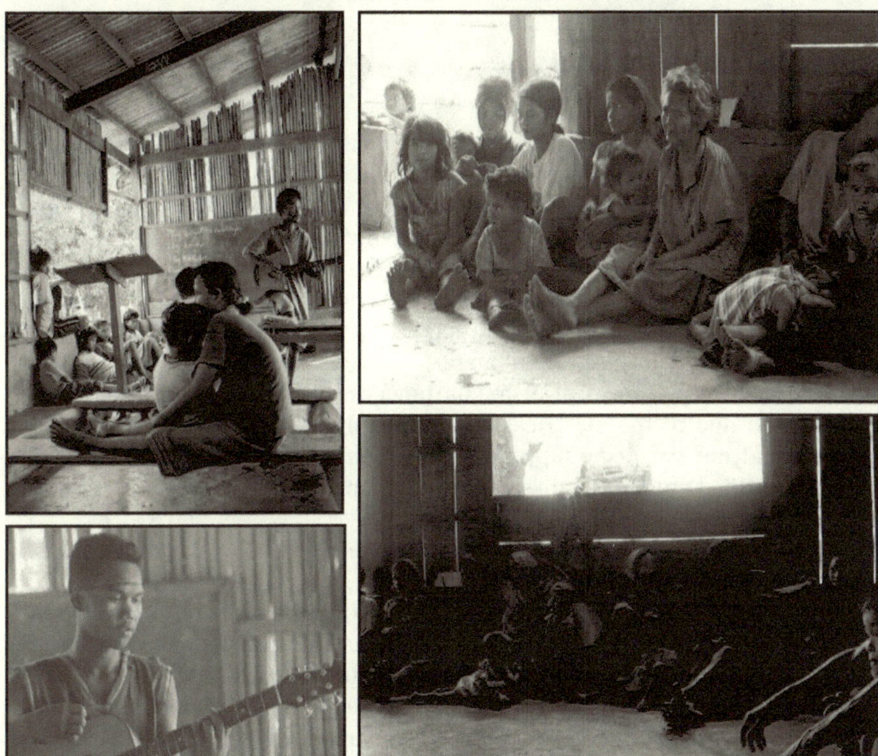

Clockwise, from top left: A member singing while youth were listening and leaning against the wall; A group of females with children attending the worship; Another group in the worship; A youth playing guitar during worship.

Among Mangyans, becoming a Christian connoted becoming acculturated and modernized. In the process of adapting modern Filipino culture among Mangyans, Christian religious institutions, both Catholic and Protestant, have become the agents of social change. Religious activities and efforts were becoming the venue for experiencing modern technology and media, while religious leaders played a vital role in social changes. It was, therefore, Christianization that has been integrated into the development of social changes that made Mangyans acculturated in the three settlements

Media Context

Media Acquisition and Use

Acculturated Mangyans in the three sitios already acquired some media gadgets and used them to connect to the outside world. Several radio receivers were already in place in the settlements, although they were still for communal rather than personal use. Tagalog movies and television series had already been introduced in some settlements with the use of old Betamax cassette players. The possession and the use of media has become a symbol of acculturation. Interestingly, the media used and consumption behavior were still significantly influenced by the religious commitment of Protestant Christians in the settlements.

The acquisition and use of media devices among Mangyans has been challenged due to the electrical energy supply. All three sitios in the research had not yet been supplied with electricity. Only three generators were identified among the three sitios as the main source of electric power supply.

Radio was the most common and favorite medium in the three sitios, although the number of radio sets in the sitios was not considerable enough. The number of radio sets identified in the course of our research was ten units in sitio Siyapo, six in Baraas, and five in Calamias. Compared to the population of the three sitios, radio acquisition was still limited. Listening patterns were still communal and shared with other members of the community such as friends and family members (see Figure 24). The radios were powered by batteries that were purchased at the local markets.

Radio was the easiest and most immediate medium that provided information, entertainment, popular culture and religious devotions to devoted evangelical Mangyans. Although there has not been systematic audience research among Mangyans, the interview informants who listened to radio could easily identify DZRH (Public AM radio by Manila Broadcasting Company), DZMM (Private AM radio station by ABS-CBN), DZAS 702 (Evangelical Protestant AM Station by Far Eastern Broadcasting Company) and Bambi FM, which were local FM stations aired from the municipality of Mambrao, as their favorite radio stations.

Daking, a 12-year-old Iraya-Mangyan girl at sitio Calamias, sang Tagalog songs fluently by listening to radio programs. She once attended a local elementary school in sitio Bagong Silang and transferred to the school at Calamias. She had also attended the Episcopal Church in the lowland a few years ago but has began attending the church at sitio Calamias. She could speak and write Tagalog due to her previous elementary education. She was somehow acquainted with radio and listened every day. Her friends in the same sitio shared similar media usage

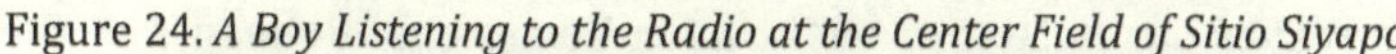

Figure 24. *A Boy Listening to the Radio at the Center Field of Sitio Siyapo*

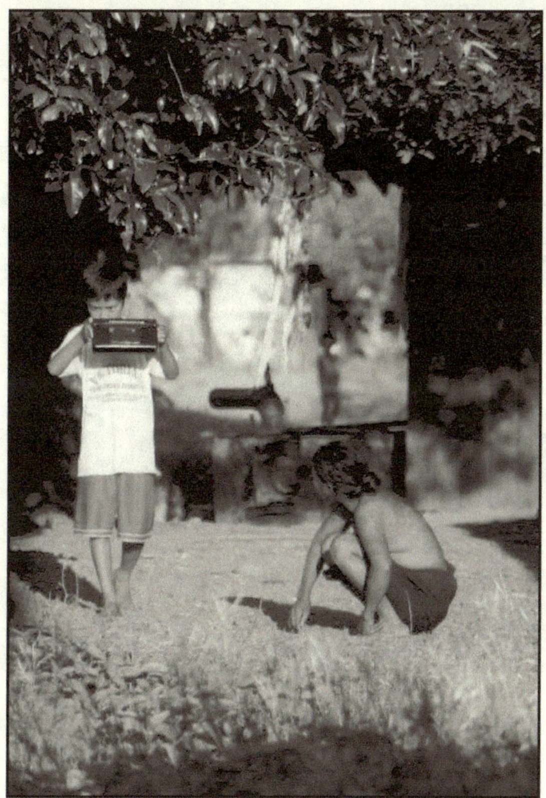

Interestingly, devoted religious members also actively used media for religious purposes. Most evangelical listeners identified DZAS 702 as their favorite channel. Some members recognized specific programs and preferences such as "Papuri" songs, which showcased a Filipino gospel-singing group and the preaching of Pastor ED Lapis of Day by Day Christian Fellowship located in Makati. Sonny, a member of ICCP in sitio Baraas said that she fixed the station channel to DZAS 702 and listened to the programs as much as she could. She expressed solid channel loyalty as a means of religious practice.

Visual Media and Television

Unlike radio, visual and television media acquisition and use were not common among Mangyans in the three sitios. This was simply due to the fact that a television set required a larger amount of money and it also required a generator to supply electric power in the sitios. The members of sitio Siyapo only possessed two television sets, and only one set at the sitio Baraas. The use of the television set was to connect with the old Betamax cassette player so that tapes could have been rented cheaply at the local market (see Figure 25).

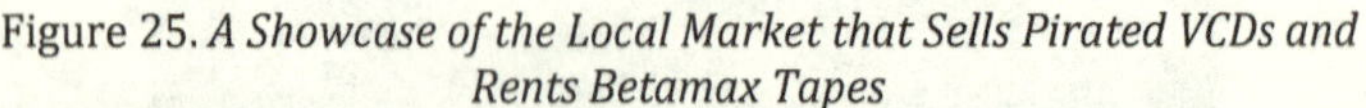

Figure 25. *A Showcase of the Local Market that Sells Pirated VCDs and Rents Betamax Tapes*

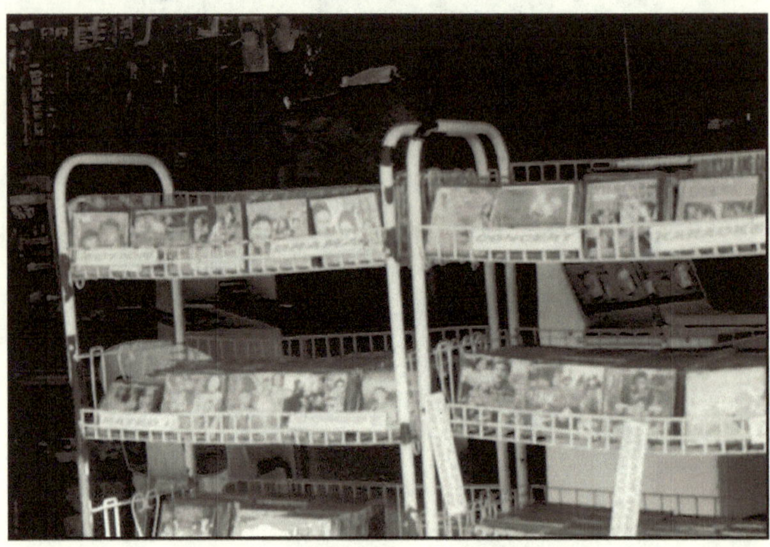

Although the availability of visual media was not common compared to radio media, its popularity goes beyond radio. In barangay Baraas, before the television set was broken, the owner of the Betamax ran various Tagalog movies and charged five pesos almost every night. It was similar to sitio Siyapo, where the owners of the television sets often called up community members to watch Tagalog tapes, either charging five pesos per person or letting them in for free if they brought gasoline to run the generators. Tagalog titles that were shown included action, drama and even X-rated movies. Community members preferred to watch movies after dinner, dependent upon the availability of cash for the entrance fee.

Media possession in the Mangyan community carried various meanings. The television owners in the settlement were considered to be rich and had great influence over other members. The owners could select the media content and decide what to show in the settlements. The media showing could also create income by charging five pesos per viewing, allowing owners to continue to dominate society.

Among the younger Mangyans, television was experienced in different ways and means than adults. Some children who used to attend the lowland elementary school had contact with a store along the way back to their settlements. They also had a chance to watch Tagalog television series through lowland contacts. Besides radio use, Daking, a young girl at sitio Calamias, also had experienced watching TV in the lowland sari-sari store.

She and her friends sometimes walked down to the lowland for 30 minutes just to watch Tagalog TV fantasy series. She remembered that their favorite series was "*Lastikman*".

Another media use came from religious and evangelical purposes. Through the Christianization process, foreign missionaries and local pastors had brought movies with religious content to show in the three sitios. Many of the *Jesus* film audiences had experienced similar or the same Jesus-figure films previously. The *kuyay* from the sitio Dapdap told us that he had watched the same film five times in different times and places. Some of the respondents said that they have also watched the recent film "*The Passion of the Christ*" through efforts of the local pastors for evangelistic purposes. Other Jesus-figure film showings became community gatherings regardless of the members' religious affiliations. The visual exposure was enough to attract the Mangyans in the acculturated settlements.

It is important to note that even Mangyan religious members had strong media preferences. The members of ICCP in both sitio Siyapo and Baraas refused to watch the usual movie showing in the settlements. They believed that secular media exposure did not positively affect their spiritual lives as Christians. Also, devoted believers, such as the pastor of sitio Baraas, perceived negative effects of media among children in the settlements from exposure to Tagalog movies. He thought that the ones who were fonder of watching videos were rude, violent and rebellious. As he believed the greater effects of the visual media on both the members of ICCP and others in the settlement, ICCP and its members deeeveloped strict regulations on media consumption.

Mobile Phone

The most notable use of modern technology in the settlements was that of the mobile phone. Only two pastors of ICCP possessed mobile phones in the three settlements during the research period. Ptr. Santi and I communicated through texting during preparations for the field research, and he continued to use his mobile phone as a means of communicating with outsiders, such as supporters and internal members of ICCP. Although not all ICCP members possessed mobile phones, the leaders used mobile phones to communicate with each other as well as with outside supporters such as Family International and Bible League. After I returned from fieldwork, Ptr. Santi even texted me in English regarding prayer requests and typical greetings during Holy Week. As a leader of ICCP, the mobile phone was the exclusive means of communication that enabled him to mobilize outside supporters and communicate internally for social gatherings and training for members.

Graffiti as a Form of Media

In sitio Calamias, interesting social media use was revealed—that is, graffiti or scratches on the wall of the community center, *Aplan*. *Aplan* was introduced as a multi-purpose center in the early 1990's with the support of a local politician. It was a place of worship, gathering and education. With the open basketball court beside the center, *Aplan* became the center of life of sitio Calamias.

The center was constructed with a concrete floor and covered with wood-board walls. The roof was covered with aluminum tins. It would have been difficult to carry all the construction materials from the lowland to this settlement. It was quite a modern structure with unique Mangyan interiors. The roof was high and the size was large compared to that of the ordinary Mangyan house. The seats were floored without chairs in one side which represents the seating culture of Mangyans (see Figure 26).

Graffiti is a means of human expression composed of drawings and writings from mural paintings of ancient times to the modern city wall spray paintings. Many different types and styles of graffiti express creativity of the ordinary people at a particular place and time.

Written mainly with chalk and coal, the graffiti on the walls of *Aplan* expressed various meanings in various forms. Some drawings and words, both in Tagalog and a transliteration of the Iraya language, explained the current interests and happenings in the settlements, while other graffiti showed universal themes such as courting and love among members in the settlement. For instance, a guitar, which was one of the modern and foreign influences in acculturated Mangyan settlements, was shown in several drawings in *Aplan* graffiti.

Figure 26. *The Community Center Aplan at Sitio Calamias*

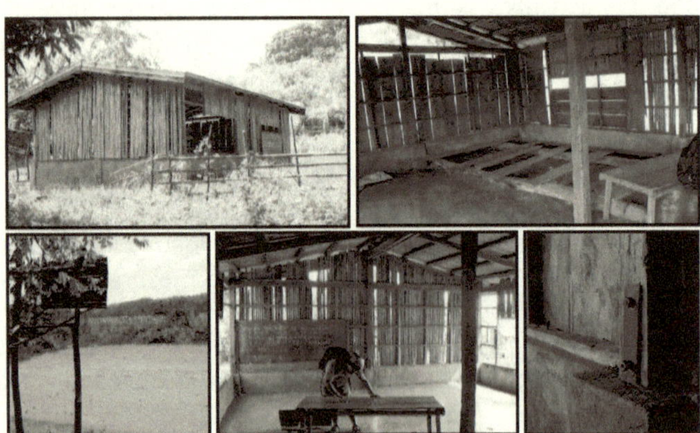

Clockwise, from top left: Full shot of the community center, Aplan; Inside view from lift of the front side; A hinge; Inside view from rear entrance; and a basketball court beside Aplan.

The Mangyans at sitio Calamias used a guitar as an instrument of worship and courtship. The drawing in the first picture of Figure 27 looks similar to the guitarists who played during worship (see Figure 22). The third drawing shows a man who plays a "*Harana*" (which means "serenade" in Tagalog) on a guitar to a lady on the other side. Although it was mainly an arrangement between parents, even traditional Mangyans used a form of serenade to court ladies for marriage (Feraro-Banta, 1985). Below this particular drawing, it says in Tagalog (see Figure 27):

SA BOGHAW NA BUHANGIN (The blue sand)

It might have been a popular song or a nostalgic place among members of the settlement because it was hard to imagine an actual place with blue sand in Mindoro.

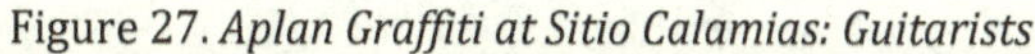

Figure 27. *Aplan Graffiti at Sitio Calamias: Guitarists*

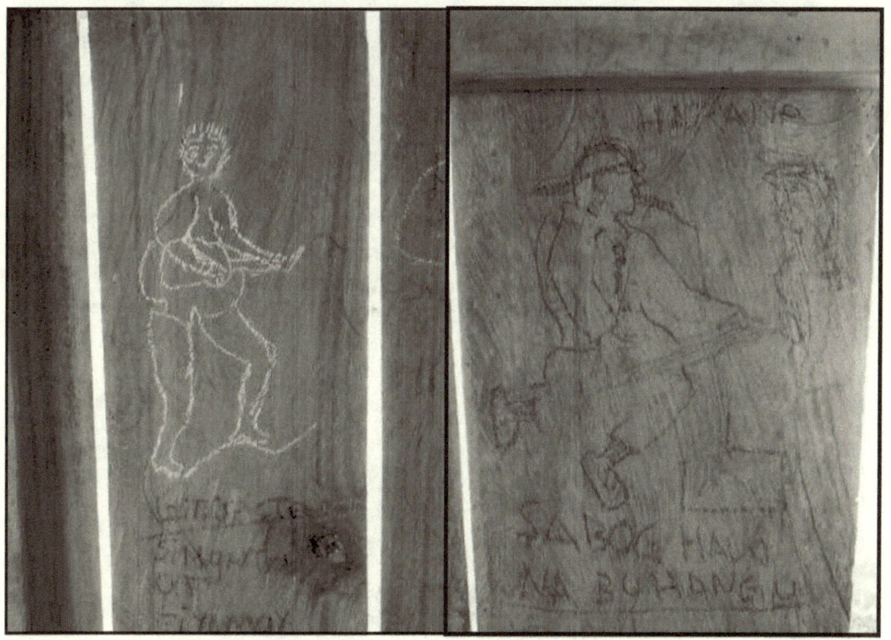

The next graffiti depicts teasing of a girl and a boy in the settlement in their personal relationship (see Figure 28). It says that EDGA (LALAKE, a boy) loves (MAHAL) ELMIB (BABAE, a girl). With the Tagalog words, the drawing depicts a boy and a girl hugging and kissing. Male and female relationships were also described in other graffiti, such words SINTA (dear one) and HALIC (kiss). Teasing love relationships among the six male and female Mangyan adolescents in the settlements was the source for the most fun graffiti in the settlement (see Figure 28).

Figure 28. *Aplan Graffiti at Sitio Calamias: Love Affairs*

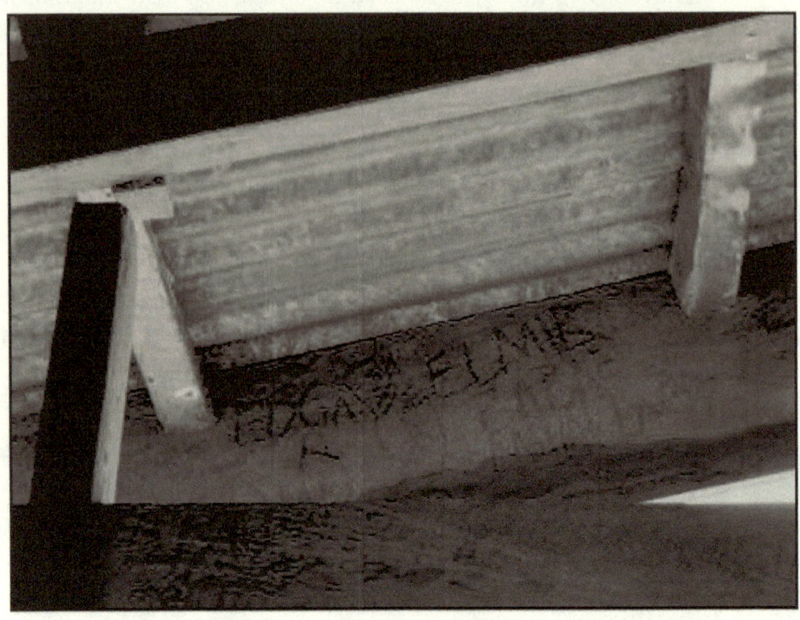

Apparently, some degrees of media influence are evident in the *Aplan* graffiti. Basketball, the favorite sport of members of the sitio Calamias, became one of the favorite graffiti subjects. The next picture depicts the graffiti of media influence (see Figure 29):

PBA IBS 5

PILIPINO BASKITBOLL ASSOSTION

This is probably a misspelling of ABC 5's Philippine Basketball Association (PBA) in Tagalog. This graffiti explained the popularity of basketball among members and their television viewing experience of the PBA on ABC 5.

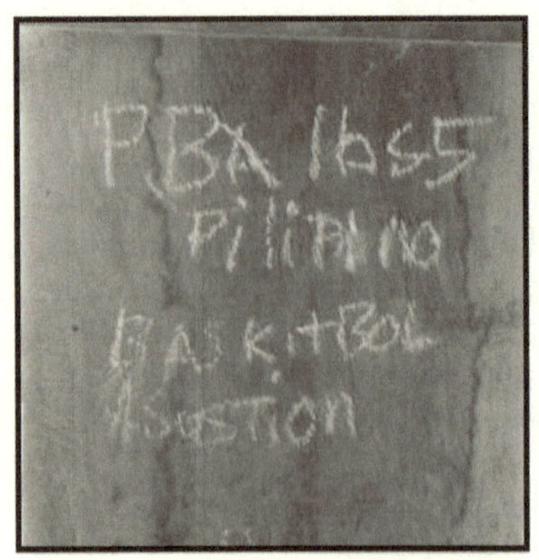

Figure 29. *Aplan Graffiti at Sitio Calamias: Media Exposure on Basketball Game*

The picture of Figure 30 (left) shows a hand holding a gun, which might be the memory of a scene in a Tagalog action movie. The picture in Figure 29 (right) depicts the famous television commercial of Gillette, Mr. Suave(a Spanish word for handsome and sounds similar to "shave"). Assuming that the graffiti writing required repetitive media viewings, these samples of graffiti explained the familiarity and extensive media use among the artists, who were mostly younger Mangyans, as well as their favorite subjects at this time and place.

Figure 30. *Aplan Graffiti at Sitio Calamias: Media Exposure on Television Commercials*

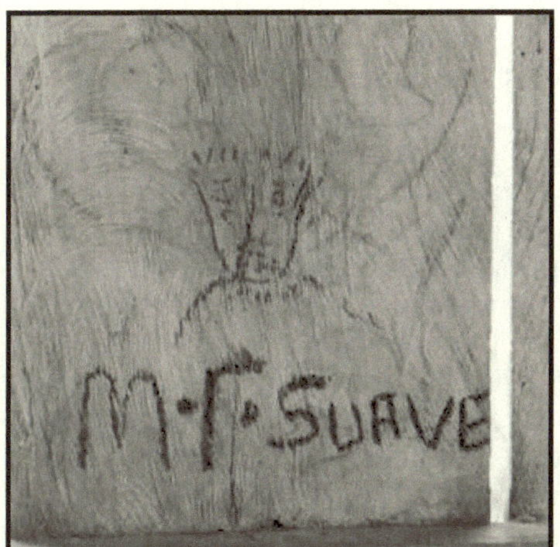

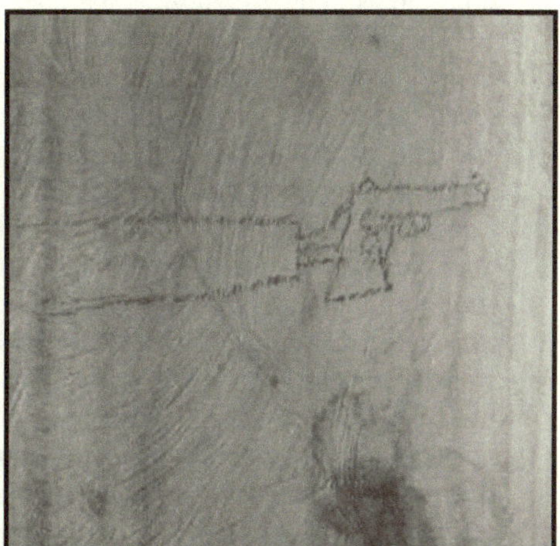

Synthesis

The contextual understanding of the research areas and informants became an integral part of this study. Based on the social construction theory (Burger & Luckmann, 1973) and media reception theories by Hall (1980), the audiences' context was synchronized in the reception of media message. The contextual understanding has served greater in this study since the informants of this study came from indigenous cultural group in the Philippines.

Social Context

Evidently, an extensive acculturation process occurred in the settlements in this research area. The settlement of the Mangyan sitios and the Mangyans' dress explicitly showed the transition of the Mangyans into a modern way of life. Second-hand cheap clothes were purchased from the lowland markets. Family and house size became smaller compared to the traditional Mangyan society. Contrary to the small size of the households, the size of the settlements tended to become larger compared to host schools, community centers and health clinics within the compound. Yet limitations in terms of media possession and use were obvious. Mangyans gained initial media exposure from the outside world. The physical metamorphosis illustrated apparent acculturation changes in the Mangyan settlements.

Notably, leadership in relation to Christianization was a part of the process of social change. Traditional magico-religious leadership merged into the socio-political leadership that intermingled with religious affiliations. In order for the leaders to maintain leadership role in the community, they were more or less forced to change their religious affiliation to Christian. Therefore, the current Mangyan leaders needed to give up their traditional position as magico-religious leaders.

The economic situation has become a positive and negative challenge for Mangyans in the acculturated settlements. The permanent settlement patterns caused by evangelization and supported by Christian groups and local government required new adaptation. Swidden agricultural and mobile methods of plantation changed to semi-permanent agriculture including rice fields. Central and local government granted the land right of native Mangyans as ancestral domain. Yet, many Mangyans exposed themselves to the greater danger of losing their land as a result of immediate cash loans from the low landers. Due to modernization, yet weak protection of the land titles from the local government, Mangyans have greatly lost their land to the lowlanders. The extensive level of interaction of the three sitios with the outside world indeed serve as a platform to confront a great challenge as they undergo more of the acculturation process in the years ahead.

Religious Context

Religious institutions such as Catholic, Protestant and Episcopal churches have extended their missions to the three Mangyan communities since the 1980s. PASAKAMI in sitio Siyapo was supported by the alliance of Mangyan missions in the Catholic Church, MTCA was supported by OMF and became more or less independent, and ICCP of Ptr. Santi was an indigenous Protestant group that stemmed from MTCA. These were the dominant Christian groups in the research areas. In addition, the Bible League of the Philippines and other independent foreign missionaries somehow significantly interacted with the indigenous Mangyan Christians.

The members of ICCP, where most of the research informants came from, showed typical conservative Christian worship and organization styles, but developed their worship styles in the presence of indigenous practices. Worship schedules were patterned after any Protestant churches in the Philippines except for dawn prayer meetings. Prayers and fasting were much emphasized with regular organizational large gatherings among the members. ICCP even extended its mission to the neighboring sitios in the inner mountain areas. Although material cultures are based on the Mangyan communities, The Protestant and conservative nature of ICCP is distinctive.

Indeed, Christianization has coincided with the acculturation process in the Mangyan communities. Various religious institutions have been active in developing the communities by donating facilities such as water pumps, schools and community centers. These religious groups actively engaged in the social development of the sitios. It is, therefore, reasonable to conclude that religion or religious institutions have become the agents of the modernization process among Mangyans in research areas.

Media Context

Modern media acquisition and use were inveriably part of the modern life of Mangyans in the three sitios. Even without a supply of electricity, Mangyans in the acculturated settlements were actively engaged in various types of media possession and use. Radio was the most popular among the electronic media, while television and movie watching were more communal. Interestingly, there was a considerable degree of graffiti in the community center of sitio Calamias, which showed much about the lives and the degree of media exposure of the members of the community.

Members of evangelical religions in the acculturated Mangyan settlements displayed conservative and selective use of the limited media available there. The devoted members of ICCP actively used DZAS 702 as a part of their religious practice and utilized the religious movies (most Jesus-figure films such as the *Jesus* film and *The Passion of the Christ*) that were brought by foreign missionaries and local pastors. Yet they strictly limited media exposure to secular media among members of the community. Viewing content such as violence, entertainment and sex were strictly prohibited for members of ICCP.

This social and religious context provided the degree of reception among the members of the research areas. Combined with the religious and social origins in the establishment in the three sitios, concealed tensions between Catholic and Protestant churches as well as MTCA and ICCP screened the film showing audiences and their reception. It provided one rationale as to why there was little conversion and follow-up after the showing, which had been reported to happen in other areas in the Philippines. Yet it was obvious that the informants were rather biased toward ICCP, towards the *Jesus* film watching. Furthermore, the cohesiveness in the religious affiliation provided strong interpretations as a community.

In addition, the previous exposure and acquaintance of visual media, though it was still limited, ensured that the film showing was not a totally new experience. Furthermore, they opted to consume various types of media, including film. Interestingly, conservative Mangyan Christians became more selective in their use of media, demonstrated by listening to religious content from the radio, which provided a level of readiness for the appreciation of the subject, the *Jesus* film. This context showed the high level of acceptance of the film medium, which was always evident in the previous film showings.

Chapter 6

The *Jesus* Film Showing

Introduction

This chapter is composed of the in-depth description of the film showing process. The process began with the initial contacts and different levels of negotiation in the decision of the showing sites. The research followed the film showing of Mangyan sitios that were already targeted in the 2008 plan. The process began to prepare the showing, actual showing and follow-up strategies.

The Mangyan film showing entailed various negotiation processes with local contacts. Ptr. Santi of ICCP and Ptr. Manad preferred and proposed to offer three different showings in three sitios, which was a different strategy from the typical three consecutive showings in one place. This adapted mode of showing was surely a considerable factor in the result of the film showing.

The film showing event turned out to be a venue for a religious gathering of the members of the ICCP. It was mainly due to the fact that the film showing was sponsored by ICCP. Yet film showing itself received great attention from Mangyan audiences as a social entertainment. The audience was composed of mixed genders and all ages. Across all the sitios, the audiences were composed of family members of all ages, often clustered in small groups. Therefore, the film showing was a genuine interpretive community reception that happened among acculturated Mangyans in Mindoro Occidental.

Obviously, the reception and the meaning-making was more on the "dominant-ideological reading" that strengthened the religious beliefs they had already accepted. Furthermore, the reception process was mediated through active leaders as "opinion leaders." And there was little evidence for perceptual and cognitive changes but rather verification of unclear biblical knowledge and strengthening of existing religious beliefs. Although religious conversion was the major purpose of this film ministry, follow-up responses did not happen in all the three sitios.

Initial Contacts and Negotiations

The scheduling process for the *Jesus* film showing was quite organized. For selection of the showing locations, the national *Jesus* film coordinator consulted with eleven District Superintendents and local *Jesus* film coordinators for possible sites for the coming year. The District Superintendent consulted the schedule with the local coordinator and, most of the time, visited the potential sites as well as met with the local pastors who would be in charge of promotion and film showing. They could negotiate where, when and with what methods they could be mobilized for the film showing. For instance, in the Southern Tagalog district, DS Tino proposed twelve sites for film showing for 2008, which were accepted by the national film coordinator, Ptr. Elmo (See Appendix E). In the list, a film showing was scheduled for barangay Baclaran in Occidental Mindoro but it was later changed to Mangyans in Occidental Mindoro, where this study was located. Following standard operational procedure, DS Tino went to Occidental Mindoro to discuss where, when and with what methods they could implement the Mangyan showings. He chose to contact Ptr. Manad instead of Ptr. Nobert, who was originally assigned for this showing in Occidental Mindoro.

Ptr. Manad became an important coordinator for this research. Born in barangay Barahan, Occidental Mindoro, he finished his A.B. in Agricultural Science and worked in the agricultural industry for a long time. He and his family had been active members of Christ is Lord, a localized Protestant group in the Philippines, for a long time. His father even once donated land and a church building for Christ is Lord. Yet, he chose to move his membership to the Church of the Nazarene due to the lack of supervision and support from the central administration in remote Occidental Mindoro. He finished his lay ministerial course to become a pastor and worked as a pastor of Harvest Church of the Nazarene in barangay Barahan, and at the same time was actively involved in establishing churches (in evangelical terms, church planting) in Occidental Mindoro. Ptr. Manad identified two Mangyan settlements for this showing, sitio Siyapo and sitio Calamias, based on his constant personal interactions with the two sitios. He continued to guide and coordinates the showings, as well as my research.

Upon contacting Ptr. Santi, members of ICCP were excited when they heard that there would be *Jesus* film showings in their sitios. They agreed to announce the film showing throughout the sitios nearby and promised to bring as many audience members as they could. The *Jesus* film team asked him about potential sites for showings, and Ptr. Santi soon sketched a rough map of the churches of his organization. He then also pointed out the five possible places for further showings for Mangyans (see Figure 8 on Chapter 4). Yet, as the team traveled to those places, Dapdap and Lanao were not included in the film showing plan.

The contact person assigned to look for locations for the *Jesus* film showing continued to visit sitio Calamias and was able to meet the community leaders, including *datu* Roding and barangay captain, *chieftain* Poming. *Datu* Roding was the traditional leader of the sitio and Mr. Poming was the official legal representative to the local government. Their presence showed the typical social and political structure revealed in the previous studies of traditional and acculturated Mangyan politics (Feraro-Banta, 1985; Kikuchi, 1973b, 1979). Ptr. Manad and the *Jesus* film team introduced their purpose of film showing in this area. Both of them warmly accepted the film showing and kindly explained the sitio's circumstances.

This Mangyan film showing was planned differently from the usual showing pattern. This showing was planned, as requested by Ptr. Santi, for three different showings in three different sitios. Usually, the film showing was planned for three consecutive days for showings in the same place to maximize the effects of the religious experience in one place. Each day, according to Ptr. Rex, the team showed an interesting secular or religious-themed movie to attract the community members. The film was shown later or on the last day, depending on the film showing plan, which was determined by the film coordinator and the local contacts. However, this particular Mangyan showing was targeted to show as widely as possible in different places to show the film to the members of ICCP and other Christian groups for potential religious experience and conversion. They wanted to see if it resulted in different reception patterns from the usual showings.

The initial contact process involved confirming the full acceptance of religious films among acculturated Mangyan groups. It was revealed that they had several experiences of religious film showings that were brought by foreign missionaries and local pastors. In a few hours of discussion and negotiation for decisions on the film showings, the local Mangyan contacts drew a plan for three different showings rather than three consecutive showings in one place. Furthermore, the film showing among Mangyans became unique in that the implementation was different from the usual showings due to the strong desire for a wider audience instead of a concentrated showing for religious conversion.

The promotion process was mainly conducted by personal contacts of the Mangyans. Ptr. Santi informed his group to visit the sites for film showing, and both *datu* Roding and *chieftain* Poming informed the settlement members of the coming activity. There were no printed promotional materials such as flyers and posters that were usually prepared by the local contacts. Yet the promotion was surely effective, as the Mangyan audiences were very attracted to the visual media and the interpersonal contacts within the ICCP organization.

Preparation for Film Showing

The team arrived at sitio Barahan on Feb. 13, 2008. Ptr. Rico J. Delos Santos (for short, Ptr. Rex), former *Jesus* film coordinator of the Southern Tagalog District, joined this trip as the main coordinator due to personal incidents that prevented DS Tino's participation. The composition of the team for film showings, according to Ptr. Rex, was flexible depending on the situation and the availability of the personnel. Standard operational procedure given by the national office indicated that the team typically contained four members. The projectionist took charge of the screening, while the secretary took care of finance, the recorder wrote a report, and a helper coordinated all of the procedures. Yet, for practical concerns, Ptr. Rex said that there would usually be one or two members to carry out a film showing with the use of buses, tricycles and boats. On this trip, Erwin and I sometimes participated, helping to carry film-showing equipment.

It was amazing to see how mobile it was to set up a film showing in a community. The equipment for showing included a portable Eiki LCD projector, a Cyber Home DVD player, a DJ-100 Fanther portable speaker and amplifier, a Yamaha EF 100 generator, a transformer, a 6 x 8 feet screen backdrop, and various electric cables and others materials that fit in a backpack (see Figure 31). It was surely more than one or two persons could carry, but it was made possible with the help of many people. In the rural areas, bus conductors helped in loading the equipment, and tricycle drivers also helped without any complaints. In this showing, the Mangyan pastors in the sitios also helped set up the film showing. It came from the very Filipino spirit called *Bayanihan,* which is a Filipino community-based support in cases of need.

Figure 31. *Loading Equipment for Film Showing*

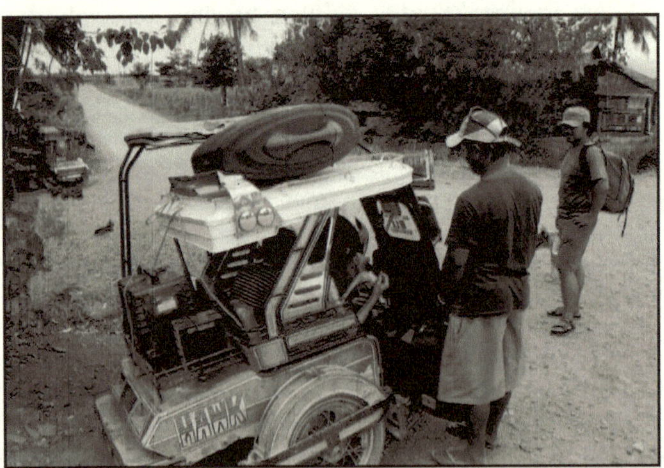

Setting up the film showing was easier than it seemed to be. Upon arriving at the three sitios, Ptr. Rex, the team leader, local coordinators and local contacts in this showing, Ptrs. Manad and Santi and his Mangyan pastors, helped transport the equipment from the tricycle to the place of showing. Ptr. Rex and others easily found resources for setting up screens in front of the church entrance. A table that was borrowed from the settlement was located usually about five to seven meters away from the screen, which is 8 x 6 feet, and set in front of the church with assembled portable speakers and amplifier. Finally, DVD players and projectors were set up and tested by generator (see Figure 32).

Figure 32. *Preparations for Film Showing*

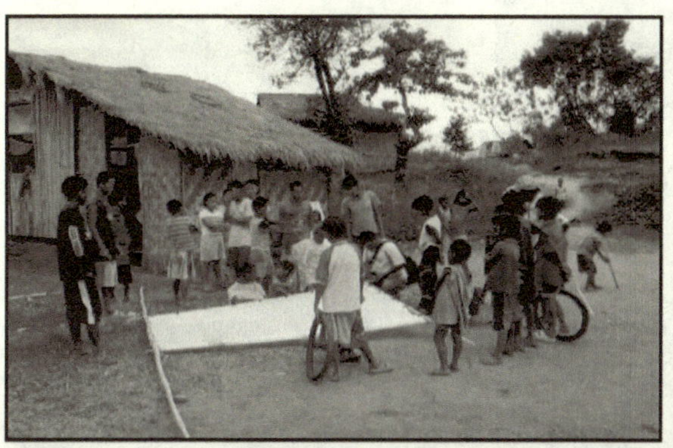

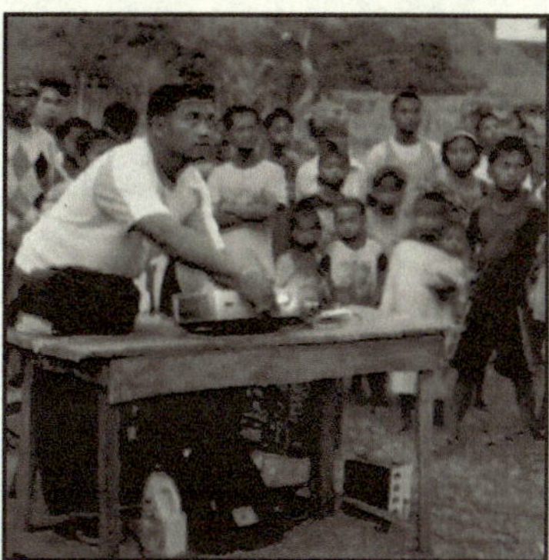

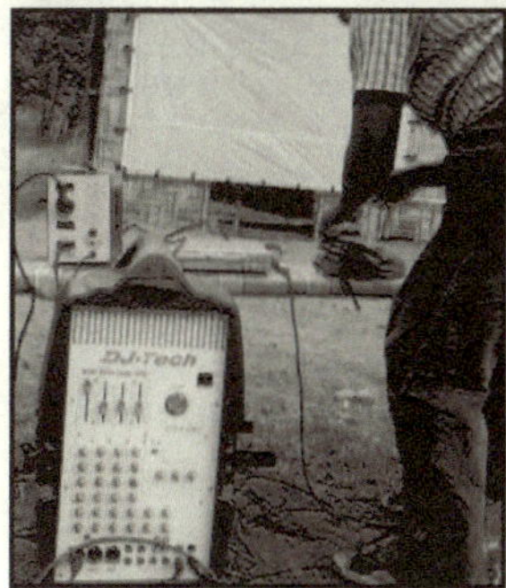

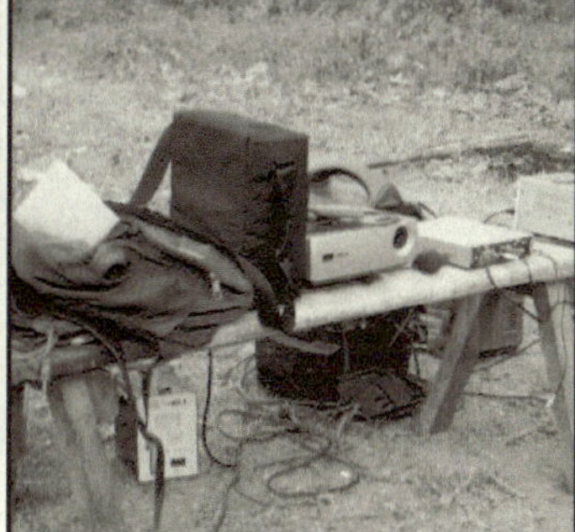

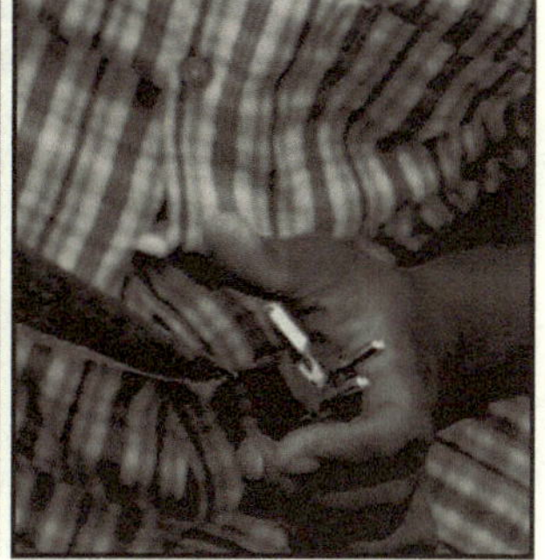

Clockwise, from top left: Children gathered around the preparation of screen at sitio Baraas; testing audio/visuals at sitio Baraas; fixing transmitter connection; equipments prepared on the bench; portable mixer; and DVD player and transmitter.

While the scene was set up, children and adults wondered about the equipment they rarely saw in daily life. From a distance, children giggled with small voices and often laughed at the changing scenes on the screen, while adults were hesitant in their full curiosity. Children often moved in and out of the place to call their friends who had not seen the rare opportunity of film preparation. When the test music began with English Christian music such as the *"Power of Love"* and *"Out of Mind into My Heart,"* the community members who came from the field and work gathered at the site to see what was going on (see Figure 33). Through the curious attraction of the media presentation, the children of the Mangyans were captured by the curious media content made in English.

Figure 33. *The Selective Response of Mangyans to the Film Showing Preparation*

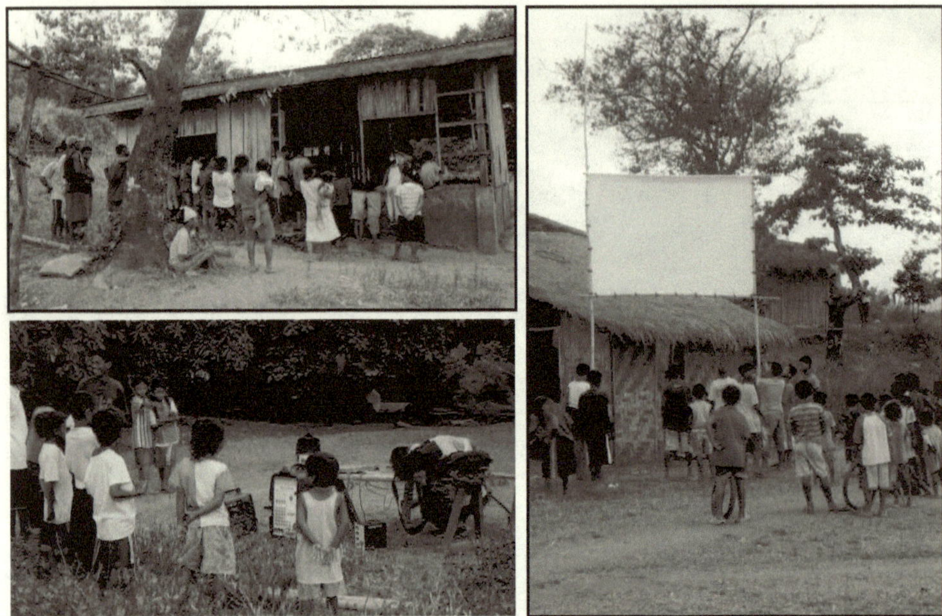

Clockwise, from top left: Sitio Mangyans hanging outside the Aplan; a group of children in the setting up at sitio Calamias; and a group of children of ICCP members at sitio Siyapo.

Although the Mangyans seemed excited by the film-showing preparation, there was a certain degree of caution and responses varied among the three sitios. The members of the ICCP churches generally accepted the event with full of excitement, whereas non-members were hesitant to enjoy the preparation in their settlements. In sitio Siyapo, due to the dominant Catholic population and strong suspicion of the activity initiated by the ICCP church, most adults were hesitant to approach the film showing in their settlements. Only a few ICCP members and their children were hanging around the preparation site, while non-members and their children were hiding behind the trees and their houses.

Although the vigilant attitude was not evident in sitio Baraas and Calamias compared to sitio Siyapo, most children and a few adults kept a considerable physical and emotional distance, standing mainly outside of the community center, *Aplan*, where preparations proceeded. Mangyans' receptive attitudes towards outsiders and film technology were somehow a significant consideration in getting responses during film showings.

Certain contingent accidents happened before and during preparation. On the way to sitio Calamias, there was an overflow of water that did not occur during the previous visit. The team members had to carry all the equipment for about a kilometer. Fortunately, two adolescent lowland Tagalogs accompanied the team and helped carry the equipment as well as push the tricycle through the flood. And in sitio Siyapo, while testing the sound, the transformer suddenly stopped functioning. According to Ptr. Rex, the transformer was important for regulating electric power because the generator could not produce enough stable electricity to run the DVD player. Ptr. Rex began testing it and took apart the transformer to diagnose the problem. The *Jesus* film coordinator, according to Ptr. Rex, needed some electrical and mechanical skills to deal with these kinds of problems in the field. It took about thirty minutes to resume test music to attract the members of the settlement to the film showing. It was good timing as the Mangyans began coming back from the field as the Western skies were aglow with the setting sun.

Actual Showing

The practice of film reception was not just a movie showing but also a collective social and religious activity. The main organizer for sitio Siyapo and Baraas was ICCP and the organization promoted and planned the showing with a gathering of the group. This was what Ptr. Santi had in mind when the film showing idea was first introduced. He greatly improvised using the film showing occasion in combination with the seminal gathering of ICCP. Due to Ptr. Santi's commitment, ICCP members became active audiences who have participated in the film showing to a great degree and mainly sat in the inner circles of the film showing compared to the passive audiences who were not members of ICCP. Yet, even the passive audiences who sat in the outer area during the showing still enjoyed this rare opportunity at the sitio. The place became a venue for social gathering and religious sharing as well as for interaction with modern technology.

The film showing event began with the preliminary showing of a dramatized Christian-theme movie, "*My Hope, Philippines.*" Produced by Billy Graham Productions in previous years, the film was aired in the Philippines, according to the *Jesus* film minister. The film describes the struggles and difficulties that can happen in the contemporary lives of Filipinos in Metro Manila. A lawyer has a nice house and good-looking family, yet his wife finds evidence of her husband's adulterous activities. By accident, the wife meets her old friend, who introduces her to the religious significance of her life by inviting her to a Protestant church. The wife finds meaning in her life through religious devotion.

This typical propagation of Christian values was intended for attracting audiences for film showing, as well as strengthening Christian values with the dramatized Tagalog movie. At first, there was suspicion about how much Mangyans in the settlement could understand regarding the situation of the movie, which was very different from the way they lived. Although the reception of this pre-showing was not in the objectives of this study, this culturally inappropriate theme and storyline, interspersed with with modern technology, might have brought them entertainment, but it was surely more evidence of a cultural force from an external religious group—that is, evangelical Protestants.

Furthermore, I wondered how the Mangyans at sitio Calamias, who have experienced conflicts with the lowlander Tagalog Protestants on matters concerning the ancestral domain, interpreted the film. Those who directly experienced incidents with lowland Protestant groups would have a negative reception of the Tagalog Christian value movie. The film did serve as a catalyst to call the attention of the Mangyans and make them come to the film showing. The film was surely aggressive evangelical religious message reinforcement by visual media on people who had not yet been exposed to the new technology.

Before the preliminary showing ended, Ptr. Rex finally asked the local contacts to determine the number of audience members. It was about seven o'clock in the evening when the film showing began, and there was a considerably large audience of 70 to 100 Mangyan individuals that gathered for the film showing. Ptr. Rex explained briefly in Tagalog about the film, its background and the story, and that the film was based on the book of Luke. Local contacts such as Ptrs. Santi and Erning signaled the start of the showing by prayer (see Figure 34).

Figure 34. *The Various Compositions of Audiences in the Film Showing*

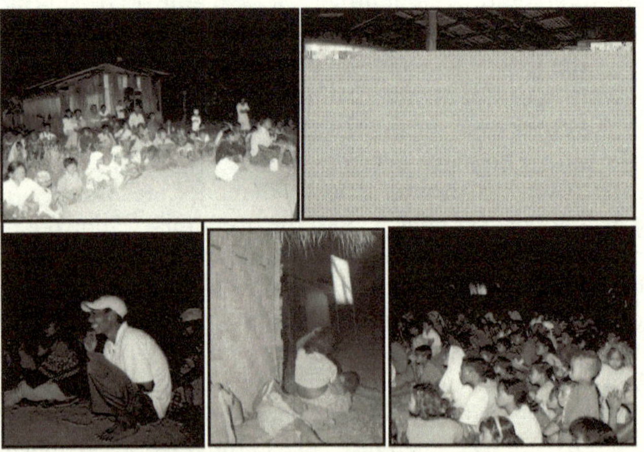

Clockwise, from top left: Audience at sitio Siyapo; audience inside Aplan at sitio Calamias; audience at sitio Baraas; a mother watching the film while breastfeeding her child; and an audience full of smiles while watching.

Moonlight illuminated the venue significantly without using electric lights, and the projector made a straight beam of light to the screen. It was bright enough to recognize facial changes and expressions as the audience watched the film. In sitio Siyapo, the beam of light from the projector provided enough light to observe the audience reception process.

The reception of the audience was of great interest. While it was obvious that some members were interested due to the fact that they traveled a few kilometers over the mountain for the film showing, others were standing behind a tree or stayed in their houses with the doors open. Mothers seemed not to want to move out when babies started crying. Those children who were tired of asking for their mothers' attention lay down and slept. Other children began to chat with their friends and amuse themselves when they lost interest in the film. Surely the children, who did not understand the Tagalog language, must have had a hard time concentrating on the show for two hours. They sometimes urinated beside the seats by simply standing up in the middle of the crowd. Similar occurrences happened in sitio Calamias, inside *Aplan*. Yet most audiences, regardless of age, did not leave but stayed for the entire show.

Composition of Audience

The film showing in the Mangyan settlement was more of a special social gathering, especially for the members of ICCP. The leaders intended to use this film showing as an opportunity for a religious meeting. Ptrs. Santi and Erning tried to organize an informal meeting with the members gathered for the showing. Most of them stayed in sitio Siyapo and Baraas with friends and relatives to continue to enjoy their special gathering in the next day. According to Ptr. Santi, ICCP occasionally brings its members together in a place for a spiritual revival or seminar on a given topic.

The showing was also open to Mangyans with the intention of a religious gathering. The audiences came from adjacent settlements with members ranging from 100 to 300 in one showing. With good communication from Ptr. Santi and his brother Erning, the Siyapo showing attracted nearly 200 audience members from the five sitios that were adjacent to sitio Siyapo, including sitio Tabag, Lamdigan, Buao and Kamanbugan. In the second showing at sitio Barras, more than 300 audience members were gathered from three different sitios, including Lanao and Dapdap, which are, respectively, six and ten kilometers away from sitio Barras. According to them, many ICCP members from other settlements including children under two years old walked over hilly mountains that usually took more than three to even five hours for this film showing. The third showing at sitio Calamias was mainly done for sitio members due to its distance from the adjacent settlements and lack of enthusiasm by the local host. Obviously, the composition of the audience included mostly family members and settlements regardless of gender and age.

The audiences could be divided into two groups. Including Ptrs. Santi and Erning, the ICCP members were actively involved in the showing. They placed their seats in front of the screen and formed a group of audience members. There were non-ICCP members (MTCA members) who were greatly interested in the film showing and traveled over the hilly mountains. This audience group began to form groups. However, there were some audience members who stayed in the outer circle during the showing. On all occasions, there were active audience members who stood or were seated a few meters away from the majority. Some stayed by the open doors of their houses.

The outer circle group was influenced for different reasons. As noted, they were not members of the ICCP group that coordinated the showing. In addition, other religious institutions such as the Catholic parish in sitio Siyapo hindered active participation in the reception of the film showing. In sitio Baraas, the Visayan ethno-linguistic group remained in the outer circle as if they were still foreign to Mangyan activities.

The showing stopped once after an hour, at the point in the film where the character of Zacchaeus was looking for Jesus under the mulberry tree, in order to switch to the second CD. The audiences began murmuring loudly among themselves to find out if that was the end of the film showing. They looked around and tried to understand what the projectionist was doing. Ptr. Rex announced that it was a short transition from the first CD to the second CD. When the light returned to the screen, the audience was relieved and excited about resuming the film.

The second half of the showing saw a shift in plot to the crisis. Soon after the Zacchaeus scene ended, Jesus began to proceed to Jerusalem to face his crucifixion and death. The pace of the movie became serious and quickly headed to the climax so that the audience did not move and chat as the climax peaked when Jesus was nailed to the cross. Some Mangyans tried to cover their eyes, afraid of seeing the torture of Jesus using whips, but they also did not want to lose the opportunity of seeing that moment. Mothers hugged their children in fear of seeing the violent scene. I felt that most of the audience was absorbed in the scene as if they were a part of the crowd in the movie. A few audience members' eyes misted over while others wiped tears while watching the crucifixion of Jesus.

Exhortation

At the crucifixion scene, Ptr. Rex paused the film again and explained the meaning of the crucifixion and death of Jesus Christ. As it was the standard operational process, he continued to explain in Tagalog that the scene was dramatized and not a direct videotaping of the actual event. According to Ptr. Rex, some audiences in rural provinces had confused the film mechanism and believed that Jesus's life was captured on film. To avoid confusion, Ptr. Rex tried to explain that this film was dramatized and scenes were performed by actors.

At the end of the showing, Ptr. Rex took to the floor for the third time and explained further to emphasize the death and the resurrection of Jesus, and encouraged audiences to respond to the film showing. He asked if any audience members had received Jesus Christ as their personal savior. He also invited the audience to come forward to receive acceptance prayers:

> Let us pray. Father, I humbly come to you this evening. Father, I am a sinner. I have sinned against you and I am sinful. That's why I come to you so that you may cleanse my heart of my sins. Forgive me for all my sins. In this moment, please come into my heart as my God and Savior. Make me into a person that follows your will. In Jesus' Name, Amen.

This was the process of confirming the film showing experience with religious conversion, which were the typical procedures in the *Jesus* film ministry. For the Mangyan showing, any explicit confession of sins or conversion by receiving the prayer was not made. There were no decision cards passed around after the showing in all occasions. When there was no conversion made, Ptr. Rex asked the audiences to pray together to receive the Holy Spirit. After the film showing ended by nine o'clock in the evening, some Mangyans who traveled from other settlements left the place and returned home, while others stayed with relatives and friends in the settlement.

Follow-up Strategy after Film Showing

As mentioned, the usual follow-up procedure for evangelical purposes was not pursued well in the Mangyan cases. In the Mangyan showings, the purpose was not evangelical but more similar to religious revival among members of the religious community. Furthermore, non-ICCP members were also religious members in either the Catholic or Protestant missions. Therefore, the follow-up that typically occurred in other occasions of the film showing was replaced with a seminal gathering of ICCP, while the rest simply enjoyed a rare film showing.

Typically, according to Ptr. Rex and other *Jesus* film coordinators, the exhortation ended by asking if members wanted to pray acceptance prayers to receive Jesus as a personal savior, and organizers and local contacts would distribute cards in case audience members made up their minds for further contact. These were called "decision cards." These cards were important for the coordinators to report the number of audience members who made decisions during film showing. They were an important indicator that could enable quantitative reports for the effects of the film showing in terms of religious converts. The personal information written on the card served as initial contact points for locals. They were developed to enable future personal contact after massive impersonal evangelistic events or film showings where interaction was limited.

In the previous film showing ministries, Ptrs. Manad and Rex emphasized that they were successful in the evangelistic follow-up after film showing. Both of the churches they were ministering in were the offspring of the *Jesus* film ministry a few years ago. After film showings, Ptr. Manad began the tedious task of making personal contact with the names on the decision cards. "It took more than two months to finish the first round of person-to-person visitation," continued Ptr. Manad. "My home church was smaller than 20 members, but after the showings and follow up, it is now more than 60 members."

Yet this strategy provided a venue for the local contacts to meet potential religious converts. Often, personal counseling was held during person-to-person contacts. Ptr. Rex also experienced a great deal of interest in the film and Christianity among audiences when he contacted them individually. Both pastors strongly agreed on the importance of follow-up after film showing, and that it was the key for success in religious conversion. The film, said Ptr. Rex, was an "opener" or "stimulator" to convert audiences into born-again Christians.

During personal contact, the local pastors often faced some personal difficulties with converts. Both Ptrs. Manad and Rex enountered many audience members who made decision cards for follow up and also expressed financial problems and family relationships. By dealing with these matters, they initiated counseling to give the potential converts comfort in spiritual revival.

Particularly in the Philippine context, they also encountered various questions on the differences between Catholic and Protestant beliefs. Those converts who were once Catholic were able to understand Protestant theological differences from ideas of Catholics such as the religious statues of the Virgin Mary. When the questions related to Catholic beliefs, the local contacts tried to explain the core theological meanings of evangelical Protestantism and were able to make Catholics understand evangelical beliefs regarding those issues. According to Filipino interviewees, the *Jesus* film was clear enough to explain the core evangelical theological meanings specifically for Filipinos, and described clearly the significance of Jesus as the Son of God and the human Mary as the mother of Jesus.

This aggressive evangelical strategy possibly contained rather dangerous potential conflicts in the community where different religious institutions are already in place. Several anecdotes described the presence of some antagonists who threatened the showing with various violations in the Philippine showings (Maano, 2000). Yet the threats were resolved and those who issued the threats became Christians. Others encouraged steadfast beliefs and strong army-like passion for evangelism. In the case of sitio Siyapo, the showing was resisted by the dominant Catholic group due to the potential threat of Catholic members converting to a Protestant church. Yet this strategy was developed by Campus Crusade for Christ, which was based on their theological conservative beliefs. The film showing became a tactic to exaggerate a fundamentalist evangelical strategy that strengthened the evangelical purpose, and at the same time, contained potential conflicts with other religions.

Synthesis

The search for the film showing location was a joint effort between the *Jesus* film team and local counterparts. It was more than just physical location but also included strategic planning with local contacts. If there was any element that was lacking, the showing would not have been possible, nor effective. This showing was a collaboration between the film team of Church of the Nazarene in the Southern Tagalog District, the Nazarene pastor, Ptr. Manad on the island of Mindoro, and the Mangyan indigenous pastor, Ptr. Santi and his ICCP. The team provided personnel to mobilize film showing equipment and Ptr. Manad and Santi worked to promote the showing in three sitios in Sta. Cruz, Occidental Mindoro. In the negotiation process and initial preparation for film showing, the local contacts played a crucial role in the success of the film showing. Pastors like Manad and Santi who personally promoted it to their communities and organizations made the showing successful.

Furthermore, it was obvious that the development of visual technology and mobility of the showing equipment accelerated the global penetration of the *Jesus* film teams. The mobile DVD equipment, sound system and generator enabled easy and quick implementation of the film showing ministry even in remote areas such as sitio Calamias. It was also possible with the support of massive funds coming from the United States to the mission fields, such as the Mangyan community. On the other hand, the audiences of the showing contradicted the modern technology and development. The film showing in Mangyan sitios surely stimulated their curiosity towards the film and modern technology.

Due to the nature of the audience group and tensions between religious groups in the three sitios, efforts to follow-up with religious converts were minimal. Most Mangyans in the three sitios were already, to some degree, members of a Christian group. In addition, the religious affiliations were not personal but rather social, which connected them with the large groups that they were associated with. In this regard, the film showing was not persuasive enough to make any religious converts among audiences. And the technological unfamiliarity with film media hindered them from believing and trusting the media message.

The reception pattern of the audiences was explicit and significant enough to understand the media reception patterns for The *Jesus* film. Mangyan audiences even traveled over mountains to watch the film. Notably, in the reception process, Mangyan audiences formed various groups for social interaction. For some uncertainties in the scene, they cross-checked the content and shared their expressions among the members of the small groups. In this process, the religious leaders such as Ptr. Santi and his followers were actively involved in explaining the stories to the members of communities, at the same time trying to impress their theological and ideological emphases of the film upon them. Therefore, the film showing was indeed a complex reception process that showed strong third-person effects on the community of Mangyan audiences.

Chapter 7

The *Jesus* Film and Its Reception

Introduction

This chapter pertains to the reception of the *Jesus* film within interpretive communities, which in this study involves Mangyan religious members. The reception pattern of *JF* showed an explicit community of interpretation, as revealed in the previous chapter. Mangyan audiences actively engaged in sharing ideas, talking, laughing and joking with each other while watching the film, as described in Chapter 6. During field research, observations were made and field notes were constructed on the audience's responses and active interactions. The jotted field notes became important data for analysis at a later time.

The observation data were later constructed based on the research framework of this study. The social construction of reality, encoding/decoding theory, ideology and discourse with interpretive community theory served to create a conceptual framework for this study to understand the meaning-making process of the Mangyan audience. The result was constructed by analyzing scenes to which the audiences actively responded, interviews about the meanings formed from the film showing, and the religious values and the perceptions on the Western figure of Jesus constructed from the film exposure. In addition, the significant scenes of the *Jesus* film were captured from the VCD format to which the audience responded to support the analyses, and this was done using VLC, a free video playback software. The captured scenes became an integral part of the reception analysis of this study.

Clearly, the film was ideologically centered and adhered to the fundamentalist evangelical standpoint of the producer. In the process, a Westernized visual image of Jesus was created, which has been the process of evangelical discursive formation. In the reception, meanings were ideological messages that were shared and reinforced by the mediation of opinion leaders in the community, such as Ptr. Santi and others. In addition, the images constructed from the film reception were patterned after typical evangelical beliefs that support the "dominant-ideological" reading in Hall's theory of reception.

Overview of the *Jesus* Film

The total length of film ran 1 hour and 56 minutes excluding the epilogue, which extended for more than five minutes. It explained the theological interpretation of the life of Jesus with the background series of still cuts from the film. Therefore, the total length of the film was approximately two hours.

The plot begins with the birth narrative and the story of a young Jesus, which serves as the prologue of the main body. The prologue and epilogue both begin with the title and the narration of John 3:16 that explicitly propose the evangelical standpoint of understanding Jesus as the Son of God and the Savior. The film ends with an epilogue that is a presentation of highlighted scenes with narration that explain the theological meaning of Jesus and His life. Besides the prologue and the epilogue, the whole film is composed of 35 scenes (see Appendix D.). The main body of the film rigidly follows the structure of the book of Luke.

Notably, the film was carefully designed to strengthen theological and historical accuracy. First of all, all artwork, costumes and props were produced based on careful archaeological research. Second, most of the dialogue and narration in the film were based on modern translations of the book of Luke. The producer intentionally avoided any creation or insertion of lines that were not based on the Bible. The main emphasis was to preserve biblical accuracy by using direct quotes from the Bible. Third, the treatment of the narration patterned after documentary genre mixed with dramatic presentation.

Various editing techniques were used to support dramatic presentations of the theological message. Music and sound effects were often used to strengthen emotions in the scenes. The plot did not always follow the order of the book of Luke, but was rearranged for the purpose of the intended message. For instance, Peter, who refused Jesus three times during his arrest, cried under a spotlight. The volume of the music rose with the overlapped image of Jesus predicting his betrayal. This scene was not explicitly described in the Bible, yet it intentionally emphasized the message of Peter's repentance.

Furthermore, the visual image of the sacredness and the authority of Jesus was intentionally accentuated using various film techniques. Most of the time, Jesus always appeared well-dressed in a way that was quite distinctive from the rest of his followers in a scene. During the whole film, Jesus wore only three white and beige costumes with matching towels. His footwear was tied and his straight hair was combed neatly to make a great contrast from the rest. These techniques were used to create the image of Jesus as sacred and holy.

Not only did the costumes and properties make clear distinctions, but the composition of scenes including the appearance of Jesus did also. Jesus usually stood two to three feet away from the rest of his followers in the scenes. And when he stood up to teach, the rest sat down. This contrast continued as he sat down when others stood up. When Jesus was teaching on the hillside, he was positioned uphill, looking down at his followers. This compositional contrasting technique was repeated throughout the film and created clear distinctive meanings of the master Jesus and the other followers.

Camera angles are another visual apparatus that highlighted the sacredness of Jesus. The camera angle posed Jesus from a low angle most of the time, whereas his followers were depicted from higher angles. For instance, when Jesus raised a girl from the dead, the shot began with Jesus looking down on the dead girl. The next shot showed the face of the girl from the perspective of Jesus. The angle shifted up to depict Jesus looking down on the girl. The camera then showed the girl rising from the bed over the shoulder of Jesus (see Figure 35). This camera composition and editing technique created the hierarchical relationship between Jesus and the rest.

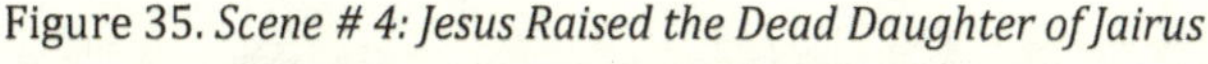

Figure 35. *Scene # 4: Jesus Raised the Dead Daughter of Jairus*

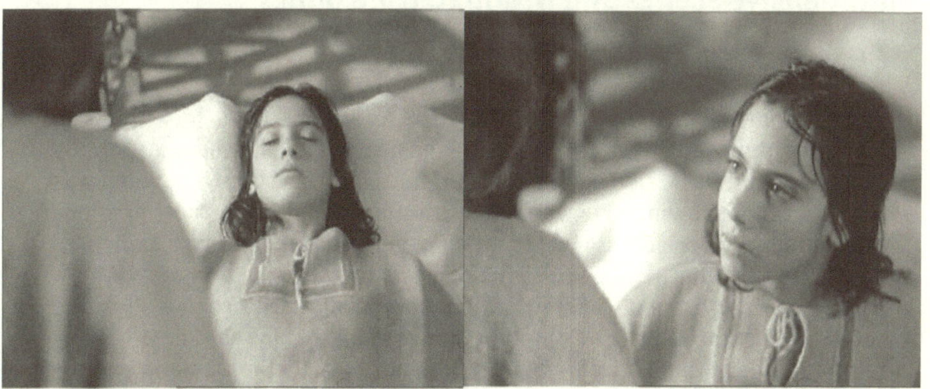

Interestingly, the film intentionally edited and rearranged the scenes to place an emphasis on anti-Semitic images that revealed the theological position of the producer as Reinhartz (2006) asserted. For instance, Jesus was baptized by John and proceeded to do the forty days of fasting and temptation, which provided a messianic view of Jesus. Yet, the next scene was followed by Jesus teaching at a synagogue and the furious Jews who rejected him. Hundreds of Jews were angry and pointed at Jesus, scolded him, and eventually cast him out of the village. The scenic composition was somewhat exaggerated in order to contrast the sacredness of Jesus and the Jews' harsh rejection of him, which eventually created the anti-Semitic meaning in the film. Furthermore, beginning from S#22 (see Appendix D), the three days of ministry and crucifixion of Jesus explicitly depicted the Jews as anti-

Christ figures, and in S#29 (see Appendix D) Pontius Pilate was depicted as intentionally avoiding sentencing Jesus to death. Boys (2004) similarly argued that fundamentalist evangelicals were ignorant in the presence of such anti-Semitic representation, a criticism that was also directed against *The Passion of the Christ* by Mel Gibson.

As mentioned in the introduction, the above-mentioned visual techniques and representation were the very apparatuses to visualize the fundamentalist belief of biblical inerrancy and Western supremacy. The film constructs the reality of Jesus that pertains to fundamentalist evangelical meanings of visual reality. Scene#1 (see Appendix D) especially literally visualized the presence of Holy Spirit as a dove (see Figure 37). Scene#12 also visualized the multiplication of food miracle in a literal sense. Furthermore, when Jesus finished praying, the baskets were filled with food (see Figure 40). These literal visualizations have reinforced the strong fundamentalist's theological standpoint. By constructing a historical Jesus in the film, the film also perpetuates the ideological Western image of Jesus in the evangelical message. With Jesus at the center of the visual message, Jesus became the Western symbol of evangelicals in the contemporary Christian era.

Responsive Scenes and Negotiated Meanings

Film-Showing Experience

The film-showing experience itself was remarkable for Christian Mangyan audiences who had limited exposure to visual media, especially religious content. Many audiences confessed that the film showing was their first film showing experience, while others could count their previous film-showing experiences. The reception experience among these audiences could itself be characterized as one of awe towards the new technology. Therefore, regardless of religious affiliation, the showing became a form of community entertainment using film media. Additionally, the film showing reinforced their theological beliefs. It was not only the appreciation of the content, but also an experience of new technology. What made it more interesting was that the technology and media could not be privately owned by Mangyan individuals.

Yet, the experience of new technology became the symbol of a desire to experience foreign culture. Post-colonial media scholars (Schiller, 1998; Hamelink, 1993; Parameswaran, 2002) pointed out that imported media content from Westernized and industrialized countries to the Third World constructs post-colonial influences. The silver screen placed in front of people who were not able to utilize the technology was a symbol of technological superiority over the indigenous Mangyan audience. They were looking up at the screen showing the film. The screen projected not only an awesome visual fantasy, but also the technological superiority of the foreigners over the Mangyans.

Visualization of the Biblical Characters

Christian Mangyans often reacted when they saw people from the Bible early into the film. When the main characters appeared on the screen, the Mangyan audiences talked and giggled in excitement when they saw the depicted biblical characters. They often confirmed the names of the characters by asking their friends and the pastors stationed nearby. They especially paid great attention to scenes such as the first appearance of the angel foretelling the virgin conception of Mary, as well as the first appearance of the adult Jesus to John the Baptist (See Figure 37). This visualization of biblical characters maintained enough interest for the Mangyan audiences to immerse in the film.

Figure 36. *Appearance of the Angel Gabriel to Mary in Prologue Scene*

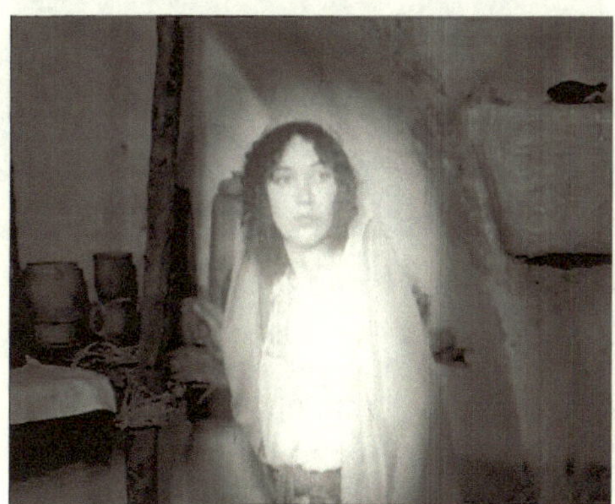

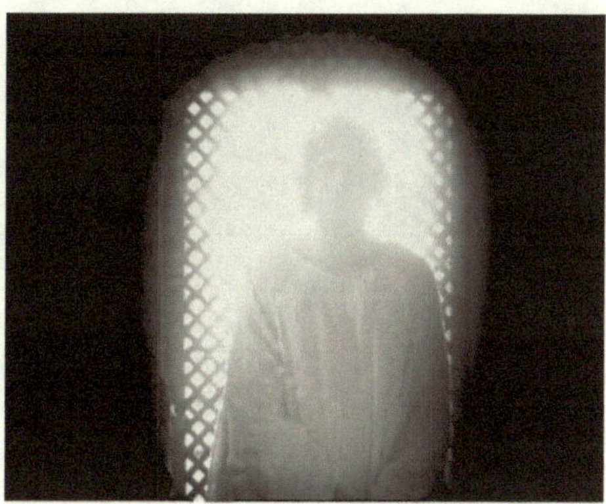

In the process of visualization of biblical characters in film form, the abstract image was now concrete enough to be imagined by audiences, especially among Christian ones. This process had a greater effect on audiences that did not have critical receptive ability. Mangyan audiences were rather excited to see the biblical characters in visual form, for example, Mary and the angel Gabriel (see Figure 33). From watching the film, the Mangyan audiences were able to visualize the biblical account in the book of Luke as well as the life of Jesus, making the event like a Sunday school class. This film-showing and reception process served to familiarize them with biblical knowledge in visual form.

When Jesus Shows Spiritual Authority

Jesus was portrayed in the film as authoritative and distinctive. These characteristics clearly differentiated Jesus from the other characters in the film. When Jesus became an adult, he sought to be baptized by John, and the Mangyan audiences began to murmur. In this scene, the distinction between Jesus and John was remarkable (see Figure 37). Jesus was neatly dressed and combed, whereas John had a full beard and had not combed his hair. In addition, when Jesus was baptized, a dove came down from the heavens to indicate the presence of the Holy Spirit. These distinctive appearances and actions signifying spiritual authority gradually enabled audiences to believe that the image was that of Jesus in the audiences' minds.

Figure 37. *Scene # 1: A Dove Representing the Holy Spirit Came Down from Heaven to Jesus (left) and John the Baptist (right)*

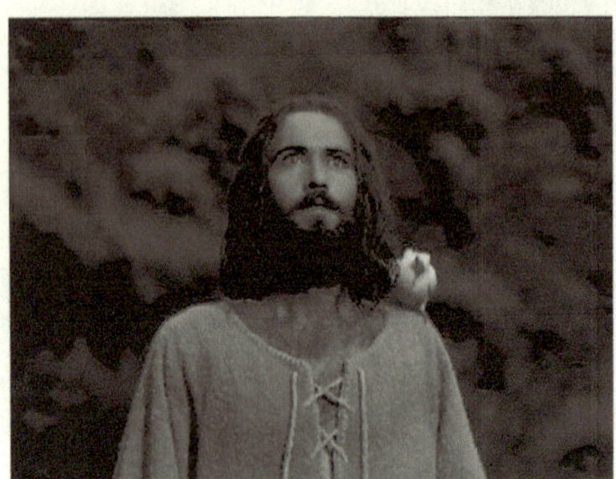

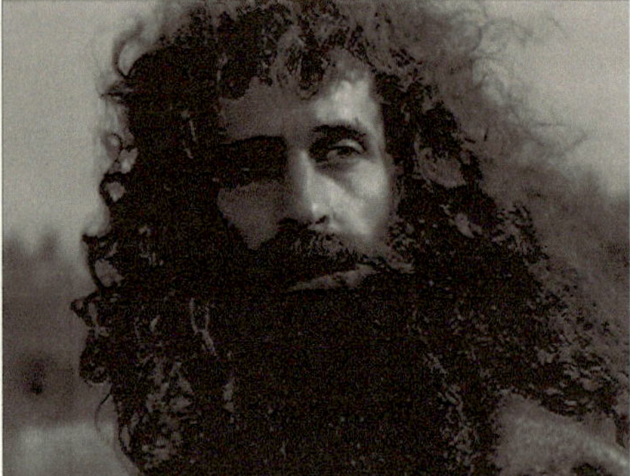

The solemn and sacred Jesus made a great impression on audiences at several points in the film. Jesus entered a synagogue in his costume and towels with neatly combed hair, making a distinct differentiation from the others in the scene. (see Figure 38, left). And in the Last Supper scene, the light was focused on Jesus, whereas the rest were exposed to dimmer lighting as they listened to His word (see Figure 38, right). In both scenes, Jesus was the central focus in the compositional design and made clear distinction as God. The composition of the scene constructed the sacredness of Jesus.

Figure 38. *Scene # 1 and 25: Jesus among the Jews (left) and Jesus with Twelve Disciples at the Last Supper (right)*

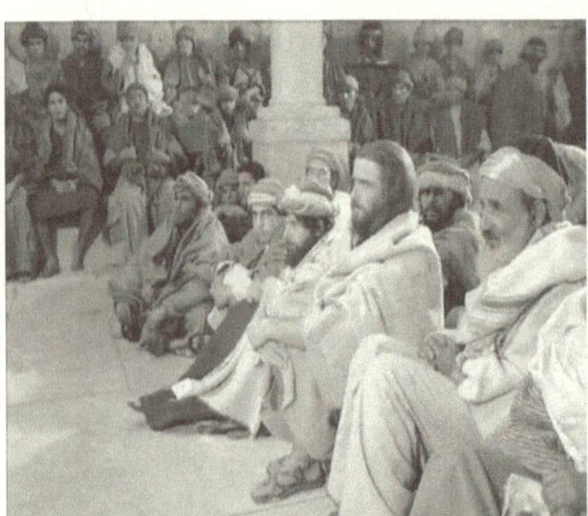

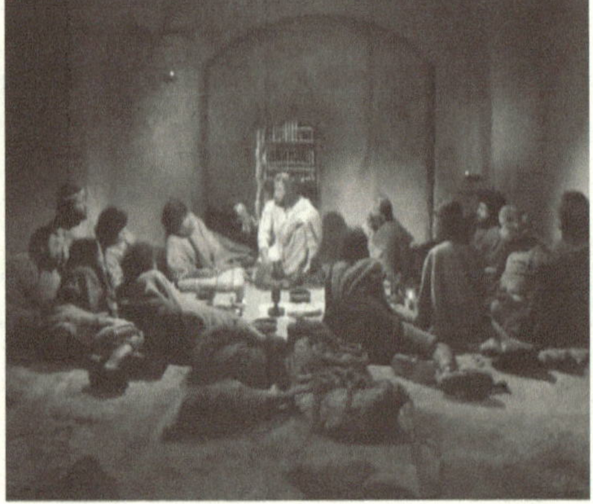

However, this relationship once again created colonial biases between the Western Jesus versus eastern disciples. Converting it to a racial framework, the Western figure became more solemn and neat, whereas the eastern disciples appeared funny and abnormal. This constructed dichotomy was repeated throughout the film and gradually drew the audience to agree with the racial typification.

When a Miracle is Performed

Healing and performing miracles were surely awesome acts to Mangyan audiences, who still retained traditional healers and magicians and did not have sufficient medical supplies. These scenes were surely evidence of a sacred Jesus. Among other miracles, Mangyan audiences laughed at the scene of casting out demons. The scene (see Figure 39, right) began with Jesus meeting a demon-possessed man just across the Sea of Galilee. A demon-possessed man moved toward Jesus and talked to him. Soon, Jesus commanded the demon to leave the man's body and to transfer to the pigs nearby. The pigs then ran into the Sea of Galilee (see Figure 39, left).

Figure 39. *Scene # 11and 16: A Demon-Possessed Man Facing Jesus (left) and Jesus Healed a Boy* Possessed by *an Evil Spirit (right)*

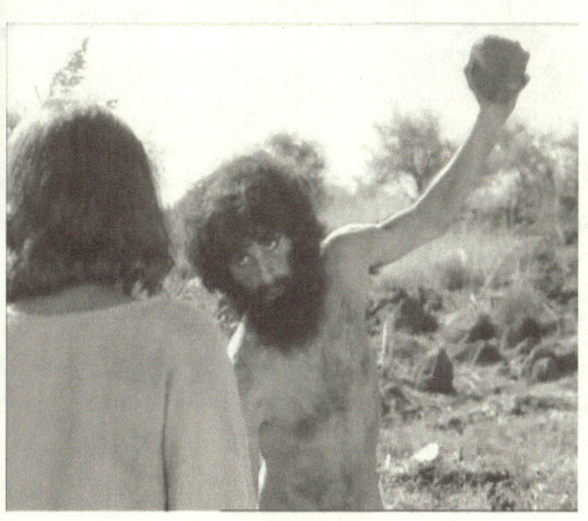

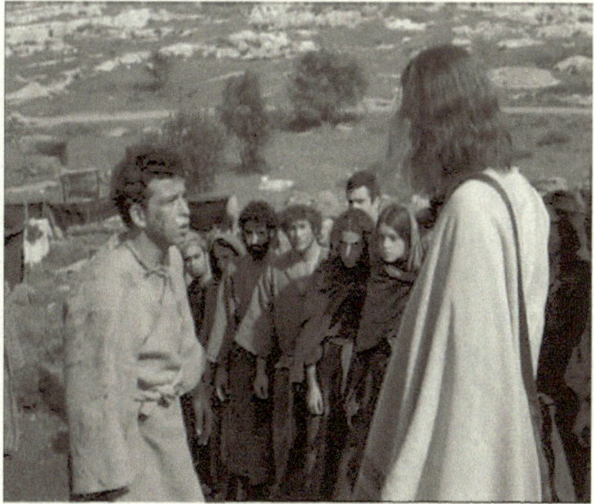

The mediated experience of the film was reinforced when the audiences had similar experiences. Ptr. Santi told that the Christian Mangyans have experienced the practice of casting out demons. There was a man in the Taguid-Mangyan near sitio Siapo. A few members of ICCP approached the man and prayed over him. Finally, the demon was cast out from the man. When the members of ICCP shared the exorcism, similar cases were personally accepted.

The miracle of Jesus took full advantage of the scene where he fed five thousand people. Jesus was teaching a large group of people on a mountain and prayed, raising five loaves of bread and two fish. Soon after he put down the baskets, the scene portrayed a continuous supply of bread and fish that was distributed among the five thousand people (see Figure 40). The "feeding of five thousand" miracle was followed right after by the raising of a girl from dead, which was purposely edited to amplify the miraculous power of Jesus. In this literal visualization of the biblical text, Mangyan audiences were astonished to see the miraculous performances of Jesus, especially in the context of food shortage in the Mangyan community, the food multiplication was more than just a miracle in the film to them.

Figure 40. *Scene # 12: Jesus Praying for Food (left) and Food Multiplied to Feed Five Thousand (right)*

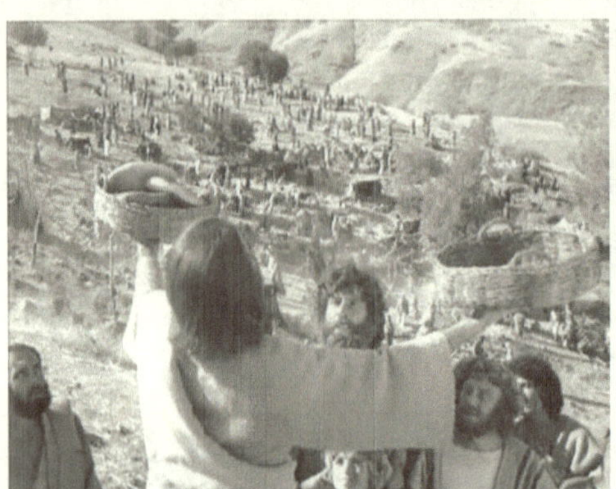

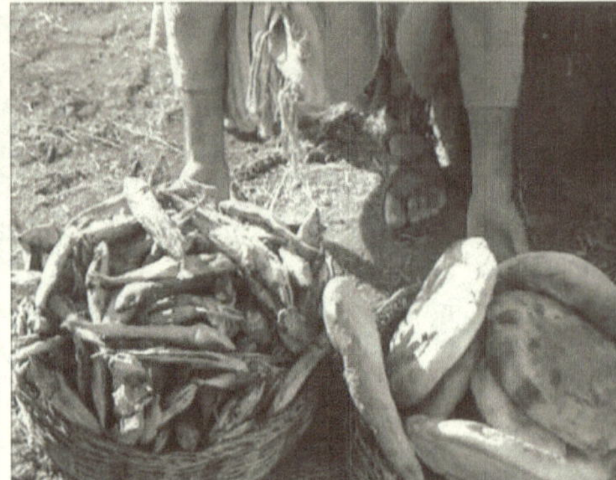

Yet, this particular miracle scene represented a fundamentalist theological stance that emphasized biblical inerrancy. The film portrayed the scenes as if they were historically correct. Yet the Bible does not clearly explain how the bread and fish multiplied to feed five thousand people. This was an intentional interpretion of the scripture in the visualizing process with the fundamentalist evangelical position of the producer and Campus Crusade for Christ (C.C.C). This visualization was evidently fundamentalist or a conservative interpretation in that there was an assumption that there was no error or the presumption that the Bible was written by direct dictation of God.

Similarity is Found in Their Lives

Interestingly, Mangyan audiences were excited to find similarities between the scenic setting in the movie and the real setting of Mangyan villages, which drew empathy for the film. The screen was set up in a village where mountains stood as a backdrop and the bare ground with rocks and soil looked like an extension from the screen. As night approached, the bright beam of light from the screen lit the dark environment, which recalled the whole setting of a village in Israel two thousand years ago (see Figure 41).

Figure 41. *Scene # 13 and 17: Peter and Two Other Disciples Lying on the Ground (left) and Jesus Teaching Disciples in the Forest (right)*

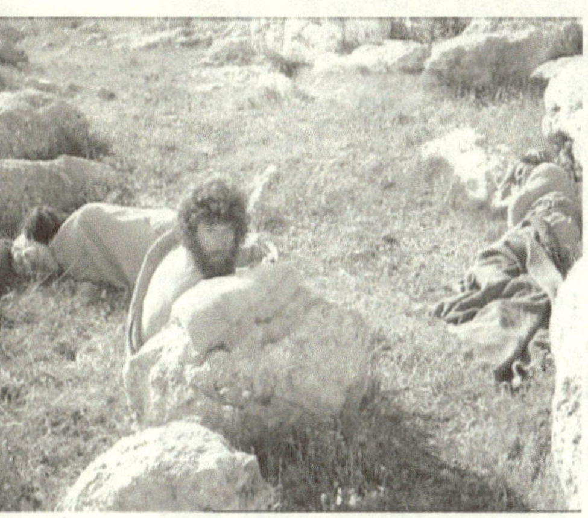

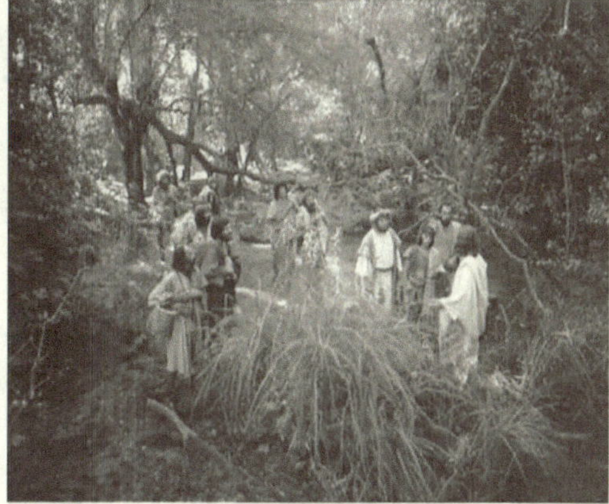

Mangyan audiences shared this empathic impression with others when they saw scenes such as dining and preaching in a field that placed a similar setting in their lives. They said, "The wilderness is almost like ours"; "Is this community like ours?"; "They have the same baskets as ours." In the environment and setting of the film, Mangyan audiences found great similarity in nature and the manner of daily living such as when Israelites sat on the ground, in the villages where pigs and goats roamed freely, and eating with bare hands.

In this reception, Mangyan audiences began to familiarize themselves with the film and to assimilate the content of the film. This assimilation process excelled in the shared religious affiliation of the audience. When Mangyan Christian audiences identified the similarity of the scenic environment to commonality in religious affiliation, the film acquired great credibility in its content and audiences paid more attention to the film.

When There is Abundant Food

The film created an illusion that was often difficult to achieve in real life. To Mangyan audiences, fully arranged food on the table was a luxury. During field work, there were often chances to eat with Mangyans, and they shared cooked rice, sweet potatoes and some canned goods that I brought with me. In the Mangyan context, the food prepared on the table of Zacchaeus was simply "abundant food" and a sign of well-being and blessing (see Figure 42).

The excitement regarding food continued in the scene of Zacchaeus and the feeding of five thousand people. They shouted, "All people have eaten," and "People are satisfied with the food." These exclamations were often repeated when Jesus helped Peter catch many fish at their first meeting. During film reception, Mangyan audiences often compared their own lives with the scenes in the film and expressed their wishes.

Figure 42. *Scene # 21: A Feast at the House of Zacchaeus*

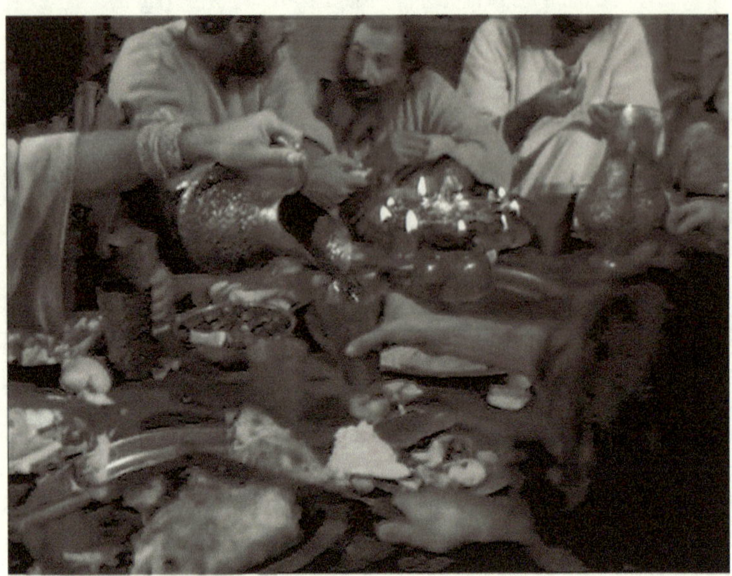

When Jesus was Crucified

The climax of the film was the crucifixion, death and the resurrection of Jesus. The crisis of the film began with the scene where Jesus was tortured by Roman soldiers. Jesus' bare body was whipped and blood was shed (see Figure 43). Mangyan audiences began to hold their breaths and watched with a great intensity that was often broken by exclamations.

As the whip hit the bloodied body of Jesus, ladies and children often covered their eyes with hands or turned their eyes down to avoid watching the screen. Adult male audiences did not avoid the scene but closed their eyes with painful feeling. Ptr. Erning shared a previous experience from a few years back when an American missionary brought the film, *The Passion of the Christ* by Mel Gibson. The crucifixion scene was too cruel to watch; many Mangyans left the scene. Some of them even avoided even this *Jesus* film showing due to the painful experience with *The Passion of the Christ.* The crucifixion climaxed with the nailing scene. Someone shouted while watching the nailing scene, "Look at his hand!" several audiences shared their experiences:

Interviewer: what particular scenes in the movie you like most?

> Mrs. Roding: The part where he healed the blind and the part that he died for the sins of men....
> Interviewer: it's like when he healed the sick and when he died and rose again... when he died...

Figure 43. *Scene # 30: The Crucifixion of Jesus*

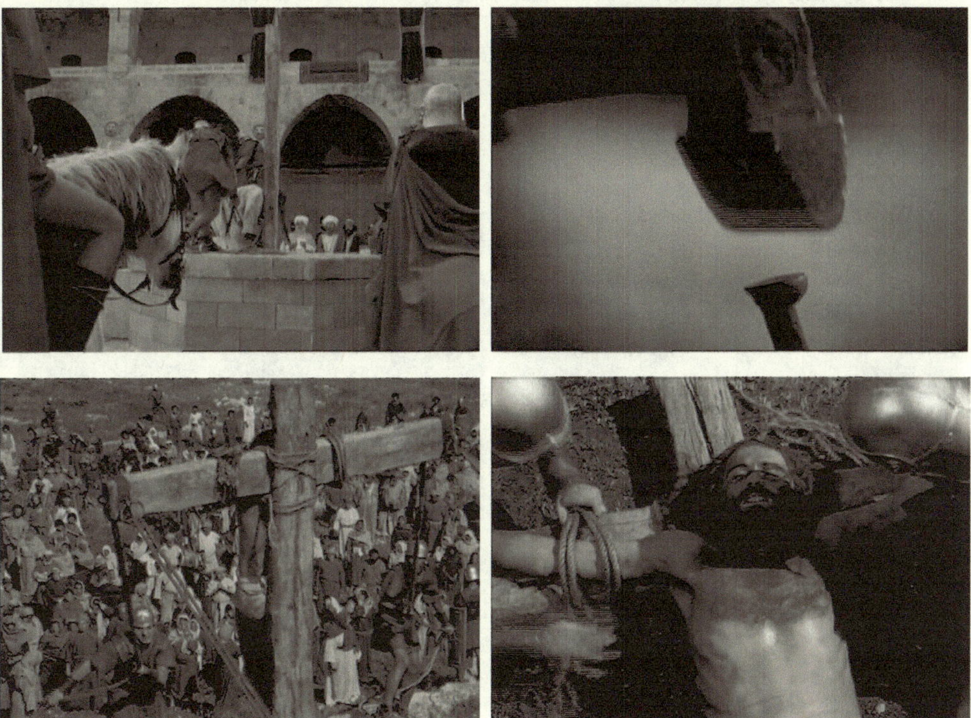

Clockwise, from top left: Jesus whipped by Roman soldier; A hammer nailing; Jesus tied on the cross; and Jesus hanging on the cross.

The crucifixion scenes were something that Mangyans had seldom experienced. In the small village, there were rare cases of fights or killings and shared blood of the human body. These were mostly mediated visual experiences, as it was often taken for granted due to the frequent exposure of violent visuals in contemporary society. Mangyans who had less media exposure were more affected and impressed by the crucifixion scenes, which caused a deep impact on their religious experience.

When Jesus was Resurrected

Soon after the astounding visual experience of the crucifixion, Mangyan Christian audiences experienced great catharsis in watching the resurrection of Jesus. Mary Magdalene and other women came to see the dead body of Jesus but soon found that the body had disappeared. In front of the astonished women, the angel Gabriel again appeared to announce that Jesus was resurrected. They ran to their friends in the village and finally saw Jesus, who appeared with a shining light around his body (See Figure 44). Upon viewing this scene, Mangyan audiences exclaimed with astonishment and joy, saying, "Jesus will be resurrected, right?" and "He is alive!"

Figure 44. *Scene # 34 and 35: Resurrected Jesus (left) and Jesus Meeting his Followers after Resurrection (right)*

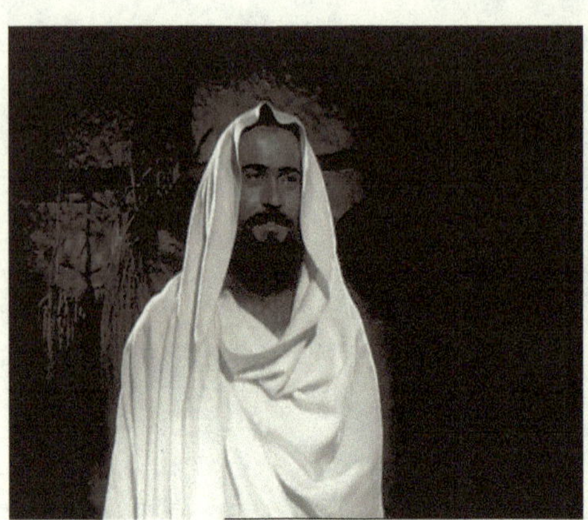

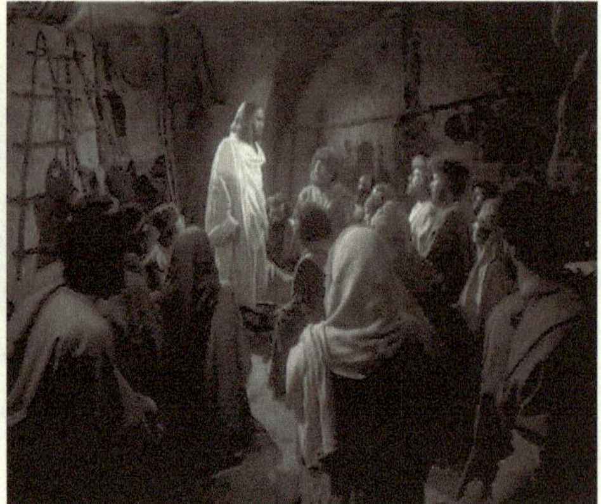

By seeing the resurrected Jesus in the film, the Mangyan Christians vividly confirmed the biblical teaching that was hard to believe. The resurrection of Jesus is one of the more hard-to-believe incidents, even in evangelical circles, but by seeing a vivid visual explanation of the resurrection of Jesus, the Mangyan audiences were able to inscribe the scene in their belief system. Visualization of the biblical text surely served as a reconfirmation of the abstract teaching of their religious beliefs.

Negotiated Meanings 1: Strengthening Religious Commitment

Mangyan Christian audiences did not remain passive as they saw images of abundant food or material prosperity but were actively engaged in the film, which strengthened their religious commitment while watching. When they saw the scene where Jesus proclaimed the tax collector, Matthew, as leader of the religious group, Ptr. Santi encouraged his members by saying, "Matthew left his job without any complaints, without money" (See Figure 45).

Figure 45. *Scene # 21: Jesus and His Disciples Called Matthew (left) and Zacchaeus Talking to Jesus from the Tree (right)*

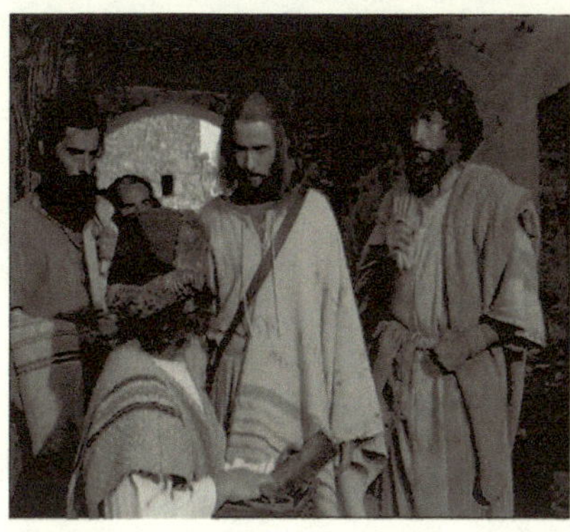

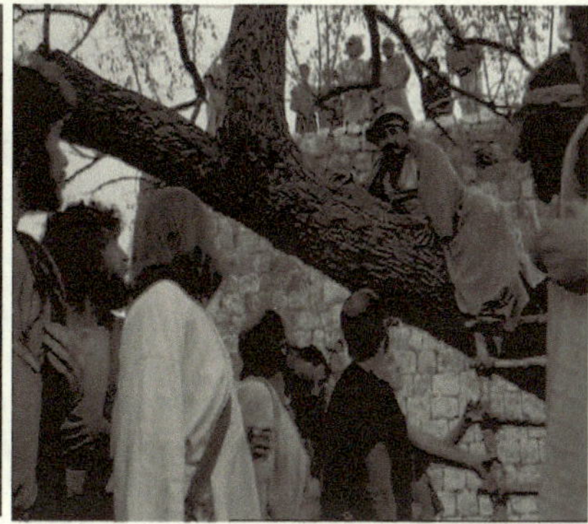

In this interaction, it was clear to see the evangelical reinforcement through the film reception. As the leader of religious community of ICCP, Ptr. Santi often used the film content to reinforce a religious standpoint and theological teachings, such as commitment in this scene. Becoming an evangelical in this Mangyan indigenous context and following the path of a newly forming religious group required great social and financial sacrifices. In response, the members of the religious community have shared the religious reinforcement through the film. Sonny and others also emphasized this reinforcement:

> Interviewer: anything that you learn or new things from the movie?
>
> Sonny : the thing i learn is that we need to all the more strengthen our faith in te Lord so that we will grow stronger more.
>
> Alex: What I learned is the same as his. Hehehehe,
>
> Nole: You should always be good to God...

On the other hand, the discipleship discourse was also one of the core emphases among evangelicals that were often followed by sacrifice. According to this view, religious commitment was more imperative than any kind of material prosperity. This also could have been an encouragement to those who were already in the commitment stage who might have suffered from material shortage. In the reception process, the leaders of the group actively used the opportunity to emphasize the importance of commitment and sacrifice in religious practices.

Matthew's narrative of following Jesus was often used among Mangyan Christians to exemplify the standard of discipleship. Loud laughs burst from the audience during Matthew's conversion. The scene was portrayed as slightly humourous and the Mangyans did not fully comprehend how difficult it would have been for a man of Matthew's status to decide to follow Jesus. In the midst of the modernization process of the Mangyans, capital was already in place to signify their mode of life. With capital, they could purchase goods, food, and even have medical services in the town of Manbrau.

In this context, leaving the position of collecting taxes was somewhat a desired commitment that needed to be impressed upon Mangyan Christians. The commitment to follow Jesus and leave material prosperity is repeated when Mary puts expensive perfumes on the feet of Jesus. Mangyan Christians raised their voices by saying, "Amen" to confirm their religious commitment.

Negotiated Meanings 2: Endurance of Hardship as a Follower

The film provided strong encouragement for firmness and boldness in evangelism in the midst of various hardships, which was exemplified in the crucifixion and ministry of Jesus. ICCP placed a great emphasis on evangelism among native Mangyans. Without much support from outside organizations, the efforts often faced serious hardship in the form of monetary shortage and rejection by non-Christian and Catholic Mangyans. Conflict between Jesus and His followers versus the Jews served as a symbol of the oppression that they have faced. This conflict was described by members of ICCP:

> Timothy: ... It's a challenge for me... God needs someone to preach the Word of ah...the Word of God, with bravery...bravery and boldness...

> Erning: The film I watched last night was a big challenge for me as a worker of God. I saw how Jesus preached amidst the storm, the hardship...I saw Jesus just like me. He has flesh, bone and skin. But I was really challenged through the film. Just as Pastor (Timothy) said, He showed boldness amidst all the hardships. He faced them all. That's why I will not grow dim in serving the Lord. I will continue to follow the will of God.

This main conflict shown in the film could be characterized as one betwen Jesus and the Jews. This conflict was interpreted as the conflict between Mangyan Christians versus non-Mangyan Christians. The rejection of Siapo ICCP church from the mainstream Catholic group could be one example, ICCP versus IMTC was another, and various rejections from non-Christian Mangyans in the process of evangelism also counted as examples. Mangyan Christian audiences empathized with the conflict narrative in the film and compared it with the situation in their ministry, using the film's narrative to encourage their members.

> Timothy: The movie became a challenge for me to preach the Word of God anytime, anywhere, in the dessert, in the river. That's why I'm challenged to preach the gospel in and out of season, even when tough days come.

Negotiated Meanings 3: Devotion to Religious Practice

The reception experience served as grounds for Mangyan Christians to reflect and recall their religious devotion to their religious practices. By showing various religious practices on film, several members emphasized the way to become true followers of Jesus. Rosena said,

> Jesus succeeded because of prayer and fasting. ... I have tried it also and it worked ... I learned to follow Christ as an example through fervent prayer and fasting.

The film reception for Rosena was an opportunity to confirm her previous religious practices, including prayer and fasting. This devotion of religious practice became firmer through the film reception experience.

Besides religious practices, some members also emphasized film reception as a means to transform ethical life. This commitment was not directly caused by the reception experience, yet was surely a product of the religious experience through film reception. One member confessed that she committed wrongdoings such as working on Sunday, adultery, gossip, anger and loss of self-control, and promised not to repeat these faults anymore. Other members also confessed their desire to change their ethical attitudes. The Mangyan audiences actively used the film experience to transform their ethics as a result of film reception.

Perceived Image of Jesus

One important question for this study was how the *Jesus* film played a role in the construction of religious meanings among Mangyan audiences through the film showing experience. At the heart of it, the perception of Jesus was imperative due to the plot and narrative of the film. The question was: How do Mangyan Christian audiences perceive Jesus from the film showing in the particular context of Mangyan villages on the island of Mindoro? How is a "negotiated" and "oppositional" reading placed in the presence of "dominant-ideological" reading of the text?

Jesus as Magician and Healer

The first and most interesting image of Jesus among Mangyan audiences was Jesus as Magician and Healer. As stated in the previous chapter, the film was intentionally produced with scenes of healing and miracles in order to emphasize biblical inerrancy. The film literally portrayed the scenes of the dead girl rising, the opening of blind eyes, the casting out of demons, the calming of storms, and the multiplication of bread and fish and many more (see Figures 36, 37, and 43). Furthermore, the composition of scenes was typical of evangelists who did healing ministry on television. During interviews, some informants strongly expressed interest in the healing ability of Jesus by saying, "He heals any kind of diseases." They were still in a reflective mood from the previous night's film showing. In this visualization, Mangyan audiences were astonished to witness the healing of the sick, and even the dead.

The miraculous power of Jesus is not only found in his healing abilities but also in how he deals with natural phenomena such as in the calming of the storm (see Figure 46). Evidently, manipulating natural phenomena has long been a desire of human beings who imagined that there are spirits in nature, as do the Mangyans. In this context, these visual presentations of miracle scenes surely provided concrete evidence of the miraculous power of Jesus to which Mangyan audiences aptly responded.

Figure 46. *Jesus Performing Miracles*

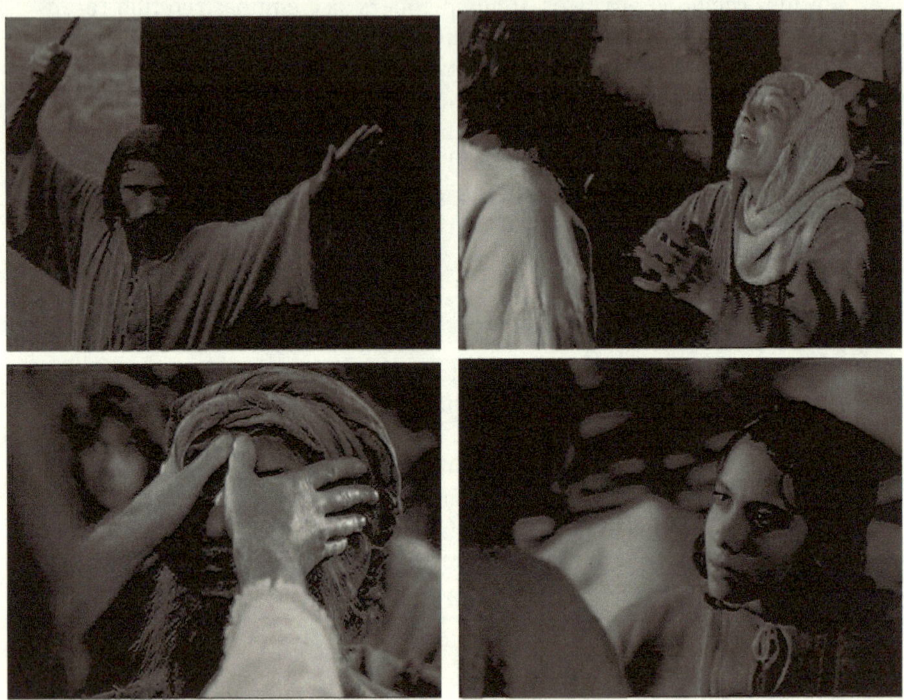

Clockwise, from top left: Jesus calming down storm; healing a crippled woman on the Sabbath; raising the dead daughter of Jairus; and a blind man recovering his sight.

Jesus as Teacher

Closely related to the miraculous power of Jesus, Mangyan audiences perceived Jesus as Teacher. In the perception, the teacher provided religious truths with charismatic authority. The teacher, in the Mangyans' perception, was the one who provided religious and socio-political guidance to the community. This religious authority was significant in the context of Mangyan culture. Traditional magicians were often bi-vocational with the role of social leader in the community. The socio-political role of *kuyay* performed religious rituals in case of sickness, funeral, birth and wedding. In their perception, the teacher and healer were often assimilated such as in the portrayal of Jesus in the movie.

The film explicitly constructed scenes to express the authority of Jesus by differentiating him from his disciples and other followers. For instance, when Jesus was teaching, he was sitting while others were standing. When Jesus was protecting Mary Magdalene, he was walking and using hand gestures while others were just staring at him. Those scenes significantly supported the image of Jesus as teacher. In various ways, Mangyan audiences exclaimed, "Jesus is preaching." In their understanding, the distinctive features and authoritative teaching were impressive in constructing the image of Jesus. This distinction effectively supported the image of Jesus as a teacher in the film (see Figure 44).

Jesus as Humble Man

In addition to the image of an authoritative teacher, Mangyan audiences also constructed the image of Jesus as humble when as he protected socially marginalized people. In an interview, a participant expressed, "Jesus talks to anyone, no matter who they are." These images were constructed by reflecting on the scenes of Jesus talking to a Samaritan woman, Zacchaeus and others (see Figure 47). Different from the traditional *kuyay*, the images of Jesus from the scenes were different by emphasizing his caring aspect, which was a more revolutionary image that could care for marginalized indigenous people like Mangyans. In this process, the Mangyan audiences assimilated the socially marginalized, whom Jesus took care of, with themselves. In another case, Jesus was protecting Mary Magdalene from the villagers who were about to stone her to death. These images supported the idea of a humble Jesus, which struck the audiences of the Mangyan community.

Figure 47. *Jesus with Marginalized People*

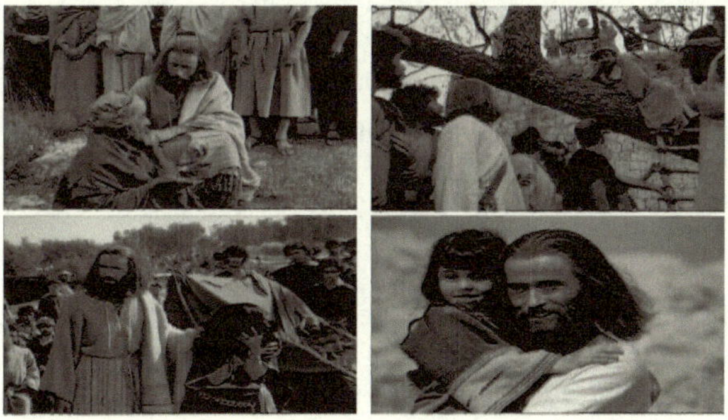

Clockwise, from top left: A blind beggar received his sight: Zacchaeus on the tree; Jesus welcomes children; and Jesus protects a sinful woman.

Loving Jesus

There was no explicit visualization of the love of Jesus in the film, but Mangyan audiences repeatedly said "the loving image of," which was the core emphasis of the evangelicals. In other words, the film effectively presented the core theology of Christianity, which was well accepted by Mangyan Christian audiences. In the interview, several informants answered, "Jesus' great love for us," "love each other," or "as Jesus loves us" as the lessons of the film.

This perception was also understood as the confirmation of reinforcing the previous knowledge of the perception of Jesus and evangelical theology. Love has been interpreted as the main motive of the sacrifice of Jesus. This theological discourse had been placed in various points throughout the film. For instance, the film ended with the narration of John 3: 16, "For God so love the world that He gave His only Son..." and the visual effects emphasizing the theology of love was well-perceived according to reception of the film.

The image of the loving Jesus also constructs the dyadic relationship between the Western Jesus and loving and caring Jesus. This evangelical emphasis, which was one of the core theological teachings, has been reinforced by the Western visualization of Jesus. Aristotelian deductive reasoning brought the simple syllogism that constructs the Western ideology.

Crucified Jesus

The crucifixion scenes made an impressive impact on Mangyan audiences. Based on their social and religious contexts, it was revealed that Mangyan Christians seldom saw violent movies in ordinary life, unlike contemporary and regular media consumers, who are accustomed to violence in visual media. During interviews, several informants recalled the vividness of the crucifixions during the showing. Jerry said, "My favorite was when he (Jesus) was crucified. It reminded me of his work of salvation (done for us)." Many of them found the depiction of torture extraordinary and even unbearable to watch. The visual effect of crucifixion connected well with the pitiable state of Jesus and the motive of his sacrifice that was his love.

Jesus as Savior

The audience also related the reception of the crucifixion scene to the message of salvation. They not only remembered the crucifixion of Jesus from the film but also related it to the theological message of salvation. The savior message was also emphasized in the film. Many of the informants stressed, "Jesus saved our lives" and "He cleansed us of our sins." Jerry also clearly expressed this sentiment:

> What I liked most (from the film) was Jesus as the savior and what he said to his disciples. Jesus will be in my life, in my heart. That was what I understood ... I got his message for me. He reigns and he reigned in my heart the moment I accepted him in my life. He will reign in heaven forever.

This reception account by Mangyan audiences was a reaffirmation of their beliefs and concretized what they already believed. The Mangyan reading of the image of Jesus as savior affirmed the previous commitment as evangelical Christians and the film showing experience provided another change to reinforce the image of Jesus as savior. It was also the confirmation process of the Protestant theological discourse on the salvation by Jesus.

Resurrected Jesus

In relation to the image of savior, the resurrection image was also clearly reinforced through the film showing. The film also patently exaggerated it by treating Jesus with glowing bright lights (see Figure 41). Jesus in the scene was somewhat vague if he was physically resurrected or appeared in a more or less fantastic illusion. Yet it seems to emphasize the special meanings of the resurrected Jesus. The reception was reinforced through their religious convictions. Mangyan Christians enjoyed seeing the resurrected Jesus on film to validate what was taught in their previous religious experience. Again, the film experience was more or less a reinforcement process of previous evangelical beliefs and the Mangyan audiences used the film showing to reconfirm their previous religious conviction.

Other Meanings

It was apparent that film showing and reception among Mangyan audiences was a shared learning process to obtain new biblical knowledge. During the film showings, various audiences asked questions and answered them within the group to verify their vague biblical knowledge. On some occasions, they often asked questions to determine whether or not their previous knowledge was correct. I observed that a five-year old child asked his father about the identity of the person who was pointing out the adult Jesus. Another time, one member asked if the lady who stood beside Jesus was mother Mary. In reply, Ptr. Santi explained that she was Mary Magdalene. Again, when Jesus was having a feast with Zacchaeus, a member asked if it was already the "Last Supper" and his friend beside him answered, "No." This learning process was evident of the interpretive community in the film reception.

Besides biblical knowledge acquisition, Mangyan audiences confirmed that the film provided a better historical understanding of Jesus and the Bible. This account was evident mainly in Mangyan ministers who did not have much theological education. Ptr. Santi shared that the film watching provided another chance for them to learn more about biblical history. For him, the setting and props were a new environment to acquire better biblical knowledge compared to reading the Bible. The visual aspects of the film surely served as learning material for him and his ministers.

Ptr. Santi's appreciation was surely one of the aims of the film. The film was intentionally researched with a group of experts to produce an image of Jesus that was as historically accurate as possible, according to the producer, John Heyman (http://www.historicjesus.com). Most of the props and costumes were researched and well-represented for a better understanding of the historical Jesus. The geographical locations were those that were the actual setting for the life of Jesus in his time. Moreover, the script of the film almost directly quoted from the book of Luke in the "Good News for Modern Man" (Today's English Version), and the book was selected in a survey of 430 seminary presidents for the book that best represented the life and work of Jesus.

Yet, the acclamation of the historical accuracy such as settings, costumes and props provided remained a risky falsification of visual interpretation as reality. Mangyan audiences who trusted the reality of the film began to accept the whole production as real, not aware of the visual and theological interpretation of the film. This process was exactly explained in the process of the construction of social reality.

Western Representation of Jesus and Mangyan Understanding

Westernized Christianity has resulted in the visual religious icon, Jesus, and contains a typical Western-centered, that is, post-colonial, metaphor. In the film, the one and true master was Jesus, and he was Western in nature. But the underlying allegory of the text was always the white and Anglo-Saxon Jesus and his work on Asians. Western Master vs. Eastern Follower has been duplicated throughout Christian history.

Apparently, Mangyans did not distinguish between the visual elements of the Western Jesus and the real Jesus. In other words, Mangyan audiences were not able to articulate the Jesus they saw was a visual construction of Jesus, which involved cultural differences. From the research data, Mangyans assumed that the Jesus in the film was the same as the historical Jesus. Furthermore, Mangyans greatly agreed upon the image of Jesus and the perception of Jesus. Those who had religious conviction were particularly easily enticed to find a relationship between the Jesus on film with their perceptions. This perception was similarly occurred both ICCP and non-ICCP members. Members of ICCP said:

Interviewer: What do you think of Christ when you saw Him last night?

all of them said " its beautiful"

b: did you recognize that Jesus was westerner

a: only a little...

b: little... ah how was he, was he something that you have imagine?

a: yeah he is.. (with emphasis)

b: how did you imagine?

I: ahh... before they only read it from the bible but now they saw him...

b: so they believe?

A: yes they believe...

Non-ICCP member, *datu* Roding also mentioned;

Interviewer: Do you think that the face of Jesus was the face you imagine before?

Roding: Yes, that was the face I had in my mind.

Interviewer: If you have one message, if you have something that you learned or felt , what is it or what is this?

Roding: I learned that men should believe whole heartedly ... Because all the words of God of Jesus is truthful...

The Awareness of Western Figure

Mangyan audiences did not have a clear understanding of the Western figure with regard to Jesus. The question about their awareness of a Western figure of Jesus was randomly asked of audiences during film showing and interviews. Yet none of the audiences learned that Jesus was a Western figure. Most of the members, including, Ptr. Santi, who was the most educated and had the most outside contacts, did not even think that Jesus was a Westerner. They did not even recognize racial differences between Jesus from the rest of his followers.

The visualization process began when the Mangyan audiences first identified the face of Jesus in the film. They began to react significantly in a deep hum of hundreds of voices when they saw the adult Jesus for the first time in the film. They began to visualize that this was "Jesus." Some audiences tried to ask questions when Jesus first appeared, "Is He Jesus?" They seemed to compare the face and image of Jesus with that of Jesus in their minds. It did not take long for audiences to identify the actor as Jesus in their perception. Soon after the assimilation process, the construction of social reality was in place, which absorbed the Jesus in the film as Jesus in their religious experience.

On the contrary, most members confirmed that the face and image of Jesus was either similar to, or the same as they had perceived. Some of them had seen the visual face of Jesus in other media, such as in pictures and illustrations. All of them confirmed that the face in the film was very similar to the faces in other visual media. Nene even confessed that Jesus had the exact same face that she had in mind because she had seen the picture of the Western Jesus in the Bible. To some of Mangyan audiences, the previous exposure to the Western visualization of Jesus became a means to confirm the continuous presentation of the Western construction of Jesus in the film reception experience.

Construction of Western Jesus through Film Reception

It was important to know that the film reception surely served as a reference to perceive the Western quality of Jesus in their religious experience to all Mangyan audiences. Even Mangyan audiences who had no visual exposure to the film or any sort of visualization of Jesus confirmed that the Jesus in the film matched their perceived images of Jesus. Jerry's experience confirmed this:

> It is my first time to see the picture of Jesus and movie. And the face of Jesus was exactly what I expected with the reading of John 18:20. His face was described there just like that.
>
> Anonymous: Before, we could only read about Him in the Bible and now we have seen Him already.

His explanation showed that his visual perception of Jesus was then inscribed with the face of Jesus from the film. In other words, the actor, Brian Deacon, became an icon of Jesus in their religious experience. This informed learning supported by visual aid served as the axis of the social construction of the racial aspect of Jesus. The film also became a reference for their religious knowledge instead of the knowledge being referenced in the evaluation of the film. In the Mangyan reception, the actualization process of film with the personal religious experience signifies the assimilation of the film in the religious practices.

The film reception over religious experience became significant because the material representation played important role over spirituality among indigenous groups such as Mangyans. Mangyan Christian audiences who passively acquired the reception of film media assimilated their religious beliefs with the content of the film. They began to inscribe the images from the film into their biblical knowledge and reinforce their theological understanding. The process can be interpreted as a materialization of religious beliefs constructed by visual representation. The process has been accelerated by the exposure to the visual as well as entertainment media.

This filmic visualization of Christianity has a new phase in that the assimilation process continues in the formation of a Western Jesus. The Western identity of Jesus was significant for firm visual and dramatic differentiation from the rest. The Jesus constructed through dramatic apparatuses such as costumes, props, camera angles and the composition of scenes that were described above. This visual apparatus made patent visual distinction by providing the cultural identity of Jesus, which is "Western" (See Figure 48).

Figure 48. *Scene # 13 and 32: The Faces of Jesus*

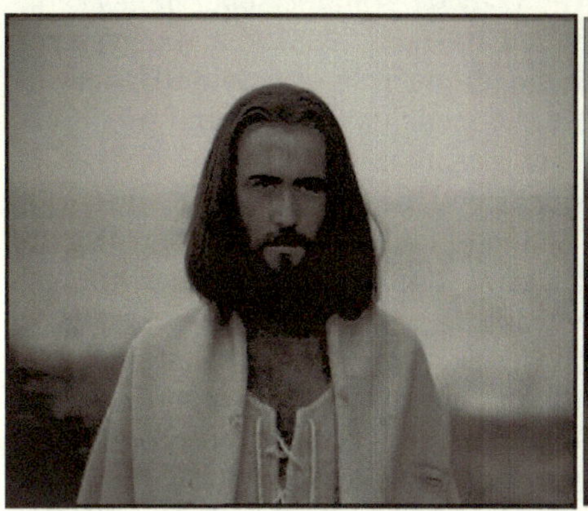

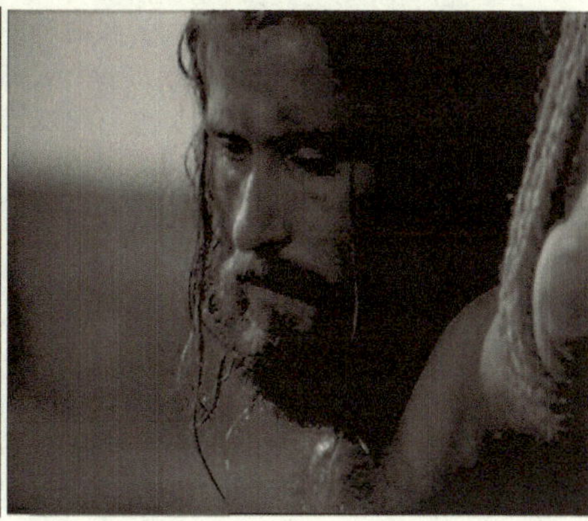

Synthesis

The *Jesus* film was created as a means of delivering Western hegemony in the historical continuation of a Western Jesus. Western hegemony in Christianity was beyond the superstructure that Mangyan Christians could resist. Furthermore, the film was centered in a fundamentalist evangelical standpoint that emphasized the concept of biblical inerrancy in Western-centered evangelical zeal. The film was actively accepted reinforced by the religious experiences of the audiences through the process of the evangelical discursive formation.

Yet, in the reception process, Mangyan audiences actively constructed religious meanings within the community of interpretations from watching the film. This process of meaning construction was not separated from, but interplayed with, their religious beliefs and practices as so-called evangelical" or "born again" Christians. The major meanings of Jesus created from the film exposure were that of healer, teacher, humble man, lover of Children, and resurrected savior. These images were similarly patterned after the plot of the film and the evangelical emphases. Understanding Hall's variations of reception patterns, this reception process was a primarily "dominant-ideological" reading that reinforced the dominant ideological meanings of the text. Little was received in the evidence of a "negotiate" or "oppositional" reading.

Significantly, this reception process was reinforced by so-called opinion leaders interceded on behalf of the visual texts for the audience during the reception process. The religious leaders of the group ICCP also emphasized the theological or organizational emphases by pointing out the scenes of the film. In this case, the film watching was an affirmative process for existing beliefs. This proved that the reception of the film was more a confirmative reception rather than the enlightened learning process of new religious meanings. It was evident that the Mangyans were actively observed in the construction process as accepting the Jesus in the film as a way of deepening religious practices. Supporting the theory of *Interpersonal Influence* in the early media effects studies (Katz & Lazasfeld, 1955), the Mangyan reception patterns clearly showed the significant role of opinion leaders in the meditative reception process. Yet the mediation served the reinforcement of current knowledge through film reception.

However, the reception exposure provided the Mangyan audiences with new experiences such as the visualization of biblical knowledge, which affirmed their previous beliefs at the same time. Audiences interactively learned and shared the biblical knowledge upon viewing the film by asking questions about vague scenes. In this process, some members of the audience groups actively shared their biblical knowledge, while others just followed others' explanation. The audiences were sometimes surprised by watching similar settings of their lives in the film. This reception often provided a unique opportunity for Mangyan audiences to empathize with the content of the film. Once the audiences found themselves in the movie, they were more receptive toward the film content.

It was evident that the Mangyan Christian audiences were not able to distinguish the Western identity of Jesus in the film. It was rather easy to determine the racial differences between the Western Jesus and his eastern followers by dramatic representation. As opposed to print media in previous history, film has posed a different phase in the racial relationship between the Western versus non-Western dichotomy. It was in the context of dramatic representation and it created much more realistic to a massive audience compared to the traditional painting or printing. For instance, the face of Jesus by Sullivan (see Figure 2) was the portrayal of Jesus without much background. Although it has great impact, it was limited to the individual Jesus. Yet the film has drama and it is interconnected with racial dichotomy in the *Jesus* film; that is, Western versus eastern. The dichotomy brought a new set of post-colonial dichotomized racial relationships compared to the traditional means of visualization.

Chapter 8

Summary and Conclusion

Summary

This study explored the analysis of constructed religious meanings from reception of the *Jesus* film by the Mangyan Christian group. The study asked, "How do Alangan and Iraya Christian Mangyans in Sta. Cruz, Mindoro construct religious meanings from the reception of the *Jesus* film?"

Guided by Hall's dominant, negotiated and oppositional readings, the research conducted a film reception analysis of the *Jesus* film that contained very Western ideological discourse. Derived from Weberian subjective meaning, *"verstehen"* (understanding), Berger's notion of "subjective meaning" was constructed through the interaction and shared practice within the religious society.

In the study, it was assumed that the constructed and practiced meanings were integrated within the social, religious and media contexts to which the audiences belonged. The collective reception of the interpretive community was intertwined with the pre-structured social and religious experience, which resulted in a new religious experience and meanings for Jesus and Christian beliefs.

Employing an ethnographic method of observation of participation (Tedlock, 2000), interviews and observations were conducted during the film showing and in the houses of the audience members on the following day after the film showing. Participation in the film showing was also intensively used during three consecutive film showings in the community and during field work. Careful observation was done on the interactions, and even of the gestures of the people. In this process, Ptr. Santi and Erwin gave support as assistants and key informants in the interpretation of the interactions. During vague situations, Erwin also helped in translating Tagalog into English during the film showing.

Social, Religious and Media Context

To understand the current social, religious and media context of the Iraya and Alangan Mangyan tribes, the study delved into the physical site, as well as social, religious, and media contexts.

Social Context

An extensive acculturation process occurred in the settlements in the research areas. The three settlements explicitly showed the transition of the Mangyans into a modern way of life. Second-hand cheap clothes were purchased from the lowland markets. Family and house sizes have become smaller compared to those in traditional Mangyan society. Contrary to the small size of the households, the sizes of the settlements were large enough to include an elementary school, a community center and a health clinic within the compound.

Notably, leadership in relation to Christianization was a part of the process of social change. Traditional magico-religious leadership merged into the socio-political leadership that intermingled with religious affiliations. In order for the leaders to maintain leadership roles in the community, they were more or less forced to change their religious affiliation to Christianity.

The changing economic situation presented both a positive and negative challenge for Mangyans in the acculturated settlements. The permanent settlement patterns supported by Christian groups and local government required new adaptation. Yet, many Mangyans exposed themselves to the greater danger of losing their land through immediate cash loans from the lowland lenders. The extensive level of interaction of the three sitios with the outside world indeed serves as a platform on which to confront a great challenge as they undergo more of the acculturation process in the years ahead.

Religious Context

Religious institutions such as Catholic, Protestant and Episcopal churches have extended their missions to the three Mangyan sitios since the 1980s. The alliance of the Mangyan mission in Catholic Church, called PASAKAMI, was deeply involved in the establishment of the sitio Siyapo; MTCA, supported by OMF, ran a church in sitio Baraas; and ICCP of Ptr. Santi provided typical evangelical services in the three sitios. Besides the three institutions, the Bible League of the Philippines and other independent foreign missionaries somehow interacted with the indigenous Mangyan Christians.

The members of ICCP explicitly demonstrated typical evangelical patterns of worship and organization but developed their worship styles in the presence of indigenous practices. Their worship style was patterned after common evangelical churches in the Philippines. Indeed, Christianization has coincided with the acculturation process in the Mangyan sitios. Various religious institutions have been active in developing the communities by putting up a water pump, school, and construction of community. It was, therefore, apparent to conclude that the religion or religious institutions had become the agents of the modernization process for Mangyans in the research areas.

Media Context

Modern media acquisition and use were an inevitable part of the modern lives of Mangyans in the three sitios. Even without an electrical supply, Mangyan settlements were actively engaged in various types of media possession and use. Radio was the most popular among the electronic media, while television and movie watching were more communal activites. Interestingly, there was a considerable degree of graffiti in the community center of sitio Calamias, which showed much meaning in the lives of people as well as the degree of media exposure of members of the community.

In addition, the previous exposure and acquaintance of visual media, though it was still limited, assured that the film showing was not a totally new experience. Interestingly, conservative Mangyan Christians had become more active but more selective in their use of media, as demonstrated by only listening to the radio for religious content. This religious and media context showed the high level of acceptance toward the *Jesus* film.

The *Jesus* Film Showing

The in-depth film showing ministry that took place in the particular three sitios:

> The search for the film showing location was the result of a series of participatory negotiations between the film showing team and the local counterparts. It was more than just looking for a physical location but also involved strategic evangelical planning with local contacts. The mobilized DVD equipment, sound system and generator enabled easy and quick implementation of the film showing ministry even in remote areas. The film showing in Mangyan sitios surely stimulated the curiosity of indigenous people towards the film and modern technology.

Due to the nature of the audience group and tensions between religious groups in the three sitios, meaningful follow-up for the religious converts was not conducted. In addition, most Mangyans in the three sitios were already, to some degree, members of existing Christian groups. The religious affiliations were not personal, but rather social, which connected them with the large groups with which they were associated.

Yet the film showing and audience response were significant enough to understand the media reception patterns for the *Jesus* film. Mangyan audiences even traveled over mountains to watch the film. Notably, in the reception process, Mangyan audiences formed various groups for social interactions. For some uncertainties in the scene, they cross-checked the content and shared their expressions among the members of the small groups.

Construction of Religious Meanings

To analyze how the film reception constructed religious meanings among the members of religious communities in the three sitios, the research revealed that:

Mangyan audiences strengthened their previous biblical and theological understanding of Jesus through the film reception. The major emphases of conservative evangelical organiation, such as Campus Crusade for Christ, were similarly shown through the constructed meanings among Mangyans. Spiritual authority was strengthened by presenting the performance of miracles literally and the meanings of the crucifixion and the resurrection of Jesus as savior was well-received.

Mangyan audiences articulated the constructed and negotiated meanings that came from the film reception. For them, the film showing provided a venue to strengthen religious commitment, faith through the various hardships they often faced through evangelical efforts, and devote their lives as followers of Jesus Christ. Similarly, the reception of the film provided strong reinforcement of the existing beliefs and practices among Mangyan Christian believers.

Interestingly, media consumption was an exclusive opportunity that connected Mangyans' appreciation of modern technology and material culture. Especially for conservative Christian Mangyans who had established program preferences regarding secular media, Christian content such as Jesus-figure films were more favorable content. These media consumption opportunities were not only for the purpose of entertainment or religious experiences, but also served as social gatherings among religious members and biblical lessons. These opportunities were holistic events that integrated personal, social and religious purposes.

The question shifted from the meanings regarding the film to specifically the images of Jesus among Mangyan audiences. The first and foremost impressive images of Jesus for Mangyan audiences were as a miracle-performing savior. The spiritual authority of Jesus was mainly shown in activities such as healing sickness, raising a girl from the dead, casting demons out of people, and subjugating natural phenomena such as storms. The emphasis on the literal visualization was on the *Jesus* film.

Jesus was surely seen as a savior who was crucified, died and was resurrected, which emphasized core fundamentalist theology. In addition, Mangyan audiences also mentioned Jesus as loving, kind and humble because he took care of the marginalized people such as beggers, children and prostitutes such as Mary. The film showing provided few opportunities for the Mangyan audiences to gain biblical and historical knowledge.

Western Representation of Jesus

In analyzing the Mangyan perceptions toward the Western figure of Jesus, the research revealed:

> Mangyan audiences have not had a clear understanding of the Western figure of Jesus. Importantly, most members have confirmed that the face of Jesus was either similar to or the same as what they had perceived. Yet, it was significant that the film reception surely served as a reference to perceive the Western quality of Jesus in their religious experience.

Mangyan Christian audiences who acquired the image of Jesus through reception of the film began to incorporate their religious beliefs with the content of the film. They began to assimilate the image from the film into their previous perceptions of Jesus. The process could be interpreted as materialization of religious beliefs constructed by the film.

Conclusion

The *Jesus* film and its global distribution was the product of the marriage between the efforts to promote fundamentalist theology and the strong evangelical spirit of world mission in the United States' mainstream Protestantism in the late 1970s. Bill Bright, the symbolic figure of American evangelicalism and a conservative Republican among evangelicals, dreamt of a visual tool for world evangelism and initiated the Jesus story in film. The *Jesus* film, which he produced, became a significant platform from which to propagate the fundamentalist theological stance, such as biblical inerrancy and the narrow meaning of Jesus as Christ throughout the world. With successful funding from conservative evangelicals in United States businessmen, Campus Crusade for Christ was able to raise funds for film production and strategized world distribution over four decades.

The film production was a continuation of the Western ideological superstructure in which the Western quality of Jesus has been constructed. The figure of Jesus reflected the constructed image of Jesus that has built up through Christian history. Clearly, the visual image of Jesus in the eyes of Westerners and the image of Jesus that they have received is a Westernized Jesus separate from the reality of Jesus. Western superiority and the spirit of the pax-Americana was high in the 1970s among evangelicals; for the role of Jesus the producer naturally selected a Anglo-Saxon actor, Brian Heyman, whose image was in continuation of the Western construction of the image of Jesus. Furthermore, the constructed moving image of Jesus containing fundamentalist theological stands have been massively reproduced and delivered the Western image of Jesus, which has reinforced the Westernized construction of Christianity to the rest of the world.

In the film showing ministry, the three sitios (Siyapo, Baraas and Calamias) on Mindoro Island, Philippines showed relatively modern settlement patterns. Religious institutions have become a major agent of the acculturation and modernization process in addition to the local government. Settlement size was relatively large compared to traditional villages, with the numbers between 200 and 300 individuals.

An extensive acculturation process has significantly changed their traditional way of living. Traditional magico-religious leadership merged into the socio-political leadership that intermingled with religious affiliations. The acculturation process was due to the extensive level of interaction of the three sitios with the outside world. In relation to the social changes, Catholic and Protestant Christian intervention have been significantly changes in the religious landscapes of the community. Various religious institutions have been active not only in religious activities, but also in social transformation, such as putting up a water pump, the establishment of indigenous schools for Mangyan children and other children. Religious institutions have become the agents of the modernization process for Mangyans. Mangyan settlements began to acquire and use media gadgets for amusement and religious purposes. The religious film showing, such as Jesus-figure films, was implemented on some occasions. Interestingly, conservative Mangyan Christians have become more active but selective in their use of media, such as listening to the radio for religious content.

In this context, the *Jesus* film showing was done as a result of a series of participatory negotiations between the film showing team and local counterparts. Film showing served for information giving and confirmation of existing evangelical beliefs.

The reception of the Mangyan religious audiences affirmed what the visual text of Jesus that contained significant Western ideology and fundamentalist theology meant among non-Western Protestant audiences. Since Hall's encoding/decoding theories (1980), many researchers have tried to argue that the audiences have become more active in the reception process and that they do not receive the hypodermic messages from the texts.

Yet in this study, the ideological Western superiority discourse revealed from the the film was dominantly re-constructed through the eyes of Mangyan audiences. The meaning of Jesus in the film was similarly reflected from the mainstream emphasis among conservative evangelicals. Mangyan audiences perceived Jesus as a religious authority, a loving, kind savior who was crucified, died and was resurrected to save souls. Mangyan audiences have received the "ideological-dominant" reading of the text without much resistance.

The "dominant-ideological" reading was firmly strengthened when Mangyan audiences empathetically found cultural cues that closely connected the audiences to the film context. Mangyan audiences found much cultural proximity watching scenes similar to their lives, which was also different from those of the lowlanders in their surroundings. Mangyan audiences burst into smiles and laughter upon seeing Jesus and the disciples sleeping in the field, eating with their hands, as well as pigs wandering around, which could be easily found in any Mangyan settlement.

Mangyan evangelical Christians used the *Jesus* film to confirm their religious beliefs and vague biblical knowledge. This process was mediated by active opinion leaders, in this case Mangyan pastors who promoted the film showing and directed the social gatherings among ICCP members. Mangyan audiences strengthened their theological beliefs, strengthened organizational commitment, and confirmed religious practices in their lives through the film showing. This process clearly affirmed that the film showing was more affirmative in that the reception reinforces the existing knowledge of evangelical Mangyan audiences.

More importantly, Mangyan evangelical audiences began to experience the visualized signification process that transformed the abstract and personal religious beliefs into more concrete and material visualization through film media for the life of Jesus and its Western quality. For Mangyans, the process occurred to the degree that they began to assimilate the contextual local beliefs on the religious experiences with the external intervention of a ready-made film. In a previous interview with a theological student who had once participated in the *Jesus* film ministry in Thailand, he confirmedthat the visual effects of the film were an example of the materialization of his religious beliefs.

This signification process became the ideological and constructed process of the Western quality of Christianity, particularly in that the visual signifier of Jesus, the center of the salvation and truth in the evangelical beliefs, was represented as a Westerner. The long Westernization process of Christian beliefs was in the context of the appearance of the Western Jesus in the film. In the particular religious visual text, the *Jesus* film continued in the objectification process of Western Christianity and served as the signifier that constructed fundamentalist evangelical beliefs and reinforced the Westernized image of Jesus among Mangyan religious audiences.

Chapter 9

Implications and Recommendations

Implications

Theoretical Issues

This study was a critical and cultural analysis of the *Jesus* film and its showing among members of Protestant Mangyan communities. It was clear that Mangyan reception was situated and guided by their conservative evangelical beliefs and practices. At the same time, the visual representation of Jesus in particular was a confirmation process of their beliefs about him visually. The process was clearly explained in the social construction process of the reality making.

In the process, there was little evidence of the "negotiate" and "oppositional" readings that might have occurred in a secular media reception. The Westernized visualization of Jesus as a discursive formation in Christianity has been taken for granted as truth. It was, therefore, reasonable to conclude that religious audiences do not participate in "negotiate" and "oppositional" readings toward religious materials, especially Mangyan indigenous audiences. This study showed that the Mangyan audiences and their reception were considerably different from the television audiences in a British context. The level of media exposure and familiarity toward film, comprehension level of Tagalog as a medium of language of the film, and the level of biblical understandings were considerable factors in the various readings toward the visual materials.

Furthermore, the "dominant-ideological" reading of the text could be interpreted in the acculturation process among modernized Mangyan Christians. Helbling and Schult (2004) argued that because the peaceful relationship with Christian lowlanders was due to the coping strategies in the face of outside intrusion, Mangyan Christians were more apt to grant the Christian missions' expansion to the sitios. The acculturated and evangelical Mangyans more actively relied upon external support and aid in the development of the sitios and the churches as well. Oftentimes, the evangelical mission efforts and support was the only major aid to the communities. Therefore, the major "dominant-ideological" reading could have resulted in the dependency on evangelical missionaries and on the content that they brought. Although the manifest evidence was not revealed from the account of the Mangyan audiences, this socio-religious context could be further studied.

It was, therefore, suggested that the theory of negotiate and oppositional reading on the ideological texts was to be considerable in the particular context such as this study. Low level of media and language literacy, and exposure to media texts, as well as religious affiliations, actually significantly affect their authentic reading of the text. It was also valuable to observe how the religious affiliations dictated the encoding process. Therefore, research further suggested that reception studies can be investigated in relation to the ICT and media literacy level.

In the reception of this context, audiences depended more upon the personal informants in the interpretive communities that were developed in the previous psychological tradition in media effects (Katz & Lazasfeld, 1955). This current study is limited to answering the specific media effects which is dominantly guided and made through ICCP leaders and members. Therefore, further studies can be made on the polygamy media readings of religious media texts such as the *Jesus* film in relation to the interpersonal influence. Additionally, a comparative reception studies can be done between Mangyans and lowlanders.

Methodological Issues

The ethnographic in-depth qualitative methods on the reception of the *Jesus* film audiences were useful in understanding the audience and its context. Especially in the context of indigenous Mangyan audiences, their social organization in the modernized new settlements, Protestant influences in the presence of other and indigenous religious practices that interconnected with the social and cultural aspects of the society, and media exposure and use became parameters for the level of media acceptance in the study.

This study provides new methodological implications on both theological studies and media studies in cross-cultural context. Theologians in recent studies have focused on the media, especially film, as a text of theological exegesis focused on the textual film analyses, which naturally ignored the reception process of the film. At the same time, media scholars lack interest in the emerging cultural forces on religious communities as a social entity. This in-depth ethnographic study provides insights on how religious media have penetrated the society and how religious groups consume the religious texts as significant social and religious interventions that interact in the construction of contemporary culture.

This study hopes to stimulate some theologians and biblical scholars to begin scholarly exegeses on religious films. Although several research studies have been done on the descriptive analysis on the Jesus-figure and

Christ-figure films, there has been little study done on the actual theological and biblical studies of film text such as the *Jesus* film. Such fundamentalist interpretations of the film could be systemically examined by the biblical and theological scholars.

Yet, the anticipated multiple meanings, especially on the perception of Jesus as a Western figure, would not be sufficiently revealed through the methods implemented. The cross-cultural reception of the Jesus-figure film among the indigenous audience group was limited due to the language and cultural understanding of the researcher and the team. This barrier was stated in the limitations of this study and recommendations were given to the future researcher on similar topics.

Practical Issues

This study posed significant questions on the effects of a globalizing, media-oriented and massive capital-oriented mission strategy. The basic assumption was that the media has a great effect on the perceptions of the non-Christian population, and the *Jesus* film has propagated the argumentations through more than three decades of ministry. Yet, this study turned the media effects to the cultural aspect that Horsfield (2005) suggested. Instead of forcing the instrumentalist media use in the Christian mission, this study's findings question the ideological implications on the religious visual materials in the mission field. This study could contribute to moving the evangelistic endeavor from an instrumentalist position and turning it instead to the cultural and ideological understanding of the media's effect on the mission strategy.

The findings clearly show that Western ideological discourse has been structured in the production of visual media, the *Jesus* film. Western ideological forces have penetrated the works of foreign missions with the massive financial support of global mission organizations. Besides statistical data on the conversion and establishment of the churches through the film team, the deeper cultural and ideological effects should be examined by missiology scholars and practitioners, in order to avoid a Western takeover of the world by Christ-figure films.

I also suggested that the in-depth ethnographic studies can be done in cross-cultural settings. As reported, the *Jesus* film has had worldwide penetration and it would be imperative to understand the same ministry in different cultural and social settings. The receiption would be different from the result if the film showing sites are different than Philippine settings or upon crossing borders, such as to South East Asian countries. By doing comparative studies, these interpretations might provide more synthetic or multiple understandings of the *Jesus* film from wider audience groups.

Recommendations

Based on the implications mentioned above, several recommendations have been proposed to conservative and evangelical missionaries, scholars, policy makers and community workers.

To Evangelical Christians and Missionaries

Evangelical missionaries and mission agencies that are currently using the *Jesus* film, or that will consider the film showing, should review their strategy based on the ideological implications of the film showing. The film showing ministry has been unaware of the deeper Western ideological implications. Based on these findings, missionaries and mission agencies should consider their film showing strategies to avoid the ideological impact that could be created by the film's use in the mission field.

The findings also benefit the evangelical media producers in terms of the deeper cultural and ideological effects of media productions for religious purposes. The Western productions are being imported cross-cultural borders without much consideration of the relevancy of the material. The study provides the legitimate rationale for the ideological examination upon the multimedia productions in the cross-cultural mission.

To Scholars

This study provides insights for the missiology researcher regarding the political and ideological aspects in dealing with cross-cultural missions. Although the media effects in this case were deeply related with the missiological achievements, few missiological studies have been done on the use of media and its effect in a cross-cultural context. This study, therefore, finds new ways of missiological studies in a technologically centered society.

As was mentioned in the delimitation of the study, the reception heavily depended upon the interview informants who happened to be ICCP members. The results remained dependent on the series of questions on the receptions of non-ICCP members, non-Christians, and that of lowlanders. Therefore, further study on the various groups in the film showing is suggested to compare and contrast the results of this study.

This study also provided up-to-date data regarding the current communication and information technology and mass communication situation among Mangyans in Occidental Mindoro. Surprisingly, the data presented reveals that there is still very minimal development in terms of technology and social development among Mangyans in Occidental Mindoro. Communication scholars and development communication scholars can further research media and social development in indigenous groups in the Philippines, such as the Mangyans.

This study also contributes to scholarly endeavors in Mangyan studies; Alangan and Iraya Mangyans in Occidental Mindoro have received less attention from Filipino and Mangyan scholars. The data generated from this humble cultural reception study hopes to provoke further studies in various topics in this area.

Policy Makers

The previous literature and current data clearly show that Mangyans in the research area (Northern part of Occidental Mindoro) have been greatly neglected in terms of modern technology development and information sharing. Even basic infrastructure, such as electricity and television signals, has not reached Mangyan settlements of the three sitios. This study suggests that policy makers propose various community development projects as a part of ICT development for the social integrity and welfare of cultural minorities.

In addition to ICT and media infrastructure for social changes, this research also discovered the need for urgent government intervention to preserve Ancestral Land titles from the lowlanders. Based on the field research, Mangyans have lost their Ancestral Domain Land to the lowlanders by borrowing cash from them. Mangyans have suffered from a lack of livelihood skills in the modern settlements, such as rice cultivation, crops and labor skills. In this research, it was clear that Mangyans need government intervention in securing land titles when obtaining cash loans and must be provided with sufficient livelihood skills and education for children to sustain their lives in the settlement.

Besides policy makers, similar challenges face the community development social workers from both government and non-government social organizations. Mangyans still have been struggling with the loss of their ancestral domain due to the lack of basic needs such as food and health care. Schools need to re-open to educate the children of Mangyans in preparation for the future. Culturally relevant Mangyan teachers were another concern in children's education. These were just a few aspects on the list of their social struggles that need to be taken care of immediately.

Appendix A-1

Focus Group Discussion Guide (The *Jesus* film Ministers)

A. What is the role of the *Jesus* film in the religious experience of audiences in your ministry site?
    i. Religious confession through the *Jesus* film
    ii. Do they feel close to God and Jesus as a savior when you watched the *Jesus* film?
        1. How much change did the *Jesus* film put in effect?
        2. Was the movie relevant for the context?
    iii. Do they directly feel certain religious experiences during film showing?
        1. What specific religious experience can you recall?
        2. Was there any specific moment or scene in which you feel close to God?
        3. Was the translation relevant and understandable?

B. How do they understand the Western figure of Jesus in the film?
    i. What meaning that you feel from the figure of Jesus?
    ii. Do you notice that Jesus in the film is a Westerner?
    iii. Does the Western figure of Jesus help more or less in your religious experience?

C. How does the religious experience and social context interplaying with the *Jesus* film contribute to the religious meaning?
    i. What was your religion before?
        1. How religious were you?
        2. How much did you devote to your religion before?
        3. How was it similar to or different from your religion?
        4. Others
    ii. What is your social context?
        1. Education, family, job, income, and Experience with media

Appendix A-2

Focus Group Discussion Guide (APNTS Students)

1. Regarding the *Jesus* film itself...
2. Have you watched or known the film before? And how?
3. Is it helpful in understanding the gospel? How?
4. How about your friends and the experience in your ministry?
5. What do you think of the film itself?
6. Formats, currency... etc...
7. Do you think it is good to be used for evangelism purposes?
8. In what aspect do you think so?
9. What are the strong points in the Film?
10. What are the weak points in the Film?
11. What is your general and specific opinion of this film?
12. Regarding the Westernized visual text...
13. What do you think of Jesus; what nationality do you immediately imagine?
14. Why do you think so?
15. Have you thought about the Western representation of Jesus before?
16. In this Film, Jesus was portrayed as a Westerner. Do you think Jesus is Western or Caucasian?
17. Did you think about that when you watched the *Jesus* film?
18. Why do you think that the film was made with a Caucasian actor instead of a Middle Eastern actor to represent Jesus more historically?
19. Do you think that the skin and nationality affects the understanding of Jesus through this film?
20. What do you think of the white skin of Jesus?
21. Any negotiated meanings created...
22. When you watch... what do you get from the text?
23. What meanings do you get from the film?
24. Reflection or implication...
25. How is the visual text relevant to your culture?
26. In the construction of Christianity...

27. Does the film help your spirituality or someone else's...?
28. How?
29. In what aspect?
30. In relation to the visual representation and the Christianity...

Appendix A-3

Focus Group Discussion Guide (Mangyans Community members)

A. What is the role of the *Jesus* film in the religious experience of Mangyan people in Baclaran, Mindoro?
   i. Did you confess that Jesus is your savior through the *Jesus* film?
      1. How do you understand Protestant church?
      2. How active are you in the Protestant church?
   ii. Do you feel close to God and Jesus as a savior when you watch the *Jesus* film?
      1. How much change did the *Jesus* film put in effect?
      2. Was the movie relevant?
   iii. Do you directly feel certain religious experiences during the film showing?
   iv. What specific religious experience can you recall?
   v. Was there any specific moment or scene in which you feel close to God?
   vi. Was the translation relevant and understandable?
   vii. Others...

B. How do you understand the Western figure of Jesus in the film?
   i. What does the Jesus from the film mean to you?
   ii. What meanings can you feel from the figure of Jesus?
   iii. Do you notice that Jesus in the film is a Westerner?
   iv. Does the Western figure of Jesus help more or less in your religious experience?

C. How does the religious experience and social context interplaying with the *Jesus* film contribute to the religious meanings?
   i. What was your religion before?
      1. How religious were you?
      2. How much did you devote to your religion before?
      3. How was it similar to or different from your religion?
   ii. What is your background?

1. Education, family, job, income, and Experience with media

Appendix B

Observation Guide

A. Social, religious and media context of the three Mangyan sitios in Sta. Cruz, Mindoro
   i. Social context of the three Mangyan sitios in Sta. Cruz, Mindoro
      1. Demographic profile respondents and/or informants
      2. Age, gender, civil status, religion, occupation, income etc...
      3. Current family life, Current organization leadership in community, Current economic situation of the Community
      4. Interaction with outsiders
      5. Current educational situation
   ii. Religious context of the three Mangyan sitios in Sta. Cruz, Mindoro
      1. Catholic religion beliefs and practice
      2. Protestant religion beliefs and practice
      3. And pagan religious beliefs and practice
   iii. Media context of the three Mangyan sitios in Sta. Cruz, Mindoro
      1. TV, Radio, Movie and other media acquisition
      2. TV, Radio, Movie and other media availability
      3. TV, Radio, Movie and other media use
   iv. The *Jesus* film showing placement in the three Mangyan sitios in Sta. Cruz, Mindoro
      1. The composition of the team members
      2. Contact and negotiation process
      3. The *Jesus* film showing preparation in the three sitios
      4. The *Jesus* film showing practice in the three sitios
      5. The *Jesus* film follow-up in the three sitios

v. Observation of the *Jesus* film showing
    1. The demographic of the audience of the film showing
    2. Positions of the audiences during the film showing
    3. The audience's reaction to the film showing
    4. The audience behavior during the film showing
    5. Social interaction during the film showing

Appendix C

Letter of Approval

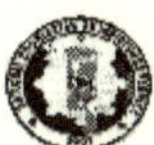

Republic of the Philippines
OFFICE OF THE PRESIDENT
National Commission on Indigenous Peoples
REGIONAL OFFICE NO. IV
2/F, A.B. Sandoval Building, Corner Shaw Blvd. and Oranbo Drive
Pasig City
Telephone Number 632-17-84

11 April 2008

Professor DONG HWAN KWON
Director of Fairbanks
School of Communication
Ortigas Ave., Extension
Kaytikling, Taytay,
920 Rizal

Dear Professor Kwon:

This has reference to your letter-request, dated 17 March 2008, seeking NCIP permission for the conduct of your dissertation research in the IP community of the Alangan-Mangyans, Occidental Mindoro. We take this opportunity to express our deep appreciation for selecting an IP area as a venue for your study. This endeavor would greatly contribute in the determination how indigenous cultural communities respond to the introduction of westernized visual image of Christianity amidst a flourishing culture. Please be informed, however, that the proper entity to grant that permission is not the NCIP but rather the IP community where you are conducting your study.

In view thereof, we will be referring you to our Provincial Officer, Engr. Narcisa Eder- Acting Provincial Officer, NCIP Occidental Mindoro for the assistance that you will need. You can coordinate with her at our Provincial Office at San Jose St. Payompon, Mamburao, Occidental Mindoro.

Thank you very much.

Very truly yours,

Atty. **ARTHUR K. HERMAN**
OIC-Regional Director

cc:
NCIP Mamburao Provincial Office
-TMSD
-File/Records

/cmn/kpl/

Appendix D

The *Jesus* Film Description

S. Num.	T. C	Scene Name	Description
Prologue	1:00 - 5:59	Prologue	Narration goes along the succinct presentation of the Appearance of an angel Gabriel to Mary, the birth of Jesus, and the youth.
S#1	6:00 - 10:03	The baptism of Jesus	Jesus was baptized by John. After the baptism, a dove representing the Holy Spirit came down from heaven to the shoulder of Jesus.
S#2	10:04 - 15:39	Jesus was rejected at Nazareth	After forty days of fasting and temptation, Jesus visited a synagogue and presented himself as the son of God. Jews were furious and cast him out of the synagogue.
S#3	15:40 - 21:08	Seashore of Galilee	Jesus taught villagers while sitting in a boat. Peter became a disciple.
S#4	21:09 - 23:25	Jesus raised the dead daughter of Jairus	Jesus bought back to life the daughter of the leader of synagogue, Jairus, at his home.
S#5	11:26 - 24:47	Matthew became a disciple	Matthew, who was collecting taxes, became a disciple.
S#6	24:48 - 32:44	Twelve disciples	Jesus called twelve disciples to follow his teachings.
S#7	32:45 - 34:23	The perfume of Mary	Mary came to Jesus and poured perfume on his feet.
S#8	34:24 - 36:04	John in the prison	A few disciples came to John in the prison and shared the story of Jesus.
S#9	36:05 - 39:41	The teaching of Jesus	Jesus continued to teach with various parables.
S#10	39:42 - 41:37	Jesus in the storm	Jesus performed a miracle to calm down the storm in the sea.
S#11	41:38- 44:03	Jesus casting out a demon	Jesus cast out a demon from a man.
S#12	44:04- 47:19	Jesus feeds five thousand	Jesus performed a miracle to feed 5,000 people with five loaves of bread and two fish.
S#13	47:20 - 48:26	Jesus predicts his death	Jesus predicted his death in the near future. This scene becomes a transition to the tragic crucifixion and death of Jesus.
S#14	48:27 -	Jesus predicts the	Jesus predicted that one of his disciples

	49:32	betrayal of Judah	would betray him during the last supper.
S#15	49:33-50:57	Jesus at Gethsemane	A few disciples watched the transformation of Jesus standing beside Isaiah and Moses in Gethsemane.
S#16	50:58-53:20	Jesus heals a demon-possessed man	Jesus healed a demon-possessed man
S#17	53:21-1:00:41	Jesus' teaching	Jesus taught his disciples while walking in the mountains and villages
S#18	1:00:42-1:03:46	The rich ruler	A rich ruler was asking about the means of salvation.
S#19	1:03:47-1:06:21	Good Samaritan	Jesus tells his followers the story of the Good Samaritan.
S#20	1:06:22 - 1:08:22	Jesus heals the blind	Jesus healed the blind.
S#21	1:08:23-1:11:18	Zacchaeus and Jesus	Jesus approached Zacchaeus, the tax collector
S#22	1:11:19-11:13:42	The entry of Jerusalem	Jesus entered into Jerusalem with a colt.
S#23	1:13:43 - 1:15:59	Jesus at the temple	Jesus entered Jerusalem and saw the merchants selling goods in a place of worship. He was angry and threw them out.
S#24	1:16:00 - 1:20:48	Jesus and the teachers of the law at Jerusalem	Jewish priests asked difficult questions to test Jesus.
S#25	1:20:49-1:24:20	Last supper	Jesus had a last meal and prayed over them.
S#26	1:24:21-1:24:31	Betrayal of Judas	Judas betrayed Jesus by revealing his location.
S#27	1:24:32-1:28:10	Jesus arrested	Jesus was arrested by Roman soldiers and Jews at Gethsemane.
S#28	1:28:11-1:30:11	The denial of Peter	Peter denied Jesus three times as predicted.
S#29	1:30:12-1:35:10	The trail of Jesus	Jesus was standing in front of Pilate and Herod for the judgment of his trial.
S#30	1:35:11-1:37:32	The crucifixion of Jesus	Jesus was beaten up by Roman soldiers
S#31	1:37:33-1:42:13	On the way to Mt. Golgotha	Jesus headed to mount Golgotha with his cross.
S#32	1:42-14-1:49:25	Jesus on the cross	The longest scene in the movie, Jesus was nailed to and died on the cross.
S#33	1:49:26-1:50:26	Jesus at the tomb	The dead Jesus was brought to his tomb. The stone door was closed.
S#34	1:50:27-1:52:49	Resurrection of Jesus	Women found that the body of Jesus at the tomb was lost. Soon, an angel from heaven revealed that Jesus had resurrected.
S#35	1:52:50-1:56:03	Jesus in front of His disciples	Jesus appeared in front of his disciples and rose up to heaven.
Epilogue	1:56:04-2:01:34	Highlights	Series of still pictures from the film with a narration of the life of Jesus and salvation.

Appendix E

Southern Tagalog District *Jesus* Film Team Registration Plan 2008

Month Of Minis-try	**Num-ber of Presen-tations Planne d**	**Mother or Existing Church Loca-tion** (if applicable)	**Church Plant-ing Area**	**New Mission Church Loca-tion**	**Who will help the pastor organize this church?**	**Ap-proved by (DS):**
Jan	3	Calamba Church of the Nazarene	Brgy. San Cristobal, Ca-lamba City, Laguna	Brgy. San Cristobal, Calamba City, Laguna	Ptr. Man-ganang	Ds. Faustino Roranes
Feb	3	Harvestime Church of the Nazarene	Baclaran, Min-doro	Baclaran, Mindoro	Ptr. Nobert	Ds. Faustino Roranes
Mar	3	GMA Church of the Nazarene	Brgy. Malia, GMA, Cavite	Brgy. Malia, GMA, Cavite	Bro. Bennie	Ds. Faustino Roranes
Apr	3	Agape Church of the Nazarene	Tagaytay City, Cavite	Tagaytay City, Cavite	Ptr. George Junio	Ds. Faustino Roranes
May	3	Calamba Church of the Nazarene	Brgy. San Cristobal, Ca-lamba City, Laguna	Brgy. San Cristobal, Calamba City, Laguna	Ptr. Man-ganang	Ds. Faustino Roranes
Jun	3	Harvestime Church of the Nazarene	Baclaran, Min-doro	Baclaran, Mindoro	Ptr. Nobert	Ds. Faustino Roranes
Jul	3	GMA Church of the Nazarene	Brgy. Malia, GMA, Cavite	Brgy. Malia, GMA, Cavite	Bro. Bennie	Ds. Faustino Roranes
Aug	3	Agape Church of the Nazarene	Tagaytay City, Cavite	Tagaytay City, Cavite	Ptr. George Junio	Ds. Faustino Roranes
Sep	3	Calamba Church of the Nazarene	Brgy. San Cristobal, Ca-lamba City, Laguna	Brgy. San Cristobal, Calamba City, Laguna	Ptr. Man-ganang	Ds. Faustino Roranes
Oct	3	Harvestime Church of the Naza-rene	Baclaran, Min-doro	Baclaran, Mindoro	Ptr. Nobert	Ds. Faustino Roranes
Nov	3	GMA Church of the Nazarene	Brgy. Malia, GMA, Cavite	Brgy. Malia, GMA, Cavite	Bro. Bennie	Ds. Faustino Roranes
Dec	3	Agape Church of the Nazarene	Tagaytay City, Cavite	Tagaytay City, Cavite	Ptr. George Junio	Ds. Faustino Roranes

Reference List

Books

Abinales, P. N., & Amoroso, D. J. (2005). *State and society in the Philippines* (2nd ed). Pasig City: Anvil Publishing.

Adewuya, J. A. (2001). *Holiness and community in 2 Corinthians 6:14-7:1: Paul's view of communal holiness in the Corinthian correspondence.* New York: Peter Lang.

Ang, I. (1985). *Watching Dallas: Soap opera and the melodramatic imagination.* London: Methuen.

Arthur, C. (Ed.). (1993). *Religion and the media: An Introductory reader.* Cardiff: University of Wales Press.

Badaracco, C. H. (Ed.). (2005). *Quoting God: How media shape ideas about religion and culture.* Waco, TX: Baylor University Press.

Ball, M. S., & Smith, G. W. H. (1992). *Analyzing visual data.* London: SAGE.

Baran, S. J., & Davis, D. D. (1995). *Mass communication theory: Foundations, ferment, and future.* Belmont, CA: Wadsworth.

Barthes, R. (1972). *Mythology.* Translated by Annette Lavers. London, Paladin.

Baugh, L. (1997). *Imagine the divine: Jesus and Christ-figures in film.* Kansas: Sheed & Ward.

Berger, P., & Luckmann, T. (1966). *The social construction of reality: A treatise in the sociology of knowledge.* Harmondsworth, Middlesex, England: Penguin.

Brooker, P. (2003). *A glossary of cultural theory.* (2nd ed.). London: Oxford University Press.

Buddenbaum, J. M., & Mason, D. L. (Eds.) (2000). *Readings on religion as news.* Ames, IA: Iowa State University Press.

Clark, L. S. (2003). *From angels to aliens: Teenagers, the media, and the supernatural.* New York, Oxford Press.

Curran, J., Morley, D., & Walkerdine, V. (Eds.). (1996) *Cultural studies and communications.* London: Arnold.

Dawson, L. L., & Cowan, D. E. (Eds.). (2004). *Religion online: Finding faith on the internet.* New York: Routledge.

Denzin, N. K., & Lincoln, Y. S. (Eds.). (2000). *Handbook of qualitative research.* (2nd ed.). Thousand Oaks, CA: SAGE.

Durkheim, E. (1995). *The elementary forms of religious life.* (K. E. Fields, Trans.). New York: The Free Press. (Original work published 1912)

Engel, J. F. (1989). *Getting your message across: Applied principles in gospel communication.* Mandaluyong City: OMF.

Fish, S. (1980). *Is there a text in this class?* Cambridge: Harvard University Press.

Fox, R. W. (2004). *Jesus in America: Personal savior, cultural hero, national obsession.* New York: Harper.

Foucault, M. (1984). *The history of sexuality: The use of pleasure.* New York: Vintage Books.

Foucault, M. (1988). *The history of sexuality: The care of the self.* New York: Vintage Books.

Foucault, M. (1990). *History of sexuality: An introduction.* New York: Random House.

Foucault, M. (2002). *Archeology of knowledge.* London: Routledge.

Foucault, M. (2003). *Discipline and punish: The birth of the prison.* (S. K. Oh, Trans.). Seoul, Korea: Nanam. (Original work published 1975)

Freedberg, D. (1989). *The power of images: Studies in the history and theory of response.* Chicago: University of Chicago Press.

Geertz, C. (1973). *The interpretation of culture.* New York: Basic Books.

Go J., & Foster, A. L. (Eds.). (2005). *The American colonial state in the Philippines: Global perspectives* (2nd ed.). Pasig City: Anvil Publishing.

Goda, T. (Ed.). (1999). *Political culture and ethnicity: An anthropological study in Southeast Asia.* Quezon City: New Day Publishers.

Goda. T. (Ed.). (2003). *Postcolonialism and local politics in South Asia.* Quezon City: New Day Publishers.

Gramsci, A. (2005). *Selections from the prison notebooks.* New York: International Publishers.

Gurevitch, M., Bennet, T., Curran, J., & Woolacott, J. (Eds.). (1982). *Culture, society and the media.* London: Methuen.

Hardt, H. (1992). *Critical communication studies: Communication, history & theory in America.* London: Routledge.

Hays, R. B. (1996). *The moral vision of the New Testament.* San Francisco: Harper Collins.

Helbling J., & Schult, V. (2004). *Mangyan survival strategies.* Quezon City: New Day Publishers.

Hesselgrave, D. J. (1989). *Contextualization: Meanings, methods, models.* Grand Rapids, MI: Zondervan.

Hidalgo, C. P., & Patajo-Legasto, P. P. (Eds.). (2005). *Philippine postcolonial studies: Essays on language and literature* (2nd ed.). Quezon City: The University of the Philippines Press.

Hiebert, P. G. (1985). *Anthropological insights for missionaries.* Grand Rapids, MI: Zondervan.

Hobson, D. (1982). *Crossroads: The drama of a soap opera.* London: Methuen.

Hoggart, R. (1958). *The Uses of literacy.* London: Penguin.

Hoover, S. M., & Lundby, K. (Eds.). (1997). *Rethinking media, religion, and culture*: Thousand Oaks, CA: SAGE.

Hoover, S. M., & Clark, L. S. (Eds.). (2002). *Practicing religion in the age of the media: Explorations in media, religion, and culture.* New York: Columbia University Press.

Horsfield, P., Hess M. E., & Medrano, A. M. (2004). *Belief in media: Cultural perspectives on media and Christianity.* Aldershot, England: Ashgate Publishing.

Hunchcroft, P. D. (2000). *Booty Capitalism: The Politics of Banking in the Philippines.* Quezon City: Ateneo De Manila University Press.

Johnston, R. K. (2000). *Reel spirituality: Theology and film in dialogue.* Grand Rapids, MI: Baker Academic.

Katz, E., & Lazarsfeld, P. (1955). *Personal influence.* Glencoe, IL: Free Press.

Kraft, C. H. (1986). *Christianity in culture: A study in dynamic biblical theologizing in cross cultural perspective.* MaryKnoll, NY: Orbis Books.

Littlejohn, S. W. (2001). *Theories of human communication* (7th ed.). Belmont, CA: Wadsworth.

Lopez, V. B. (1976). *The Mangyans of Mindoro: An ethnohistory*. Quezon City: University of the Philippines Press.

Maano, N. (2000). *Jesus on the road: Reel stories of real people*. Paco, Manila: Lighthouse Inspirational.

Marsh, C., & Ortiz, G. (Eds.). (1997). *Explorations in theology and film*. Malden, MA: Blackwell Publishing Ltd.

Marvasti, A. B. (2004). *Qualitative research in sociology*. London: SAGE.

Marx (1977). *A contribution to the critique of political economy* (2nd ed.). (S. W. Ryazanskaya, Trans.). Moscow: Progress Publishers. (Original work published 1859)

Marx, K., & Engels, F. (1995). *The German ideology*. New York: International Publishers. (Original work published 1846)

McDannell, C. (1995). *Material Christianity: Religion and popular culture in America*. New Haven: Yale University Press.

Merton, R. (1948). *Mass persuasion*. New York: Free Press.

Miles, M. R. (1996). *Seeing and believing: Religion and values in the movies*. Boston, MA: Beacon Press.

Mitchell, J., & Marriage, S. (Eds.). (2003). *Mediating religion: Conversations in media, religion and culture*. London: T&T Clark.

Miyamoto, M. (1988). *The Hanunoo-Mangyan: Society, religion, and law among a mountain people of Mindoro island, Philippines*. Osaka, Japan: National Museum of Ethnology.

Modelski, T. (1984). *Loving with a vengeance*, London: Methuen.

Morgan, D. (1998). *Visual piety: A history and theory of popular religious image*. Berkeley, CA: University of California Press.

Morgan, D., & Promey, S. M. (2001). *The visual culture of American religions*. Berkeley, CA: University of California Press.

Morley, D. (1980). *The Nationwide audience*. London: BFI.

Morley, D. (1986). *Family television: Cultural power and domestic leisure*. London: Comedia.

Morley, D. (1992). *Television, audiences and cultural studies*. London: Routledge.

Nida, E. A. (1954). *Customs and cultures: Anthropology for Christian missions*. Pasadena, CA: William Carey Library.

Nida, E. A. (1960). *Message and mission: The communication of the Christian faith* (Rev. ed.). Pasadena, CA: William Carey Library.

Nida, E. A. (1968). *Religion across cultures: A study in the communication of the Christian faith*. Pasadena, CA: William Carey Library.

Payne, G., & Payne, J. (2004). *Key concepts in social research*. London: SAGE.

Pernia, E. E. (2004). *Communication research in the Philippines: Issues and methods*. Quezon City: University of the Philippines Press.

Postma, A (1981). *Mindoro Mangyan mission*: A pictoral. Manila City: Arnoldus Press.

Postma, A. (Ed.). (1988). *Annotated Mangyan bibliography 1570-1988*. Manila: Arnoldus Press.

Radway, J. (1984). *Reading the romance*. Chapel Hill: University of North Carolina Press.

Schiller, H. I. (1976). *Mass communications and cultural dominance*. White Plains, NY: International Arts and Science Press.

Schult, V. (1991). Mindoro, *a social history of a Philippine island in the 20th century: A*

case study of a delayed developmental process. Manila: Divine Word Publications.
Stern. R. C., Jefford, C. N., & DeBona, G. (1999). *Savior on the silver screen*. New York: Paulist Press.
Stone, B. P. (2000). *Faith and film: Theological themes at the cinema*. St. Louis, MO: Chalice Press.
Stout, D. A., & Buddenbaum, J. M. (Eds.). (1996). *Religion and mass media: Audiences and adaptations*. Thousand Oaks, CA: SAGE.
Tatum, W. B. (2004). *Jesus at the movies: A guide to the first hundred years* (Rev. and Exp. ed.). Santa Rosa, CA: Polebridge Press.
Thomson, E. P. (1978). *The making of the English working class*. London: Penguin.
Walsh. R. (2003). *Reading the gospels in the dark: Portrayals of Jesus in film*. Harrisburg, PA: Trinity Press International.
Waters, M. (1995). *Globalization*. London: Routledge.
Weber, M. (1963). *The sociology of religion*. (Trans.). Ephraim Fischoff. Boston: Beacon Press.
Williams, R. (1975). *The Long revolution*. London: Penguin.
Williams, R. (1977). *Culture and society 1780-1950*. Harmondsworth, Middlesex: Penguin Books.
Williams, R. (1983). *Keywords* (Rev. ed.). New York: Oxford University Press.

Chapters in a Book

Adorno, T., & Horkheimer, M. (1977). The culture industry: Enlightenment as mass deception. In J. Curran, et al. (Eds.), *Mass communication and society* (pp. 120-167). London: Edward Arnold.
Althusser, L. (1971). Ideological state apparatuses. In L. Althusser, *Lenin and philosophy and other essays* (pp.121-173). London: New Left Books.
Barsotti, C. M., & Johnston, R. K. (Eds.). (2004). *Finding God in the movies: 33 films of reel faith*. Grand Rapids, MI: Baker Books.
Bobo, J. (2003). *The color purple: Black women as cultural readers*. In W. Brooker, & D. Jermyn (Eds.), *The audience studies reader* (pp. 305-314). London: Routledge.
Buddenbaum J. M. (1996). The role of religion in newspaper trust, subscribing, and use of political information. In D. A. Stout, & J. M. Buddenbaum (Eds.), *Religion and mass media* (pp. 123-134). Thousand Oaks, CA: Sage.
Clark, L. S., & Hoover, S. M. (1997). At the intersection of media, culture and religion: A bibliographic essay. In S. M. Hoover (Ed.), *Rethinking media, religion and culture* (pp. 15-36). Thousand Oaks, CA: SAGE.
Clark, L. S. (2002). The "protestantization" of research into media, religion, and culture.
In S. M. Hoover, & L. S. Clark (Eds.), *Practicing religion in the age of the media: Explorations in media, religion, and culture* (pp. 7-36). New York: Columbia University Press.
Clark, L. S. (2004). Reconceptualizing religion and media in a post-national, postmodern world: A critical historical introduction. In P. Horsfield, M. E. Hess, & A. M. Medrano (Eds.), *Belief in media: Cultural perspectives on media and Christianity* (pp. 7-22). Aldershot: Ashgate Publishing Limited.
Conklin, H. C. (1969). An ethnocological approach to shifting agriculture. In P. V.
Andrew (Ed.), *Environment and cultural behavior* (pp. 221 – 233). New York: The Natural History Press.

David, R. (1978). Manila's street life: A visual ethnography. In K. Hidetoshi (Ed.), *A comparative study of street life: Tokyo, Manila, and New York* (pp. 19-44). N.p. Research Institute for Oriental Cultures.

Gibson, T. (1994). Childhood, colonialism and fieldwork among the Buid of the Philippines and the Konjo of Indonesia. In J. Koubi, & J. Massard-Vincent (Eds.). Enfants at societis en Asie du Sut-East (pp. 183-205). Paries: L'Harmattan.

Hall, S. (1980). Encoding and decoding. In S. Hall, D. Hobson, A. Lowe, & P. Willis (Eds.), *Culture, media, language* (pp. 128-138). London: Hutchinson.

Hall, S. (1997). Subjects in history: Making diasporic identities. In W. Lubiano (Ed.), *The house that race built* (pp. 289-99). New York: Pantheon Books.

Hamelink, C. J. (1993). Globalism and national sovereignty. In K. Nordenstreng, & H. I. Shiller (Eds.), *Beyond national sovereignty: International communication in the 1990s* (pp. 371-393). Norwood: Ablex.

Harper, D. (2000). Reimagining visual methods: Galileo to Neuromancer. In N. Denzin, & Y. Lincoln (Eds.), *Handbook of qualitative research* (2nd ed.) (pp. 717-732). London: SAGE.

Harper, D. (2004). Photograph in research. In M. S. Lewis-Beck, A. Bryman, & T. F. Liao (Eds.), *SAGE encyclopedia of social science research methods,* (pp. 821-2), (vol. 2). London: SAGE.

Hoover, S. M. (2003). Religion, media and identity: Theory and method in audience research on religion and media. In J. Mitchell, & S. Marriage (Eds.), *Mediating religion: Conversations in media, religion and culture* (pp. 9-20). London: T&T Clark.

Hoover, S. M., & Park, J. K. (2005). Religion and meaning in the digital age: Field research on Internet/web religion. In P. Horsfield, M. E. Hess, & A. M. Medrano (Eds.), *Belief in media: Cultural perspective on media and Christianity* (pp.121-136). Aldershot: Ashgate Publishing Limited.

Horsfield, P. (2005). Theology, church in media: Contours in a changing cultural terrain.

In P. Horsfield, M. E. Hess, & A. M. Medrano. (Eds.). *Belief in media: Cultural perspectives on media and Christianity* (pp.23-32). Aldershot: Ashgate Publishing Limited.

Jhally, S., & Lewis, J. (2003). Enlightened racism: The Cosby show, audiences and the myth of the American dream. In W. Brooker & D. Jermyn (Eds.), *The Audience studies reader* (pp. 279-286). London: Routledge.

Kwon, D. H. (2007). Westernized visual representation of Jesus and the construction of religious meaning: Jesus film and its' reception among Asian audiences. In S. D. Kim (Ed.). *Media culture and industry in Asia* (pp. 223-235). Chuncheon, Korea: Hallym University.

Langmuir, E. (2000). Sign and symbol. In. G. Finaldi (Ed.), *The image of Christ* (pp.8-44). London: National Gallery Company Limited.

Liebes, T., & Katz, E. (2003). The export of meaning: Cross cultural reading of Dallas. In W. Brooker, & D. Jermyn (Eds.), *The audience studies reader* (pp. 287-304). London: Routledge.

Lindlof, T. R. (1996). The passionate audience: Community inscriptions of the last temptation of Christ. In D. A. Stout, & J. M. Buddenbaum (Eds.), *Religion and mass media: Audiences and adaptations* (pp. 148-168). Thousand Oaks, CA: SAGE.

McIntyre, C. T. (1984). Fundamentalism. In W. A. Elwell (Ed.), *Evangelical dictionary of theology* (p. 433-435). Grand Rapids, MI: Baker Book House.

Morgan, D. (2002). Protestant visual practice and American mass culture. In S. M.

Hoover, & L. S. Clark (Eds.), *Practicing religion in the age of the media: Explorations in media, religion, and culture* (pp. 37-62). New York: Columbia University Press.

Morgan, D. (2004). Visual media and Ethiopian Protestantism. In P. Horsfield, M. E. Hess & A. M. Medrano (Eds.), *Belief in media: Cultural perspectives on media and Christianity* (pp. 91-106). Aldershot: Ashgate Publishing Limited.

Pennoyer, F. D. (1979). Shifting cultivation and shifting subsistence patterns among the Taubuid of Mindoro. In P.B. Naylor (Ed.), *Contributions to the study of Philippine shifting cultivation* (pp. 43 - 54). Los Banos: University of the Philippines.

Pink, S. (2004). *Visual research.* In M. S. Lewis-Beck, A. Bryman, & T. F. Liao (Eds.), *SAGE encyclopedia of social science research methods* (pp. 1185-6), (vol. 3). London: SAGE.

Postma, A (1994). Sickness, death, and after-death: The Mangyan experience. In Henry W. Kiley (Ed.), *Filipino tribal religious experience: Sickness, death and after-death* (pp.3-25). Quezon City: Giraffe Books.

Schiller, H. I. (1998). Striving for communication dominance. In D. K. Thussu (Ed.), *Electronic empires* (pp.17-26). London: Arnold.

Stout, D. A., Scott, D. W., & Martin, D. G. (1996). Mormons, mass media, and the interpretive audience. In D. A. Stout, & J. M. Buddenbaum (Eds.), *Religion and mass media: Audiences and adaptations* (pp. 243-258). Thousand Oaks, CA: SAGE.

Tedlock B. (2000). Ethnography and ethnographic representation. In N. K. Denzin, & Y. Lincoln (Eds.), *Handbook of qualitative research* (2nd ed.) (pp. 455-486).Thousand Oaks, CA: SAGE.

Journals, Conference Proceedings and Monographs

Conklin, H. C. (1949). Preliminary report on field work on the island of Mindoro and Palawan, Philippines. *American Anthropologist, 51*, 268-273.

Conklin, H. C. (1958). Betel chewing among the Hanunoo. Proceedings of 8th Pacific Congress, Nov 1953, Quezon City: National Council of the Philippines. Estel. L. A. (1952). Racial types of Mindoro. *Journal of East Asiatic Studies, 1,* 21 - 29. Estel. L. A. (1953). Racial origin in northern Indonesia. *Journal of East Asiatic Studies, 2,* 1-20.

Gibson, T. (1985). The sharing of substance versus the sharing of activity among the Buid. *Man 20,* 391 - 411.

Katz, E., Blumler, J. G. & Gurevitch, M. (1973). Utilization of mass communication by the individual. Paper presented at the meeting of the Veriges Radio Audience and Programme Research Department Hulfen, Sweden.

Kikuchi, Y. (1973a). Cosmology in Hanunoo society Mindoro, Philippines: Panaytayan group. *A Quarterly Record of Social Anthropology, 6,* 1 - 26. Kikuchi, Y. (1973b). The emergence of the formal political leadership among the Batangan in Mindoro, Philippines. Paper presented at the 9th International Congress of Anthropological and Ethnological Sciences. Chicago.

Kikuchi, Y. (1974). Lack of ethnic symbiosis in the Philippines. *A Quarterly Record of Social Anthropology, 12,* 35 - 41.

Kikuchi, Y. (1979). Political leadership and the corporate group in cognatic society:

Mindoro swidden agriculturalist. Research report to the Philippine studies program, The Institute of social sciences, Waseda University. Tokyo.

Kikuchi, Y. (1982). Perspectives on the Filipino kinship system. *Social Science Review, 80,* 1 - 18.

Maceda. M. N. (1967). A brief report on some Mangyans in northern Oriental Mindoro. *Unitas, 40,*102 - 155.

Mandia, E. H. (2004). The Alangan Mangyan of Mt. Halcon, Oriental Mindoro: Their ethnobotany. *Philippine Quarterly of Culture & Society, 32,* 96 - 117.

Miyamoto, M. (1978). Hanunoo-Mangyan social world. *Senri Ethnological Studies, 2,* 147 - 195.

Miyamoto, M. (1985). Disputes among the Hanunoo-Mangyan of Mindoro Island: A case study in Wasig local community. In *Filipino Tradition and Acculturation: Research Report 3*: 119 - 157.

Osteria, T. S. (1985). The health and nutritional status of the Hanunoo Mangyan: Implications for a community based health delivery system. Occasional paper no. 10. Manila: De La Salle University Research Center.

Parameswaran, R. (August 2002). Local culture in global media: Excavating colonial and material discourses in national geographic. *Communication Theory, 12,* 287-315.

Pennoyer, F. D. (1976). Spirits, specialists, and the Taubuid cosmos, *Folk, 18,* 247-261.

Pennoyer, F. D. (1977). *The Taubuid of Mindoro, Philippines. Philippine Quarterly of Culture and Society, 5,* 21 - 37.

Pennoyer, F. D. (1980a). Buhid and Taubuid: A New subgroup in Mindoro, Philippines. In P.B. Naylor (Ed.), Papers to the 2nd Eastern Conference on Austronesian Languages (pp. 265 - 271), Ann Harbor: University of the Michigan.

Pennoyer, F. D. (1980b). Ritual in Taubuid life (Mindoro, Philippines). *Anthropos, 75,* 693 - 709.

Postma, A. (1974). Development among the Mangyans of Mindoro: A privileged Experience. *Philippine Quarterly of Culture and Society, 2,* 21 - 37.

Postma, A. (1977). Mindoro missions revisited. *Philippine Quarterly of Culture and Society, 5,* 253 - 265.

Pernia, E. E., Pascual, M. S. and Kwon, D. H. (November, 2006). Religion in the box: Religious television programming and viewership in the Philippines. *The Journal of Communication and Religion, 29,* 484-510.

Webster, J. G. (Spring 1998). "The Audience." *Journal of Broadcasting and Electronic Media, 42,* 190-207.

Theses and Dissertations

Afagbegee, G. L. (1994). *Values as cultural determinants of interpersonal Communication behavior among the Hanunoo-Mangyans: An ethonocommunication approach.* Unpublished master's thesis, University of the Philippines, Los Banos.

Arinto, M. T. B. (1999). *A study on the survival of religious programs on Philippine television.* Unpublished undergraduate thesis, University of the Philippines, Quezon City, Manila.

Caraan, R. A. (2001). *Community-based rattan utilization and management: A case study of the Alangan Mangyan and the depletion of rattan in their concession.* Unpublished master's thesis, Ateneo de Manila University, Quezon City, Manila.

Feraro-Banta, L. (1985). *Changes on the socio-cultural life of the Alangan-Mangyans: A comparison of the traditional Alangan and the marginal Alangan in Mindoro Oriental.* Unpublished master's thesis, University of the Philippines, Quezon City, Manila.

Gibson, T. (1983). *Religion, kinship, and society among the Buhids of Mindoro, Philippines.* Unpublished doctoral dissertation, London School of Economics. London.

Ispuruyanto, Y. (1999). *A case study of TV for evangelization: The SAV PUSKAT Catholic programs on Indonesia.* Unpublished master's thesis, University of the Philippines. Quezon City, Manila.

Leykamm, M. (1979). *Sickness and healing among the Alangan Mangyans of Oriental Mindoro.* Unpublished master's thesis, Ateneo de Manila University, Quezon City, Manila.

Jonson, D. M. (1994). *The role of television in increasing the religious consciousness of the Filipino people.* Unpublished undergraduate thesis, University of the Philippines, Quezon City, Manila.

Kooran, G. K. (2000). *Media, religion, society.* Unpublished master's thesis, University of the Philippines, Quezon City, Manila.

Mandia, E. H. (1987). *An ethnobotanical study of the Alangan Mangyans of Northeastern Mindoro.* Unpublished master's thesis, De La Salle University, Manila.

Miyamoto, M. (1975). *The society and folk-beliefs of the Hanunoo-Mangyan in Southeastern Mindoro, Philippines.* Unpublished master's thesis, Metropolitan University, Tokyo.

Navarro, R. P. (1993). *Providing for an implementation law in the constitutional provisions on ancestral lands: The case of the Alangan Mangyans.* Unpublished doctoral dissertation. Ateneo de Manila University, Quezon City, Manila.

Obordo, M. E. M. (2001). *The mass mediated church: The Catholic religious programs' use of traditional and new media and its effects on the Filipino religious culture.* Unpublished undergraduate thesis, University of the Philippines, Quezon City, Manila.

Pennoyer, F. D. (1975). *Taubuid plants and ritual complexes.* Unpublished doctoral dissertation, Washington State University, Washington D.C.

Quiaott, J. S. (1997). *The changing patterns in the man-land relationship of the Alangan Mangyans of oriental Mindoro.* Unpublished master's thesis, Xavier University, Cagayan de Oro.

Turner, J. G. (2006). *Selling Jesus to modern America: Campus Crusade for Christ, evangelical culture, and conservative politics.* Unpublished doctoral dissertation, University of Notre Dame, Notre Dame.

Velarde, V. C. (1999). *Communication patterns and strategies of different religions Philippines.* Unpublished undergraduate thesis, University of the Philippines, Quezon City, Manila.

Electronic Sources

Backker, F. L. (2004). The image of Jesus Christ in the Jesus films used in missionary work. [Electronic version]. *Exchange, 33*, 310-333. Retrieved October, 25, 2007, from Communication and Mass Media Complete.

Boys, M. (2004, Spring). I Didn't See Any Anti-Semitism: Why Many Christians Don't Have a Problem with The Passion of the Christ. [Electronic version]. *Cross Currents, 54*(1), 8-15. Retrieved September 8, 2009, from Religion and Philosophy Collection database.

Deacy, C. (2006, Summer). Reflections on the uncritical appropriation of cinematic Christ figures: Holy other or wholly inadequate. *Journal of Religion and Popular Culture 13.* Retrieved January 8, 2008, from http://www.usask.ca/relst/jrpc/art13reflectcinematicchrist.html.

Israel A. C. (2009, June). Bill Bright and Campus Crusade for Christ: The Renewal of Evangelicalism in Postwar America. [Review of the book] *American Historical Review, 114*, 787-8. Retrieved September 8, 2009, from Religion and Philosophy Collection database.

Flesher, P. V. M. & Torry, R. (1998). Filming Jesus: Between authority and heresy. *Journal of Religion and Film* 8. Retrieved December, 6, 2007 from http://www.unomaha.edu/jrf/2004Symposium/FlesherTorry.htm.

Harvey, V. (1976, October 6). Political piety of Bill Bright. *Christian Century, 93*, 828-828. Retrieved September 8, 2009, from ATLA Religion Database with ATLA Serials database.

Jesus Film. (2003, June 30). Jesus film project. Retrieved July, 19, 2003, from www.jesusfilm.org.

Kozlovic, A. K. (2004, Fall). The structure characteristics of the cinematic Christ-figure.

Journal of Religion and Popular Culture 8. Retrieved December, 15, 2007, from http://www.usask.ca/relst/jrpc/art8-cinematicchrist.html.

Lang, C. (2007), *A brief history of literary theory.* Retrieved January, 5, 2008, fromhttp://www.xenos.org/essays/litthry8.htm.

Melton, J. G. (2009). "Evangelical church." In *Encyclopædia Britannica.* Retrieved September 08, 2009, from Encyclopædia Britannica Online: http://www.britannica.com/EBchecked/topic/196819/Evangelical-church

Reinhartz, A. (2006). History and pseudo-history in the Jesus film genre. *Bible*

Interpretation, 14, 1-17. Retrieved October, 25, 2007, from Religion and Philosophy Collection.

Reysen, S. (2006, Spring). Secular versus religious fans: Are they different?: An empirical examination. *Journal of Religion and Popular Culture, 12.* Retrieved December, 17, 2007, from http://www.usask.ca/relst/jrpc/art12-secularvsreligious.html.

www.ingramcontent.com/pod-product-compliance
Lightning Source LLC
LaVergne TN
LVHW090947080826
845145LV00003B/922

* 9 7 8 1 6 0 9 4 7 0 6 8 5 *